Iran Since
the Revolution

Sepehr Zabih

93-632

THE JOHNS HOPKINS UNIVERSITY PRESS
BALTIMORE, MARYLAND

First published in the United States of America, 1982,
by The Johns Hopkins University Press,
Baltimore, Maryland 21218

First published in Great Britain, 1982,
by Croom Helm Ltd, 2-10 St John's Road, London SW11

Library of Congress Cataloging in Publication Data

Zabih, Sepehr.
   Iran since the revolution.

   Bibliography: p.
   Includes index.
   1. Iran — Politics and government — 1979-
I. Title.
DS318.8.Z32   955'.054   82-7735
ISBN 0-8018-2888-0   AACR2

Printed and bound in Great Britain

CONTENTS

PREFACE

Since the turn of the century Iran has experienced three major political upheavals in her relentless, but so far unsuccessful, struggle to democratize her political system. The 1906-11 constitutional revolution attempted to introduce a Western-style liberal parliamentary monarchy to Iran, but instead led to the rise of the first Pahlavi dictatorship by 1925. The nationalist movement of the Mossadegh era in the early 1950s sought to secure Iran's economic independence as a precondition for a popularly based constitutional democracy, but resulted in the emergence of the second Pahlavi dictatorship. The authentic revolution of 1978-9 tried to terminate all forms of dictatorship once and for all, and instead paved the way for an even more despotic theocracy. The last revolution inaugurated an era of such unprecedented turmoil that in some ways it may be regarded as not one, but three consecutive and on-going revolutions. The first overthrew the Shah, the second utilized anti-American radicalism to institutionalize an Islamic Republic, and the last transformed the republic into a one-party fundamentalist theocracy.

While a consensus on the need to overthrow the Pahlavi dynasty emerged by the autumn of 1978 among the overwhelming majority of politicized Iranians, revolution meant different things to the different groups which had coalesced around that goal. Consequently, the anti-Shah coalition broke up as soon as the Shia fundamentalists started establishing a theocracy rather than a pluralistic democracy or a Marxist People's Republic, as at least two other claimants to power had contemplated. In a real sense of each of the last two revolutions was waged not only to deny them a share of power, but also to divest them of the right of challenging the authority of the Shia fundamentalists.

In the process the secular forces, some of which had spearheaded the insurrectionary seizure of power in 1979, began to be devoured by the revolution itself. The progressive elimination of the opposition forces culminated in the ousting of the first President of the Islamic Republic in June 1981, and the subsequent armed struggle against the regime by the more militant of these forces. This struggle continues to date. The prospects of its success depend as much on the ability of these forces to attract massive public support as on the Islamic Republic's determination to retain power.

To develop the above themes, this study will begin by raising the question of why and how Khomeini succeeded. Chapter 1 will try to provide at least a partial answer to this question. The American connection with the revolution and the disintegration of the armed forces will be considered in the answer. The process of the institutionalization of the revolutionary regime, despite the lack of consensus on its ideological and constitutional foundation preceding the enactment of the Islamic Constitution, will be the focus of Chapter 2. The hostage crisis which interrupted that process, the leadership of the militant students and the phases of evolution of the crisis, with an emphasis on its internal ramifications, will be examined in Chapter 3. A closer look at the presidency and the Majlis will be attempted in Chapter 4, along with the first manifestations of political disputes between these top institutions of the new regime. Chapter 5 will focus on the resurgence of the opposition, which though dating back to the dispute concerning the constitution, had been temporarily submerged during the hostage crisis. Under separate headings the Shia opposition, the Kurdish insurrection and the intellectual alienation will be probed. Since the left emerged as a dominant political force in the year-long revolutionary upheaval and began to disagree on the legitimacy and viability of the Islamic Republic, Chapter 6 will be devoted to the parties of the left — both those which are presently in the forefront of opposition to Khomeini as well as those persisting in their support for him.

The political rift between secular and fundamentalist forces which culminated in the demise of the Islamic Republic's first President is considered in Chapter 7, while Chapter 8 focuses on the outbreak of armed struggle against the regime. The acts of political terrorism and the brutal response that they evoke, as well as a realignment of opposition forces both inside and outside the country, will be emphasized. Chapter 9 will discuss changes in Iran's relations with the world at large beginning by a discussion of US–Iran relations since Khomeini's accession to power, and ending with the Islamic Republic's international outlook. Iran's changing threat perception both before and after the Iraqi invasion, along with the ramifications of that war, will constitute the main inquiries of this chapter. A prognosis of the prospects of the opposition forces and the chances of the viability of the Islamic Republic will be offered in the concluding chapter.

Research for this study was begun immediately after the revolution. A deliberate effort has been made to rely, as much as possible, on original Iranian sources. Over the last few years I have travelled extensively in the USA, Western Europe and the Middle East to collect data and to conduct interviews with scores of Iranian writers, diplomats, civilian and military officials and politicians representing all shades of political opinion. Of particular value to me has been the vast collection of Farsi newspapers and other publications originating from Iran, Europe or the USA. Together with those put out by various exile groups, these constitute the bulk of the original sources used in this study. Equally indispensable to me has been the availability of powerful short-wave radios to monitor Iranian state-controlled broadcasts directly, rather than relying on the summary of their English transcripts available in several Western countries and often used exclusively by non-Farsi-speaking authors.

Many sources and individuals from all walks of life have contributed to my research. Those who could be identified are cited in the text. Others must remain anonymous for compelling personal or family safety reasons. The valuable co-operation of still others who gave me numerous useful and extended off-the-record interviews must also be acknowledged.

To Robert Hershman, formerly of the MacNeil-Lehrer Report of the Public Broadcasting Service, Washington, DC, I owe special thanks for putting at my disposal much-needed communication facilities at the height of the uprising in Tabriz in December 1979. Equally significant were the contributions of Dr Mehdi Rouhani, the leader of the Iranian Shiite community in France, and Mahmoud Khayami and Hossein Khodadad for their understanding of the intricacies of intra-clerical relations among the Shias in Iran and Iraq. To Charles Naas, John Stempel, formerly of the US embassy in Tehran; Ralph Lindstrom, presently the US State Department's Country Director for Iran; and Professor Geoffrey Kemp of the National Security Council staff go special thanks for their generous time and frank co-operation regarding US–Iranian relations during both the Carter and Reagan Administrations.

Some of my former and present colleagues should be mentioned also for extended and often beneficial exchanges over the past few years. Amongst them: Amos Perlmutter of the American University, Washington DC; Paul Seabury, Chalmers Johnson and George Lenczowski of the University of California, Berkeley; Adeed Dawisha of the Royal Institute of International Affairs, London; Ahmad Ghoreishi and Ghassam Motamedi, formerly of the National and Tehran Universities; Nasser Amini and Ahmad Mirfendereski, formerly of Iran's foreign ministry; Yusof Mazandi, a foreign journalist of long standing; and last but not least, Parviz Raeen of the Associated Press and *Time-Life* magazine. Robert Moss and Brian Crosier of *The Economist* and *Journal of Conflict*

Resolution respectively, were most helpful in sharing information with me. Needless to say, responsibility for the contents of this book remains exclusively mine.

To my family I owe the usual gratitude for putting up with my frequent absences and unavoidable interruptions of our family life to which, they assure me, they have by now become accustomed. Judi Weisgraber of Saint Mary's College, California has been most gracious and competent in typing both drafts of this manuscript and performing other tedious tasks commonly involved in such an enterprise. Saint Mary's College and the Institute of International Studies, University of California, Berkeley were also most forthcoming with much-needed support.

S.Z.
Moraga, California, April 1982

1 WHY AND HOW KHOMEINI SUCCEEDED

Although the focus of this book is on Iran since the 1979 revolution, an understanding of how and why that revolution succeeded in bringing Khomeini to power is indispensable for putting events since 1979 into their proper perspective. Much has been written on the causes of the 1979 revolution by scholars, journalists and diplomats alike. Some who played a critical role from its inception until the deviation from its original course some time in December 1979, when a controversial Islamic constitution was adopted, have also publicized their accounts. To evaluate the academic worth or the objectivity of all these accounts is beyond the scope of this study. What is evident is that the whole true story of the revolution remains to be told. More time needs to elapse before a definitive account of the revolution can be offered. Thus, for example, former President Carter and his National Security Adviser, Zbigniew Brzezinski, are still to be heard from. On the Iranian side, Mehdi Bazargan, Generals Gharabaghi and Fardoust, Banisadr and the late Beheshti, men who have or had intimate knowledge of the critical events between 16 January and 11 February 1979, have, by and large, been silent or their knowledge has been inaccessible to researchers and specialists.

To contend that the full story of this momentous event cannot yet be told does not mean that aspects of the revolution cannot be studied. This writer and many others have attempted to do so over the last few years.[1] Some of the American diplomats serving in the field or in various intelligence and State Department agencies have also disclosed their personal knowledge of these events.

For the purpose of this study, instead of reviewing the totality of circumstances and causes which gave birth to the revolution, the author intends to ask a different set of questions under the general heading of 'How Khomeini Dominated the Revolution'. This is done because one of the author's chief assumptions is that Khomeini's total leadership was unplanned and avoidable. It is further contended that barely three months after his seizure of power, the majority of the anti-Shah political groups and personalities began to realize their errors in pledging loyalty to him, and one after another deserted him.

By the revolution's first anniversary Khomeini had already lost the support of secular-liberal forces. By the end of another year

1

non-fundamentalist Islamic groups and anti-Soviet leftist organizations had joined the opposition. More significantly, towards the end of 1979 four of the grand Ayattolahs began to oppose him with varying degrees of vehemence. Put differently, what began as an authentic and anti-dictatorial popular revolution based on a broad coalition of all anti-Shah forces was soon transformed into an Islamic fundamentalist power-grab, in the process of which that coalition disintegrated irreversibly.

This was not merely a peaceful and democratic transfer of power from one group to another. It entailed a particular form of radicalization of the revolution. It had to do with the form and substance of the new Iranian political system. Who could rule the country, in the interest of whom and with what degree of accountability, were the critical issues at stake. The absence of a consensus of response to these and similar issues, and more significantly the failure to develop a legitimate mechanism to resolve the existing differences of perception of Iran's new social and political system, have heavily affected the course of events since 1979.

With regard to Khomeini's seizure of control of the revolutionary coalition and his subsequent transformation of the course of the revolution, attention should be paid both to external and to internal causes.

Since the deposed Pahlavi regime relied heavily on the USA, the American connection with events in Iran in 1978-9 must be probed. By the same token, since the disintegration of the armed forces enabled the revolutionary forces to change the power transition from a fairly peaceful one into a violent insurrectionary one, the collapse of the Imperial Army requires careful scrutiny.

The American Connection

Most accounts of American behaviour, particularly in the latter phase of the year-long revolutionary turmoil, seem to agree on several cogent factors:[2] first, the incoherence and confusion of the Carter Administration; secondly, a State Department seemingly hypnotized by an abstract model of human rights; thirdly, a weakened and undermined intelligence community which was incapable of predicting the crisis or, when it began to unfold, of making a correct assessment of what it portended. These three factors combined to produce a débâcle for the United States in Iran, with far-reaching ramifications, many of which have not yet been fully comprehended.

The American authors Michael Ledeen and William Lewis offer one of the best analyses of the American dilemma in the Iranian revolution.[3] According to them, not only had high government functionaries such as Brzezinski made their opposition to the Shah known before they joined the Carter Administration, but important Democratic senators like Kennedy, Mondale, Cranston, Church and Fraser had gone on record criticizing various aspects of US–Iranian relations. Within the staffs of these senators, influential advisers in international affairs had long before joined anti-Shah groups: among them was Robert Hunter, the former foreign-policy adviser to Senator Kennedy. When accompanying Kennedy as a guest of the Shah, he was denied an audience with the Iranian ruler in order to present his misgivings about human rights violations in Iran.

Within the National Security Council (NSC) Brzezinski and Hunter were not the only ones with reservations about the Shah. David Aaron, deputy assistant to the President for national security affairs and a close collaborator of Vice-President Mondale, had declared that 'This administration is different. If the Shah thinks that he will get all the arms that he wants, he shall have surprizes.' This view was shared by other members of the Council and it accurately reflected that of Mondale.

Kennedy, Mondale, Cranston, Church and Fraser, known as the 'Vietnam era' senators, supported these critics of the Shah in the NSC. They felt it was immoral for the USA to provide an uninterrupted flow of arms to a ruler who was guilty of grave violations of human rights. But among the close associates of Carter's foreign-policy establishment there was neither unanimity nor consistency concerning the Iranian crisis.

At the outset reports from the embassy in Iran were by and large optimistic. William Sullivan, who replaced Richard Helm as US ambassador, reflected the views of his predecessor by portraying basically a monarch who exercised total control and a military sufficiently strong to resist attack from any radical neighbours. Did it, therefore, follow that the Shah could continue his liberalization policies? If there was a link between the Shah's strength and his ability to liberalize Iranian society, would it not follow that the US should simultaneously enhance the position of the Shah?

Few in the USA realized the inherent contradictions between these two factors. Liberalization for the educated Iranians meant the loosening of the Shah's grip on power. It meant genuinely free elections, a constitutional democracy, a free press, and in short the transformation of the Iranian political system from a dynastic autocracy to a responsible democratic state. For these Iranians, those who thought this transformation might be achieved without an erosion of the Shah's power were simply uneducated or myopic.

Why the US embassy could not comprehend the contradictions between the two propositions is the subject of much speculation. Ledeen and Lewis feel that the two ambassadors, each for personal and career reasons, were reluctant to unsettle their superiors in Washington with facts which they were not ready to accept.[4] Other sources indicate that the two were as much victims of the perplexity of Iranian politics and the complexity of the Shah's personality as were many perceptive Iranian insiders in close contact with the American officials.

The beginning of 1978 was thus marked by a formal US policy which relied on the premise that the Shah's strength would not be sapped by progressive liberalization. President Carter had set the tone by his infamous New Year toast in Tehran in which he observed that Iran, 'under the Shah's enlightened leadership', had become 'an island of stability'. The best estimate of the expectations of US officials about the Iranian situation was that once the President had set the main tone of the policy it should be permitted to proceed, and if it generated undesirable results then it could be re-evaluated and revised if necessary.

Within the foreign-policy establishment there were those who wished that the policy would not succeed, for its failure would simply prove them right. There were others who thought it was essential to persuade the Shah to implement such liberalization policies as would eventually democratize the Iranian political system and make the Shah dispensable.

The period between January and August was a period of 'wait and see' for the United States. Major upheavals in Qom in January, and in Tabriz in February when for two days it was in the hands of insurgents, had been successfully contained. Daily the Shah would announce the release of more political prisoners, and the controlled media was given a little more freedom in news coverage. At the end of June a confident Shah was quoted as saying that he would simply not permit a second Tabriz as long as he was alive.[5] US embassy reports were by and large positive. Ambassador Sullivan decided to leave on his summer vacation and was physically absent until late September. Every indication disproved the alleged contradiction in a dual policy towards Iran which sought simultaneously to strengthen the Shah and to liberalize Iran's political system.

This optimistic view was verified in testimony before various congressional committees. Thus, in late August the Central Intelligence Agency (CIA) could estimate that the country was neither in a prerevolutionary nor a revolutionary situation. The Defense Intelligence Agency (DIA) in its 28 September estimates could foresee another ten years of rule by the Shah.[6]

Bearing in mind that the events of August and September were the turning point in Iranian political developments, these optimistic estimates would seem, to say the least, outdated by about sixty days. Blaming over-reliance on the SAVAK (A Farsi acronym for State Security and Information Organization) or restrictions on CIA and DIA activities due to President Carter's objection to secret operations for this massive intelligence failure, would not suffice either. By the time the US ambassador returned to his post in Tehran in late September, he had sufficient time and reliable sources to ascertain the gravity of the Iranian developments. As will be seen later, at the end of October the ambassador still believed that his Iranian contacts, both inside and outside the government, were unnecessarily panicky and that the dual policy of backing the Shah and his liberalization policies would succeed.

Were the American officials the only foreign observers guilty of misinformation and misconception about Iran in the summer of 1978? Ledeen and Lewis have credited the French and Israeli diplomatic and intelligence services with a more accurate and perceptive analysis of the Iranian situation. This author had the opportunity of talking to a number of Israeli officials including Uri Lubrani, head of Israel's mission to Tehran, during a flight out of Tehran on 17 July 1978. The Israeli officials were most knowledgeable about two interrelated aspects of the Iranian scene. One was the activities of the religious opposition, and the other was the political mood of the Bazaar. Relying on a community of fairly well-integrated Iranian Jewish merchants, they predicted rightly that the Bazaar would play the critical role in the outcome of the ongoing struggle. Liberalization policies were immaterial for them. These policies might influence the students and the Western-educated secular upper middle classes, but the lower classes, the small Bazaar traders who were subjected to Islamization by the Shia clergy, would not be impressed by the effects of the political Westernization of Iran.[7]

When pressed for a prognosis, the Israeli diplomats appeared not to be of the same mind. Some gave the Shah another two or three years; others thought his departure would be voluntary, in favour of his son and by a peaceful transition of power. None underestimated the Shah's ability to use the military to safeguard his reign. By the same token none even conceived the slightest notion that the Shah's determination would become progressively paralysed to the point that he would become a victim of political and personal fatalism. As a precautionary measure, however, in August the chief Israeli diplomat, Dr Karni, informed the Iranian Jewish community that they should be aware of the progressive Islamization of the lower-class Bazaari population and maintain a low profile in their commercial activities. In point of fact that advice was not well heeded. The Jewish community proved no more prescient as to the exact course of the Iranian turmoil than other segments of the population.

At any rate, as the tempo of public agitation increased and the regime failed to show any determination in coping with the crisis in a measured and well-thought-out manner, the United States too began to show signs of reassessing the Iranian situation. As far as the Shah was concerned, however, this process had begun not in mid autumn but in mid summer of 1978. His testimony on America's withdrawal of support is unambiguous. 'I did not know it then – but it is clear to me that the Americans wanted me out', he wrote shortly before his death.[8] By the time the leaders of the Western democracies met on 4 January 1979 in Guadeloupe, the Shah believed that France, West Germany and Britain had come to accept the American position. Nor was this totally unprecedented. The Shah felt that the withdrawal of US support evolved gradually. Thus, the student demonstrations in Washington in November 1977 were part of an organized effort to discredit him and his government to which the oil companies and the CIA contributed financially and otherwise. It was inconceivable to the Shah that the US government could not have prevented a student rally within the earshot of the president if it had really wished to do so. The suspicion that the USA might have been in collusion with the Soviets also worried the Shah: he related a conversation with Nelson Rockefeller in which he wondered whether it was conceivable that the Americans and the Russians had divided the world between them.

President Carter's concern for human rights is blamed for playing a considerable role in the Shah's downfall. Puzzled at US insistence that there was no contradiction between supporting him and pushing for liberalizing his regime, he tried hard to secure America's unequivocal support for his regime. Nearly all accounts agree that instead of unconditional support he received mixed signals. His dilemma was aggravated further, on the one hand, because he felt US support was conditional on continuous liberalization policies in Iran and, on the other, because he feared pursuing such policies in the midst of an economic crisis was bound to undermine his regime. Numerous attempts were made by the Shah to ascertain the real intentions of the USA during the crisis in the autumn of 1978. One particular attempt early in October involved former Prime Minister Amir Abbas Hoveyda (later executed), US Ambassador William Sullivan and a special envoy with close ties to the latter. Frustrated at the failure of diplomatic and official channels to secure an ironclad guarantee of US support for the Shah, Hoveyda, who had been just recently dismissed as Minister of the Imperial Court, summoned a former chancellor of the National University whom he believed to have close ties with the United States, to find out what Washington was really up to.[9] When the former chancellor assured him that he did not believe the USA was fomenting public protest against the Shah, Hoveyda expressed agreement with his analysis but thought that the Shah should accept US non-involvement in the worsening turmoil. Hoveyda asked the former chancellor to get in touch with Ambassador Sullivan and report back to him so that he could try once more to assure the Shah that the Americans were not behind the opposition campaign. In a lengthy discussion with Sullivan, the former chancellor was told that he had full authority to express total US support for the Shah.

> Here is a copy of a top-secret (for your eyes only) report that I just sent to Washington to say that the Shah was irreplaceable and that the US should go all the way with him. The trouble with you guys is that you panic easily. Our people report that the opposition meetings are poorly attended and organized haphazardly; and therefore they should be regarded as a nuisance and not a threat.

Reassured by the ambassador, the former chancellor reported back to Hoveyda, who arranged an immediate audience with the Shah to assure him that the USA, based on all available evidence, was not supporting the opposition. Hoveyda's emissary found it most difficult to convince a suspicious Shah who would either listen in dazed silence or cite some recent examples of American setbacks elsewhere in the world as proof of US susceptibility to vacillation in supporting traditional allies. Thus, for example, he cited the assassination of South Vietnamese President Diem, which he was certain was the work of CIA agents. The Shah was convinced also that the rise to power of Fidel Castro was greatly facilitated by American agents working against the former

Cuban dictator Batista.

But that was not all. He knew that some US embassy officials were in touch with the opposition leaders, especially those of the National Front and those of Bazargan's Iran Liberation Movement. When Hoveyda's emissary pointed out that low-echelon embassy officials traditionally contacted these personalities so that they could write objective and detailed analyses for their superiors, and that what was significant was what the ambassador would do with these reports, the Shah was not convinced. He was aware of that routine practice, but these were not normal times. Contacts with opposition groups were bound to be construed as signs of the erosion of America's support, particularly when the new administration pressed him to pursue liberalization policies.

During his meeting with Sullivan, Hoveyda's envoy was urged to assure the Shah of his, Sullivan's, and the US government's sincerity. If the Shah did not trust him, he was willing to resign. All the Shah had to do was to indicate his displeasure to the US government which, because it was so desperate to reassure the Shah, would immediately order Sullivan's reassignment. But the Shah did not believe that his troubles would be solved by changing the US ambassador. He seemed resigned to the fact that the decision to withdraw American support was a matter of high policy unlikely to be affected by changes in diplomatic personnel.

Although the Shah's mind could not be radically changed, the indefatigable Hoveyda, upon hearing the account of that audience, tried once more to secure another direct assurance from the highest US authorities. His envoy went to Washington, DC and, through Ambassador Zahedi, arranged a meeting with Brzezinski. After he was briefed about the Shah's continuing doubts, he proposed to contact the sovereign directly and without intermediaries. At the end of October President Carter's National Security Adviser telephoned the Shah to convey to him, in the strongest possible terms, America's unshakeable support. A dubious Shah listened passively. Neither citing any special grievance nor expressing unhappiness with American diplomatic personnel, he expressed his gratitude. Barely a week later Hoveyda was arrested during the Shah's 'anti-corruption' campaign. When in January he was offered freedom and exile from Iran, the deeply hurt, long-time Prime Minister refused them. In a real sense Hoveyda had become another victim of the Shah's dilemma in comprehending the real intentions of the USA towards him and Iran in the autumn of 1978. Having completed his historic mission, the former university chancellor left the country before the revolution amidst the deep sense of helplessness and despair which pervaded all officials around the Shah.

In retrospect there is little doubt that the US diplomatic mission was not of one mind in evaluating the country's internal developments. The embassy was staffed by a number of well-qualified Farsi-speaking personalities. In annual visits to Iran dating from the early 1960s, the author found the quality of the political secretaries of the embassy vastly improved. Thus a major fault that some analysts have found with the US embassy staff, namely their overall ignorance of the forces of opposition in the autumn of 1978, is not fully borne out by reliable evidence. However, Ledeen and Lewis contend that nobody in the CIA, the State Department and the academic community understood Khomeini.[10]

Some who had met him in Nejaf, or later in France, felt he was a moderate and for the most part mainly a symbol of the unity of the anti-Shah coalition. Others believed that the forces of opposition were led by the leaders of the secular National Front, men like Karim Sanjabi, Mehdi Bazargan, Shahpour Bakhtiar and Dr Gholamhossein Sadighi. A further general criticism related to the unfamiliarity of US officials with Khomeini's writings and sermons since his exile from Iran in 1963.

Several points should be made about the above. In the first place, nearly all of these critical evaluations are retrospective. The truth is that no one except those who had a blind faith in the quality of Khomeini's leadership anticipated his total domination of the Iranian revolution by the spring of 1979. Khomeini in exile was underestimated by some of his closest associates, ranging from the veteran nationalist leaders to such senior Shia Ayattolahs as Shariatmadari and Shirazi. It was only after his return to Iran and the establishment of the Islamic Republic that Iranians and foreigners alike began to study his writings and observe his political style.

Nor is it quite accurate to say that US officials were universally ignorant of the religious dimension of Iran's incipient revolutionary movement. John Stempel, a Berkeley PhD fluent in Farsi and a political secretary at the US embassy, as early as in the summer of 1977 had advised his academic colleagues of the rising influence of the clergy within the country.[11] A year later he and some of his colleagues, very much like some of their Israeli counterparts, were fully immersed in the literature of the radical clergy. Indeed Khomeini's latest sermons, widely circulated in Iran through inexpensive cassettes, were regularly transcribed by the embassy and reported to the top officials.

Had they foreseen the emergence of Khomeini as more than a symbolic leader of the anti-Shah revolution, at least by early December, they could have interpreted his role more accurately. In fact, for nearly fifteen years Khomeini had been issuing appeals and circulating sermons for a general uprising against the Shah, but with little influence on Iran's political development. The Shah's regime gave a higher priority to the urban guerrilla operations within Iran than to a clerical leader in exile in Iraq. At no time did the government contemplate banning the annual pilgrimage of tens of thousands of Iranians to Nejaf and Karbala, where many of them would meet with Khomeini and pass on to him the religious donations collected in the Bazaars of Iran. Nor did the Shah press the Iraqi government to restrict Khomeini's activity, at least after the Iraq–Iran *rapprochement* of June 1975.

If his writings and pronouncements were generally ignored, it is primarily because until late in 1978 his political significance was negligible. The Iranian revolution was born within the country and the contribution of exiled personalities, whether religious or secular, assumed significance only when its momentum had picked up by the mid-autumn of 1978.

A more plausible criticism of the USA concerns the misconceptions and at times the ludicrously benign view of Khomeini after the triumph of the revolution. Clearly, both Ambassador Andrew Young, who thought of Khomeini as a kind of saint, and the State Department's Iran Country Director Henry Precht, who believed some American newspapers were misreading and exaggerating Khomeini's early writings, proved to be wrong.[12] But here again it is important to note that in his first few months in power a majority of Iranian and foreign observers of the revolution were so enthusiastic about its authentic and popular basis that their judgements about Khomeini were coloured by wishful idealism. About a year into his tenure the true nature of Khomeini's rule, the determination to monopolize power, and his absolute conviction that a Shia theocracy was both desirable and practical, awakened even the most persistent of his former admirers.

How the United States fared with Khomeini in power will be examined later. Suffice it to say that an American connection with the Iranian revolution did exist. Whether or not this connection could have evolved differently and the exact nature of its influence on the course of the revolution are not matters of unanimous consent. As will be seen, the Iranian military leaders were acutely aware of this connection and endeavoured assiduously to utilize it, first for preserving the army and later for effecting a peaceful transition of allegiance to Khomeini.

The Huyser Mission and the Iranian Army

The dispatch in mid-January of General Robert Huyser, Deputy-Commander of US forces in Europe, has been the subject of much controversy since the overthrow of the Shah. At the time of his arrival the different forces engaged in political turmoil associated several tasks with his mission:

(1) The High Command of the Imperial Army came to believe that his mission was initially that of facilitating the departure of American military advisers from Iran and securing the safety of sophisticated American weapons, especially F14 aircraft.

(2) That initial mission assumed a political character once the Carter Administration decided, in early January, that the Shah could not retain power. Huyser and the entire American mission in Iran then became instrumental in facilitating the Shah's departure.

(3) As far as the revolutionary forces were concerned, Huyser was also capable of convincing the Iranian Generals either fully to support the Bakhtiar government once the Shah had left, or to stage a coup when Khomeini returned. However, the revolutionary forces determined that the Imperial Army should be disbanded with the minimum of dislocation and violence instead of being allowed to transfer allegiance to the new regime.

The revolutionary forces, led by such personalities as Mohammad Beheshti, Mehdi Bazargan, Dr Yaddolah Sahabi and Hashem Sabaghian, were so convinced of the total domination of the Imperial Army by the American military mission that they believed the Huyser mission could play a critical role in determining the attitude of the army in the final stage of the political upheaval. In negotiating with the General and other American officials they pursued an extremely pragmatic strategy. First, they expressed complete agreement with the USA that post-revolutionary Iran needed a well-organized army to protect Iranian territorial integrity and to ensure that no external power would take advantage of the turmoil to intervene. Secondly, they pledged that the safety of US military advisers and sophisticated US-made weapons would not be jeopardized. Thirdly, once the Shah had left the country, they concentrated all their efforts towards convincing the military of the futility of supporting the Bakhtiar government, and used Huyser as a lever to convince the armed forces that even the US government had come to recognize that Bakhtiar's government was doomed to failure. Fourthly, in the period between 1 and 12 February these representatives of the revolutionary forces pursued one fundamental objective: to ensure that Huyser would not instigate a coup, and that if the Iranian military leaders tried to do so, he would dissuade them.

In pursuance of this final goal the revolutionary leaders were aided by several factors. The safety of US military personnel, the security of the sophisticated F14 aircraft, and the welfare of American citizens in Iran as a whole were all used to convince Huyser to go along with their position. Putting it bluntly, if the United States did not wish its personnel to be harmed or to allow uncontrolled, armed guerrillas, some with pro-Soviet sympathies, to gain access to its sophisticated weapons, General Huyser had better see to it that the military surrendered to the popular revolutionary forces.

In a fascinating account during his trial before the revolutionary military court, General Amirhossein Rabii disclosed some critical aspects of General Huyser's mission.[13] On 10 January Huyser attended a meeting of Iranian commanders and told them bluntly that the Shah should go. Rabii quoted the US General as stating that the Iranian people, like many others across the world, were no longer willing to accept a political system based on individual authority. His government was in agreement with this sentiment, which was also shared by the West European allies of the United States.

Once the Shah was gone, in a third session with the military commanders, the American General was quoted as having urged the Iranian Army leaders to come to terms with the revolutionary forces. Indeed, General Huyser gave them a list of the telephone numbers of Khomeini's representatives, and implied that they were awaiting their calls and were willing to negotiate an agreement designed to prevent further chaos and bloodshed. But it is important to recall that at that stage the government of Bakhtiar was still legally in power. The US attitude towards that government changed with the progress of events in Iran. Huyser told the Iranian commanders that the military should encourage Bakhtiar to approach Khomeini's representatives.

In return the Iranian High Command requested that Huyser should demand three concessions from Khomeini's forces: one, that Khomeini should postpone his return to Tehran pending the conclusion of negotiations with his representatives; two, that Khomeini should stop issuing inflammatory communiqués addressed to the Iranians; and three, that the BBC should be persuaded not to act as a channel of communication between Khomeini and the Iranian masses.

According to General Rabii at no point, at least in his presence, did Huyser instigate any move by the Army to stage a coup. Instead, the Army generals were urged to meet at Beheshti's residence, and later at Bazargan's, to discuss a peaceful settlement of the crisis. From his testimony and the account that Dr Bakhtiar has given the author, it appears that not until the Sunday morning triumph of the revolution did the Army leaders recognize that the USA was resigned to the collapse of Bakhtiar's government. Indeed, a day before the total collapse of that government, Saturday 10 Feburary 1979, martial-law administrator General Rahimi issued a declaration imposing a 4.30 p.m. curfew on Tehran. Khomeini's representative contacted the American embassy to find out whether General Rahimi's action had the support of General Huyser and the US government. When they were assured that the United States had no role in Rahimi's actions, Beheshti and Bazargan urged Khomeini to issue a blunt appeal to the people urging them to disobey the curfew and warning the military leaders not to move against the people.

It is apparent that at that stage at least some among the leadership of the Army wanted to use the proclaimed curfew in order to crush the rebellion of the Air Force technicians and cadets, which had begun the previous day. General Rabii has testified that a plan for the use of curfew hours to put down the rebellion of the Air Force cadets and technicians was discussed between Joint Chiefs of Staff and Premier Bakhtiar that Saturday morning. General Badrei, Commander of the Army, and General Nashat, Commander of the Imperial Guard, agreed to put their forces under the command of General Rahimi, the Tehran martial-law administrator. Dr Bakhtiar advocated the use of the Air Force for precision bombing of the Air Force Cadet Academy. Resistance to this plan came from Gharabaghi, the Chairman of the Joint Chiefs of Staff, who thought the military should not take pre-emptive action while negotiations with Khomeini's representatives were under way.

According to some of the former Iranian Generals now in exile, the American diplomatic and military missions in Tehran were contacted by Gharabaghi, to inquire about potential American reaction to measures by the military. Be that as it may, the curfew could not be imposed. About a million Tehranis filled the main thoroughfare of the capital city in defiance of the curfew. Sabaghian and Beheshti told the

US embassy that if General Huyser did not dissuade the military commanders from implementing their plan, neither the safety of the American military advisers nor the custody of sophisticated US-made weapons could be assured. Gharabaghi informed the beleaguered Dr Bakhtiar of division within the Army High Command and the impossibility of imposing the new curfew. When asked if General Huyser had been informed of the development, the Iranian General allegedly responded that the USA had received all the guarantees for the protection of its personnel dispersed in two military installations in the capital, from as high an authority as Beheshti. Two weeks later when the revolutionary forces were in complete control of all army garrisons and bases in the country, they saw to it that US personnel were flown safely out of the country. Once that was accomplished the revolutionaries demanded Huyser's prompt departure from Iran. Moreover, the new leaders of the country, notably Beheshti, took steps to silence some of the participants in the recent negotiations involving General Huyser and army leaders. Two who were executed, despite pledges that their lives would be spared, were General Rabii himself and General Moghaddam, a political adviser to Gharabaghi and the last head of the SAVAK.

In retrospect it is apparent that the victors in this drama were those shrewd negotiators for Khomeini, who succeeded in achieving the disintegration of the army, managed to insure against American intervention through the presence of General Huyser, and did so by reciprocating American acquiescence to the army's surrender by guaranteeing the safety of US citizens. When Beheshti emerged as the second strongest personality of the Islamic Republic, many of his opponents with first-hand knowledge of his role in the negotiations tried to discredit him. But Khomeini has always been convinced that these critical days were saved for the revolution by the negotiating skill and shrewdness of men like Beheshti, Sabaghian, and at a later stage Dr Ibrahim Yazdi. At the minimum they had succeeded in averting a delay in the victory of the revolution and prevented countless losses in life and property. As for General Huyser, there was no doubt that he accurately reflected the vacillation and indecisiveness of his government.

In June 1981, in testimony before a sub-committee of the US Congress, General Huyser expressed the view that the Iranian military had possessed the capability of restoring order and security to the country and he was puzzled as to why they did not attempt to do so.[14] He refused, however, to answer in open hearing questions about encouraging the Iranian military commanders to stage a coup or else to occupy the oil installations. He also revealed that when the Shah had decided to leave the country, many of his generals were eager to follow suit. One of Huyser's duties had been to convince them not to do so because he was fearful that leftist guerrillas might step into the vacuum and give the revolution a leftist orientation.

There are many other accounts of his mission, many of which reflect the particular bias of their authors. What is indisputable is that his mission to Iran was accompanied by the disintegration of the Imperial Army in the final days of the revolution. Whether or not the two facts are causally related is not as important as the belief of many Iranians that the neutralization and disintegration of the armed forces played an extremely significant role in facilitating the triumph of the revolutionary forces.

The Collapse of the Armed Forces

Not all aspects of the collapse of the armed forces have been fully understood. Some details will never become public because the participants in the drama were either silenced by the firing squads of the revolutionary regime or died in June 1981, when the opponents of that regime blasted the headquarters of the Islamic Republican Party. Others, like the provisional Prime Minister Mehdi Bazargan, are either unwilling or unable to give their accounts of what actually transpired when the Army declared its neutrality on Sunday 11 February 1979.

In what follows, original Farsi-language material, such as the testimony of high-ranking officers before revolutionary tribunals, a series of articles which appeared between 22 and 28 February in the authoritative newspaper, *Ayandegan*, as well as interviews with Bakhtiar, the last pre-revolution Prime Minister, and some of the Iranian Generals now in exile, will be utilized to uncover the true story of the army's disintegration.[15]

Towards the end of the autumn of 1978 most senior army officers believed that three main forces were dominant in the country: the popular forces, then led by Khomeini, dedicated to overthrowing the Shah; the Army under the command of the Shah; and the United States, represented by its diplomatic and military missions in Tehran. Many of them were convinced that the Shah had left the country on 16 January, hoping that the last-named of these forces would succeed in reaching an agreement with Khomeini's people which would keep the monarchy intact.

Two days after the departure of the Shah, units of the armed forces in Ahwaz and Dezful in Khuzistan province, to demonstrate their loyalty to the Shah and his government, opened fire on unarmed demonstrators. However, signals from the United States began to confuse the Shah's generals. Particularly disturbing was President Carter's press statement on 17 January in which he spoke of Iran's future government and expressed the hope that once the dust had settled, Iran would remain a friend of the United States. The Iranian Generals took it to mean that America, as the third dominant force, was hesitant in joining with the army in reaching an agreement with Khomeini.

A second signal which aggravated the Army's uneasiness was Carter's request to Khomeini on 20 January, 'to give Bakhtiar's government a chance'. For the American President to appeal to the still-exiled leader of the opposition to give the Prime Minister a chance simply meant that Carter was acknowledging Khomeini's power to crush Bakhtiar's government. Even though the intention appeared to be to foil the radical elements who might take advantage of the continuing strife, the senior army officers joined Bakhtiar in interpreting that statement with suspicion. Had it been followed by a consistent and well-defined policy, the Army would have had few grievances. But a few days later, on the question of Khomeini's return to Iran the United States once again sounded the alarm, now hinting that the imminent return of Khomeini would aggravate the situation and might even lead to the seizure of power by the military. What puzzled the Iranians was that if Khomeini was regarded as the main anti-communist bulwark, why should he not return to Iran to ensure the failure of the radical forces? If he was not so regarded, why should the president of a super-power give an incredible boost to Khomeini's prestige by appealing to him to give a chance to Bakhtiar's government? Compounding the confusion were the activities of non-governmental American personalities such as Ramsey Clark, who met Khomeini in Paris on 21 January and openly declared that he would strongly recommend that the USA should promptly abandon Bakhtiar.

Once Khomeini returned to Iran on 1 February, the most authoritative account of the position of the armed forces seems to indicate that:

(1) The Army's generals did not have the capacity to stage a military coup.

(2) By the same token, without the consent of the military an Islamic regime was unlikely to be established.

(3) Regular Army officers as yet were, by and large, fiercely loyal to

the Shah.

(4) The Shah's opponents within the military consisted mainly of some of the better educated members of the lower middle classes.

On Friday afternoon 9 February there occurred the first incidents involving Air Force technicians and the members of the Imperial Guard over the showing of the film of Khomeini's arrival in Tehran on the state television. This was followed the next morning by a more serious clash at the Air Force Training School between cadets and members of the Imperial Guard. However, neither of these two clashes was large scale or conclusive. All accounts indicate that the critical battle for the control of Tehran's military headquarters and police stations took place from 9 p.m. on Saturday to 7 a.m. on Sunday, over the occupation of the machine-gun factory. The battle for the factory was now joined by the armed guerrillas, who chose the factory deliberately for they knew its arsenals contained nearly 50,000 light machine guns. The guerrillas needed the weapons to arm the civilians and to strike the final blow against the armed forces.

In retrospect it was clear that, had the Army wanted, it could have prevented the capture of the machine-gun factory and the nearby arsenal, for the Imperial Guard, numbering about 30,000 well-armed and still loyal men, was at nearby Lavizan Camp.[16] General Rahimi, the martial law administrator, and General Rabii, the Air Force Commander, both testified during their trial that they had refused to do so because they did not wish to cause countless civilian casualties. The attack and the early-morning occupation of the factory and the arsenal swelled the ranks of armed guerrillas at least ten-fold. On Sunday morning the better-organized guerrillas surrounded the main Tehran garrisons of Eshratabad and Bagheshah, and by 10.30 that morning the Council of Army Commanders signed its now famous declaration of neutrality between the government and Khomeini supporters, calling on the soldiers and officers to return to their barracks.

The timing of the announcement on the state radio was also significant. Even though the state radio was under the control of the military, this important declaration was broadcast at 2 p.m., the regular newscast time. In the 3–4-hour interval the armed guerrillas who had surrounded these army bases finally broke in and gained access to many more thousands of light weapons. Since the announcement of neutrality had not yet been made, the Imperial Guard and other units continued resistance, causing more casualties. The Chairman of the Joint Chiefs of Staff, General Gharabaghi, was later blamed for the failure to broadcast the announcement promptly, but no action was taken against him because of his critical part in paving the way for the disintegration of the armed forces.[17] Indeed, he had a firm pledge from Khomeini, given through Beheshti, that his life would be spared if he succeeded in convincing the Army of the futility of remaining loyal to the Bakhtiar government.

At any rate, the capture of the machine-gun factory proved to be of tremendous value to the armed guerrillas. To date there is no reliable method of ascertaining which of the two main guerrilla forces, the Mojahedin or the Fedayeen, was responsible for that critical decision. What is obvious is that within 36 hours the armed guerrillas had succeeded in capturing seven of the army garrisons in the capital. As a result of the delay in the announcement of the Army's neutrality by the state radio, the capture of these bases resulted in considerable demoralization among the officers and a fair number of casualties on both sides. Some analysts have attributed the delay in the announcement to a plan worked out between Beheshti and General Gharabaghi.[18] This analysis holds that Khomeini did not wish the armed forces to remain intact because he knew that as long as they did so they would continue to pose an inherent threat to his regime. So rather than announcing the decision of their neutrality, which would permit the armed forces to retain their arms and simply return to barracks, it was essential to cause the disintegration of the armed forces by inciting clashes between them and the armed guerrillas. Only when a counter-force had been created and the army completely purged, could the Islamic Republic reinstate the military as the cohesive official armed forces of the country. In sum this analysis holds that Khomeini wanted the disintegration of the armed forces and not merely their neutrality, for if their allegiance to the Shah, nourished over four decades, could be so easily transferred to Khomeini, what assurance would there be that their allegiance would not be given to anti-government forces in the future? Once the precedent of the Army's prompt change of allegiance was established, it would be difficult to prevent its recurrence. Thus, it would be preferable to reduce its power and counter it by other armed organizations so that shifting allegiances would not play a critical role in determining the outcome of the struggle for power. For this reason the Revolutionary Guards were organized, and had it not been for the war with Iraq which began on 22 September 1980, the present Islamic Republic's armed forces would have been much smaller.

Needless to say, other techniques were also used to ensure that the

Army would remain loyal to the regime. In every major garrison Mullahs were appointed as prosecutors in the Islamic revolutionary courts, issuing harsh sentences against army officers found guilty of anti-revolutionary acts. In Tehran itself Hojatolislam Reyshahri has presided over the prosecutor's office with an iron hand.

An ironic by-product of the disintegration of the armed forces had to do with the later defection of the Mojahedin and their opposition to Khomeini. The Mojahedin advocated the complete abolition of the armed forces and their replacement by a so-called People's Revolutionary Army. Though Khomeini of course had no love for the armed forces, he resisted, knowing that the abolition of the army would create a vacuum into which the Mojahedin themselves could move. When, after the ousting of Banisadr in June 1981 the Mojahedin joined Banisadr and they together appealed to the armed forces to join them, Khomeini was quick to remind the Army that the Mojahedin had advocated the total abolition of Iran's armed forces and were therefore not to be trusted by the Army.

To conclude, Khomeini's success was evidently due to many factors, two of which were the American connection and the disintegration of the Army as the main pillar of the Shah's regime. Intentionally or otherwise, the first factor contributed to the Shah's decisional paralysis, while the second allowed an insurrectionary power-seizure rather than a non-violent transfer of the army's allegiance to the revolutionary leaders. These two combined to shape much of Iran's post-revolutionary political developments. Although an analysis of the other causes of Khomeini's success is outside the scope of this study, an examination of the unprecedented turmoil which Iran has been experiencing since 1979 will, hopefully, elucidate the main reasons for his ability to seize and retain power.

Notes

1. Apart from the author's *Iran's Revolutionary Upheaval* (Alchemy Books, San Francisco, 1979), two French works are notable: Brière, Claire and Blanchet, Pierre, *Iran: La Révolution Au Nom de Dieu* (Editions du Seuil, Paris, 1979); Balta, Paul and Rulleau, Claudine, *L'Iran Insurgé* (Editions Sindbad, Paris, 1979). Barry Rubin's *Paved with Good Intentions: The American Experience and Iran* (Oxford University Press, New York, 1980) and Amin Saikal's *The Rise and Fall of the Shah* (Princeton University Press, Princeton, 1980) are also noteworthy.
2. Michael Ledeen and William Lewis, *Debacle: The American Failure in Iran* (Alfred A. Knopf, New York, 1981).
3. *Ibid.*, Excerpts of this work appeared in *L'Exprès*, No. 1564, Paris. 3 July 1981 under the title 'La débâcle americaine en Iran.'

4. *L'Exprès*, No. 1564, p. 76.

5. Personal interview with former Iranian Prime Minister Dr. Jamshid Amuzegar, Tehran, 5 July 1978.

6. *L'Exprès*, No. 1564, p. 77.

7. Data released by the government indicated the release of 2312 political prisoners of a total of 3112, between January and October 1978. *Rastakhiz*, Tehran, 21 January to 28 October 1978.

8. Mohammad Reza Pahlavi, *Answer to History* (Stein & Day, New York, 1980), p. 165.

9. Extended interview London, January 1980 and Berkeley, California, June 1981.

10. *L'Exprès*, No. 1564, p. 78.

11. Personal interview at the Institute of International Studies, University of California, Berkeley, 11 August 1977.

12. *L'Exprès*, No. 1564, p. 78.

13. Report on his trial, *Ettelaat*, Tehran, 28–30 March 1979.

14. Quoted in *Iran Post*, 1 July 1981.

15. Personal interview, Paris, 27 December 1979 and 12 April 1981. *Ayandegan* newspaper became the largest-circulation morning newspaper after the revolution but was later banned when the IRP took over its press in April 1980.

16. *Ayandegan*, 24 February 1979.

17. In April 1980 exiled Iranian groups in Paris received a handwritten letter from the general pleading innocent to the charge of betrayal of his country and the armed forces, and promising to reveal details of 'foreign plots' against Iran as soon as it was possible. Quoted in ARA (Farsi acronym for *Iran Liberation Army*, the best known of several exiled army groups in Europe) Paris, 25 April 1980.

18. *Ayandegan*, 27 February 1979.

2   THE DYNAMICS OF POWER

With the success of the revolution major political and practical problems emerged. The first basic issue had to do with the disintegration of the military and the active participation of numerous armed groups in the final days of revolution. Khomeini's assessment of the relative strengths of the various political forces led him to believe that the military, despite its disintegration, had to be considered as the most significant potential threat to the revolutionary regime. His strategy in dealing with this issue was based on a massive purge of the officers corps on the one hand, and the creation of a militia from amongst the guerrillas who had fought relentlessly in the violent seizure of power.

Neither of the two goals could be achieved with ease. Excessive pressure on the officers corps could have prompted military action against the infant regime. Forcible disarming of guerrilla groups with diverse ideologies would have required sufficiently large security forces whose loyalty had not yet been tested. Moreover, the guerrilla groups, especially those of the Mojahedin and the Fedayeen, were all claimants to power and could not easily be persuaded to surrender their arms as a symbol of their new political power.

On the morrow of revolution there were at least three more claimants to power. There were the militant Moslem clergy, some of whose members had participated in the armed struggle at the height of the turmoil. They showed neither modesty nor reservation in the scope of their claim or the justice of their cause. For them the revolution was waged in the name of, and for the sake of, Islam. If this required a complete purge or even the abolition of the Army and the disarming of the better-known guerrilla groups, so be it. The militant clergy recommended two significant measures to Khomeini immediately after 11 February. One was to punish the officer corps of the military on a massive scale, the other was an urgent plea to the public to turn in their arms at collection points set up deliberately in mosques and Islamic seminaries under the control of the clergy. They volunteered to preside over revolutionary courts and mete out swift and vengeful punishment against high-ranking officers. More will be said about the revolutionary courts later. But with regard to the disarming of the guerrillas, the best estimate is that not more than 5 to 10 per cent, of close to 300,000 weapons, in Tehran alone, were turned in.

The second claimants to power were the secular political groups who had joined Khomeini at the urging of Bazargan, and with the expectation that the secular-clerical coalition which had made the revolution a success would survive the overthrow of the Pahlavi dynasty. This group succeeded in sharing power within the Provisional Government until 5 November 1979.

A third claimant to power was the National Front and its various affiliates, which had expelled Bakhtiar from the organization when he agreed to become what was to be the Shah's last Prime Minister. It is, of course, essential to remember that all these four claimants to power had joined a broad coalition against the old regime and that the coalition had begun to crumble almost as soon as victory was achieved.

Except for the militant clergy, the other claimants to power came to believe that a primarily secular liberation movement was being transformed into an Islamic fundamentalist revolution, seeking to substitute the autocratic Pahlavi system with a theocratic Shia one, that Ayattolah Khomeini was in a real sense the creation of the revolution rather than its primary creator, and that internal conflict was unlikely to be resolved by the denial of the legitimate claims of all groups who had participated in the revolution.

Another point made by the non-clerical groups was that the revolutionary movement had begun as a protest against political oppression, economic disparity, moral and material corruption, and the close identification in international politics with the West, led by the United States. This protest movement had become progressively radicalized until it had destroyed the Pahlavi dynasty in a violent insurrection.[1] In the process opposition forces had coalesced into a broad and popularly based movement encompassing parties and groups from the entire spectrum of ideology, class, ethnic and religious affiliation. At the end it had acquired those characteristics that theorists of revolutionary change commonly associate with a genuine political revolution. That is to say, once the use of violence had been sanctioned, the momentum of the Iranian movement as a struggle to alter the political order had become irreversible.

Members of the revolutionary coalition had contributed to this struggle in accordance with their ideological dedication and organizational expertise. The non-clerical groups would not deny that the Shia clergy had rendered a vital service in broadening the popular basis of support for the revolution. Its grass-roots activity, its skilful exploitation of such Shiite concepts as *Shahadat*, martyrdom, and the just struggle against *Sultane Zalem*, an oppressive and morally corrupt secular ruler, were acknowledged.

The single most effective contribution of the Shia clergy, despite a mixed record of co-existence with the secular Shah, was recognized to be its unity on the question of the legitimacy and righteousness of passive resistance at the first, and ultimately of armed struggle against the regime. However, the secular, and in particular the guerrilla organizations, denied that the Shia clergy had either pioneered armed struggle or carried its heaviest burden. While Khomeini's advocacy of militancy was acknowledged, the positions enunciated by other Shia leaders such as Mohammad Kazem Shariatmadari and his less militant followers residing in Iran were also noted. For instance, until as late as August 1978 most of them had confined their political demands to a reinstatement of the 1906 constitution, providing for the election of a five-man Shia council to supervise the compatibility of secular laws with Islamic principles.[2]

Nor had they advocated an Islamic republic to replace the Pahlavi monarchy. It was only after the momentum of the revolutionary mobilization and the prospect of military-civilian conflict so intensely radicalizing the revolutionary coalition that they, too, had been compelled to full participation. The secular claimants of power, moreover, suspected that the espousal of the radical objectives may have been for tactical reasons, so that the unity of purpose and the coherence of action might generate maximum impact. In other words, some of the clerical leaders had been swept away by the outpouring of a massive, popular anti-monarchy sentiment, and few were able to contemplate either the short-range or long-range consequences of their actions. For all these reasons militant clerics were expected to distinguish between the committed and radical groups in proportion to their role in the successful insurrection.

As to the National Front, its claim to a share of power was above all a historical claim. The Front rightly considered itself as the most consistent opponent of the Pahlavi regime, since from as far back as the early 1950s. Yet it seemed impotent to acquire the leadership of the revolutionary movement, which Khomeini acquired almost by default.

Why was he able to impose his demands on the less militant Shia and the more secular leaders such as Dr Karim Sanjabi and Mehdi Bazargan of the National Front, who flocked to Neauphle-le-Château in France throughout November and December, in search of his sanction for courses of action they were contemplating? It is now known that Khomeini's perseverance swayed the first echelon of the National Front leadership from accepting the Shah's overtures for the formation of a coalition government.[3] It was he who refused to accept the legitimacy of any accommodating gesture toward the Shah, even for tactical purposes. And once he had returned to Iran he succeeded in instigating the insurrection which overthrew the lesser-known National Front personality Shahpour Bakhtiar for having dared to do so.

It appears that his success was largely due to the absence in Iran of any nationally recognized secular leader of the stature of the late Dr Mohammad Mossadegh. It was, secondly, due to his rapid rise as the sole fully politicized Ayattolah with an impeccable record of hostility toward the Shah. The revolutionary coalition was also in need of a dramatic leader able to interpret correctly the Shah's successive and belated concessions as signs of inherent weakness. His obstinate refusal to return to Iran unless the Shah left the country, raised the level of tense anticipation for the return of the Imam, which in turn served to complete the cycle of revolutionary change. Herein lies the explanation for the vast reserve of gratitude and support on which Khomeini has so far been able to capitalize, despite enormous adversities.

In coping with these adversities he has been prone to utilize tactics and strategies commonly practised by Iranian leaders in recent history such as Reza Khan in the late 1920s, Dr Mossadegh in the 1950s, or indeed the deposed Shah in the 1960s and 1970s. One such tactic was to consolidate one's power-base by dividing one's enemies. Once the sources of threat, imaginary or real, were perceived, the revolutionary regime would set out to destroy those which it identified as irreconcilable, and to isolate and neutralize those which it saw as less imminent or formidable.

Another traditional tactic has been the utilization of 'foreign links' for the purpose of either breaking the resistance of adversaries or maintaining a high degree of visibility for 'foreign enemies' of the revolution. Similarly, the phenomenon of 'counter-revolution' as a catch-all concept linking domestic and foreign foes was used increasingly as the revolutionary regime struggled through its infancy.

The net result of the successful utilization of a combination of these tactics by Khomeini was that one by one the last three claimants to power were removed from the scene. The revolutionary regime legitimized the exclusive claim of militant Islam through a series of institutional measures.

At the outset it tolerated a provisional government representing the third claimants to power, namely the secular political groups. This government soon became entangled in conflict with two other hierarchies of power, one in the form of the Revolutionary Council and the other in the hundreds of local committees with their own armed guerrillas acting as their enforcers.

The Provisional Government

Mehdi Bazargan, who was nominated by Khomeini on 5 February, as the first Prime Minister of the revolutionary regime even before the Bakhtiar government was overthrown, organized a provisional government which on the formal level represented the new regime.

Except for one major difference which proved quite troublesome for the provisional government, nothing in its composition or institutional foundation represented a radical departure from precedent. That major exception concerned the jurisdiction of the Ministry of Justice over the existing court system.

In two ways this exception was significant. First, the revolutionary regime had to deal with the purge of prominent figures of the former regime. Could this be done through the normal judicial procedures, notoriously cumbersome and dilatory in Iran? Did the revolutionary emergency allow for setting up revolutionary courts to mete out swift, harsh justice? Secondly, and related to the above, was a pledge by both the more devout religious personalities in the provisional government, and Khomeini himself, to revamp Iran's legal system and infuse into it as many of the traditional Islamic *Sharia* concepts as feasible. Thus, the issue of purging the country in order to entrench the revolutionary regime in power was a critical question both in its short-range and long-range repercussions.

In the first post-revolutionary phase the secular and centrist groups, while favouring the swift punishment of royalist Army leaders and some of the more corrupt civilian associates of the Shah, did not welcome a drastic Islamization of the judicial system. On the other hand, the leftist groups and the clerical elements, for quite divergent reasons, favoured a broader concept of retribution against the largest cross-section of the officials of the former regime. The left supported and indeed violently clamoured for such a purge as an ideological and tactical goal. The leftist groups appeared to believe that the more radical the transformation of the bureaucracy and other institutions, the better their opportunity to gain power, or at least to acquire a share in its exercise.

For the extremist religious groups the reason was their dedication to the Islamization of the revolution and the construction of a theocratic Islamic state. They believed that once the precedents of revolutionary Islamic courts invoking broad Qoranic injunctions, such as 'corruption on earth' and 'fighting God' to punish former enemies were established, it would be only a matter of time before the judicial system would become fully Islamicized. This issue soon became one of the incipient causes of dissension for the new regime.

Equally dissentient was the emergence of competing centres of power. Apart from the Provisional Government, Khomeini had already established a secret revolutionary council, first with five and later with twelve to fifteen members. At the outset this clergy-dominated council exercised both legislative and judicial authority, the former by enacting laws and regulations either in co-operation with the provisional government or independently from it. The latter was exercised through its overall supervision of the Islamic revolutionary courts. A further function of the council was its supervision of the process of drafting a new constitution.

In all three areas the relationship between the council and the government proved extremely uncomfortable and ultimately irreconcilable. Khomeini himself, possessing neither administrative nor responsible political experience, or intimate knowledge of contemporary Iran, failed to smooth out that relationship. Compounding the matter was the insistence of thousands of local revolutionary committees, themselves an outgrowth of the strike committees of the pre-revolutionary period, upon sharing in governmental authority.[4]

The Bazargan government was clearly doomed from the very outset. Three reshuffles and frequent threats of resignation did not improve its fortunes.

About a month before his resignation on 5 November, Bazargan made some revealing statements concerning the proliferation of power centres in Iran since the revolution.[5] Having earlier compared his government with the handle of a pocket knife whose blade was in others' hands, Bazargan declared that his government was certainly not governing Iran. Nor did Khomeini do so alone.

Formally it is my government which rules Iran, ideologically it is Khomeini, his close associates and the Pasdaran who exercise authority over the country. Additionally there are revolutionary courts and countless clerics who in the name of the continuation of the revolution have taken over the control of towns and cities and have caused the central government indescribable headaches.

Though he was reluctant to blame Khomeini for the Provisional Government's inability to govern effectively, he acknowledged that Khomeini's lack of managerial experience had been a major flaw. After being used only to acting as an opposition leader, Khomeini was suddenly entrusted with governing the entire country.

Bazargan's political relations with Khomeini were extremely difficult. 'Our difficulties date back to the time that he was still in Paris where I urged upon him a gradual strategy in our struggle against the Shah.' Bazargan had wanted to overthrow the Shah by the gradual mobilization of the masses, beginning with the schools and universities and extending to the bureaucracy and the Army. If they were not sufficiently educated in the value of freedom and democracy and a revolution was thrust upon them, a new dictator would emerge in the ensuing chaos and disorder.

According to Bazargan, Khomeini had opposed gradualism, believing that the time was then ripe for a popular revolution and that to miss the opportunity would be a serious blunder. But even he came around to Khomeini's viewpoint on many occasions. The provisional Prime Minister confessed that had they shown more patience, they would not have encountered the existing chaos in Iran. That the situation during his tenure was chaotic has been readily admitted by Bazargan.

In a memorable interview with the Italian journalist Oriana Fallaci, Bazargan singled out the promptness and decisiveness of the revolution as the major cause of the ensuing difficulties. Once the authority of the central government had been completely destroyed, it became extremely difficult to construct a new hierarchy of legitimate power. The revolutionary committees prevented the Provisional Government from consolidating its authority. On the one hand the reinstatement of the old security apparatus was frowned upon because it was reminiscent of the old regime. On the other, the new Pasdaran (Farsi for guards — Islamic Revolutionary Guards Corps) and the armed civilians who comprised the revolutionary committees were not able to maintain even a modicum of law and order.

The survival of the regime appeared to be dependent on how accurately it could identify the sources of threat to its existence and how effectively it could neutralize them. The role of the Provisional Government soon became almost irrelevant to that basic issue.

As to the most imminent sources of threat to the young revolutionary regime, foremost amongst these were the remnants of the disintegrated armed forces. Harbouring a fear bordering on paranoia of a military move reminiscent of the CIA-sponsored 1953 coup, the new regime set out to purge the Army's leadership decisively. However, the execution of several hundred Army and Security officers and the forced retirement of thousands more, left the regime with two other pressing problems.[6] First was the need to maintain some semblance of order in circumstances of extreme volatility due to the distribution of several hundreds of thousands of weapons during the final days of the insurrection. After some half-hearted attempts to recall these weapons, the regime decided on forming a militia which was later named *Pasdarane Enghelab* (Revolutionary Guards). Recruited from amongst insurgents with a variety of ideological orientations, this rag-tag army, at first numbering about 30,000, became the sole trusted arm of the government. What was left of the conventional armed forces, reduced to about one-fourth of their pre-revolutionary strength, became the object of systematic indoctrination, with the Shia Mullahs functioning like political commissars. As yet, neither the revolutionary authorities nor the officer corps of the new army of the Islamic Republic place much credence on its efficacy or loyalty.

The second issue which placed the armed forces in the forefront of Iranian politics shortly after the revolution was the outbreak of separatist ethnic minority insurrections throughout the country. The most serious of these occurred amongst the Turkomans in Gorgan, the Arab-Iranians in Khuzistan, and most significantly in Kurdistan. Five months into its rule, the regime discovered that the rag-tag militia and the dispirited and emasculated conventional armed forces could only quell the sporadic outbreaks of insurrectionary attempts in the first two instances. Their efforts in Kurdistan, on the other hand, have so far proven non-effective. Threats of severe disciplinary action, and even the execution of some officers for desertion and insubordination following Khomeini's assumption of the powers of Commander-in-Chief at the height of the Kurdish uprising in July, have had little effect. The Kurdish opposition, as will be noted elsewhere, soon acquired a broader scope, surpassing the goal of ethnic autonomy.

The other concern of the new regime was the institutionalization of its power. In April a referendum gave overwhelming support to an Islamic republic in place of the deposed monarchy.[7] Even then, the language and the options of the referendum caused considerable dissension in the ranks of the non-clerical claimants to power. The secular leftist groups were dubious about the term 'Islamic Republic,' preferring instead such alternatives as 'Democratic Islamic Republic' or

'People's Democratic Republic.' Khomeini's adamant refusal to settle for anything less than an Islamic republic forced these groups either to boycott the referendum or to accept an overwhelming defeat at the polls.

On the other hand, such centrist secular groups as the National Front and its offshoot the National Democratic Front, and some of the former guerrilla groups supported the replacement of the old monarchy by an Islamic republic. Two reasons were responsible for their support. One was Khomeini's pledge for the election of a constituent assembly to draft a new constitution, and the other was the language of the referendum, which promised another plebiscite for the final approval of this draft. Shortly thereafter these and other secular forces were confronted with another crisis when the revolutionary council publicized the secretly drafted constitution.

These forces were even more alienated when Khomeini decided against a general election for a 300-odd-member constituent assembly to review and adopt the draft. Instead, he insisted upon the election of a 75-member assembly of experts to give final approval to the draft.

By this time it had become obvious to the opposition forces that Khomeini was determined to deny them either the opportunity of demonstrating their relative political strengths through representation in a constituent assembly, or any concessions regarding the substance of the new constitution. Indeed, the fundamental reason for refusing to do so was Khomeini's awareness of the inherent misgivings of the secular forces about the theocratic essence of the proposed republic. Furthermore, he knew that the mobilization of the masses for a plebiscite was far easier than controlling a direct, multi-district election for a much larger constituent assembly.

Since the April referendum Iran's main political polarization had been centred on Khomeini and his policies. Such conventional designations like Left and Right would be relevant only in the context of the degree of support for, or opposition to him. On the issue of the first referendum, what opposition emerged stemmed from either the ambiguity of the term 'Islamic Republic' or the misgivings of the traditional leftist groups about Khomeini's unwillingness to include such words as 'democratic' or 'people's republic'. In retrospect, the nucleus of the opposition proved right in its assessment and projection of what Khomeini envisaged for the country's political future.

The new opposition had several grievances against Khomeini. Not only was he breaking his promise for an elected constituent assembly as an integral part of the process of structuring the new Islamic Republic, but he was also accusing his critics of obstructionism and non-Islamic behaviour. They were further disconcerted by the secrecy surrounding the preparation of the draft.

Once it was published, Dr Yaddolah Sahabi, a close colleague of Bazargan and Minister of State in charge of constitutional transition, emphasized its liberal-humanitarian attributes as well as its moderately interpreted Shia Islamic features. The draft was the subject of a fairly free and heated debate in the press which had not as yet become a victim of state control and Islamization. However, this situation changed in early July when the revolutionary council adopted a new press law with many restrictive features. Once this was done, the issue of freedom of the press and assembly became the second *cause célèbre* of the emerging polarization. Furthermore, with the announcement of the final draft all political groups were drawn out from their sanctuaries of neutrality and ambivalence, for this momentous event in post-revolutionary developments could no longer be ignored. The constitutional crisis, more significantly, brought into the open the rift brewing within the top Shia leadership — a rift which may yet prove to be a landmark in the realignment of the political forces in revolutionary Iran.

The Rift in the Shia Leadership

Indispensable to understanding the nature and intensity of the rift within the Shia leadership is an analysis of the divergent views of the concept of *Imamate*.[8] This concept, which has never been institutionalized since the death of the Prophet in 612 AD, relates to the scope and limitations of the authority of the Mujtaheds or Shia theologians, sometimes known by the generic term *Ulama* (learned men). One interpretation, based on *hadith*, the body of Moslem conventions and precedents, maintains that pending the reappearance of the Twelfth Imam, who went to occultation in 940 AD, the Mujtaheds can perform all functions reserved to an Imam, both in the spiritual and temporal realms. Thus a Mujtahed, particularly if recognized as the sole *Marjae Taghlid* (source of emulation) is a fully accredited agent of the Imam.

Because the spread and consolidation of Shia power has been rather uneven, there are no adequate historical data to measure the degree of acceptance of this particular interpretation of the doctrine of Imamate. Although Shia Islam was declared Iran's state religion in 1501 by the Safavid

Shah, Iran had never been ruled independently from the Shah by the Shia clergy subscribing to this concept of Imamate. Yemen, until 1962, was the only Arab Shia state in recent history which had been ruled by Imam Yahya, proudly subscribing to such a dostrine. The term Imam was bestowed on Khomeini on his return to Iran in February 1979. In a less meaningful fashion this title is used by certain Shia minority groups, of which a recent example is Imam Mussa Sadr of Lebanon, whose mysterious disappearance in Libya four years ago has prevented Khomeini's rapprochement with Colonel Khaddafy.

A less broad interpretation of the doctrine, somewhat akin to the American doctrine of strict interpretation of the Constitution, rejects the transfer of full authority of the Hidden Imam to any of the Mujtaheds. It also questions the *ex ante* deputization of Shia ulamas. Instead, it believes that the Shia clergy must be fundamentally pre-occupied with the protection and the maintenance of the faith in the spiritual realm. It could concern itself with temporal issues only selectively or when and if a clear and present danger threatened the foundation of Shia institutions. Amongst the subscribers to the latter view there are numerous interpretations, for the recognition of such a danger is extremely subjective.

As for the recent doctrinal developments within the Iranian Shia leadership, it is worth recalling that Ayattolah Borujerdi, who had been the sole Marjae Taghlid until his death in 1962 had been, generally speaking, a strict interpreter of the concept of Imamate. During his time, for instance, he did not actively participate in the political events of the Mossadegh era nor those following the reinstatement of the deposed Shah in 1953. Such political activism had been left to the lesser Ayattolahs, notably the late Abolghasem Kashani and to a lesser extent Khomeini, who frequently tried to politicize his reluctant colleagues.

With the death of Borujerdi and the absence of a consensus on a sole, qualified successor, four prominent Ayattolahs had performed the function of *modarres* or Islamic teacher and interpreter of the Shia laws. This had coincided with the inauguration of the Shah's land reform and his attempts to preside over the socio-economic trans-formation of the country. Precisely because of the absence of a sole *Ayattolah Ozma* (Grand Ayattolah), Shia leaders such as Khomeini had used the opportunity to put forward a more political interpreta-tion of the concept of Imamate. This in turn had led to the major religious uprising of June 1963 in the wake of which Khomeini was sent into exile, first to Turkey and then to Nejaf, Iraq, where there were some 3.5 million Shias. With the emergence of the Shah as a more authoritarian ruler in the early 1960s, and the influx of Western, predominantly American, technology, education and culture into Iran, it was only a matter of time until those inherent tensions between the temporal and the spiritual authorities would resurface. Thus, for example, Islamic guerrilla groups of the Mojahedin began to operate in the mid-sixties. Repeated efforts to mollify the Shia leaders, some of whom were not impervious to material and other rewards, failed. Within Iran, Shariatmadari acquired almost the same pious and enlightened reputation associated with the late Borujerdi. Indeed, the cycle of revolutionary upheaval started in January 1978 when the inner sanctum of Shariatmadari's residence in Qom was invaded by security forces, who shot to death two theological students and arrested others for refusal to end their fasts in protest against a state-sponsored news article insulting to Khomeini. It was on the 40th day after the anniversary of the death of those 'martyrs' that with the consent of Shariatmadari, the city of Tabriz, capital of Azarbayjan, in late February staged the first full-scale uprising against the Shah. In the final days of the revolution other Shia leaders, some recently released from prison, joined the campaign against the Shah.

Once the Shah was overthrown, quite a number of clerical leaders expressed views differing from those of Khomeini concerning the constitutional foundation of the Islamic Republic.[9] Even before the issue of the procedures for drafting a new constitution was raised, some of the less politicized Ayattolahs, sensing Khomeini's determination to monopolize all power in his own hands, questioned the necessity of adopting a new constitution. Notable among these was Shariatmadari, who suggested that instead of a brand new constitution the 1906 document should be revised by deletion of the clauses relating to the Pahlavi dynasty, and other amendments which had enhanced the former Shah's power. As far as he was concerned, the faithful application of the revised constitution would have been sufficient for the protection of the faith. Among other things the 1906 Constitution recognized a five-man Council of Mujtaheds to assure the compatability of Majlis-enacted laws with Shia tenets.

Khomeini was totally opposed to that formula. Just as he had insisted that the new regime should be an Islamic Republic pure and simple, he pressed for a completely new constitution to institutionalize his own concept of a Shia theocracy. Failure to do so, he warned, would endanger, 'our Islamic Republic and will be tantamount to a defeat for the Qoran and Islam.'[10]

The dispute over the constitution became the central issue of political polarization by the end of spring 1979, with Khomeini's forces proceeding systematically with their project and the opposition forces waging a losing battle to prevent its completion.

Laying the Foundations of the Republic

Once the referendum sanctioning the establishment of an Islamic Republic was approved, the revolutionary regime set out to complete the various stages of the institutionalization of its power.

The first task was to introduce a mechanism for drafting the new constitution. This could be done by one of the following methods: (a) a nationally elected constituent assembly; (b) a committee of legal experts representing all political groups which had voted for the Islamic Republic; (c) a smaller 'assembly of experts' to be elected nationally.

Khomeini opted for the third method for he was convinced a national election for a large constituent assembly of approximately 300 members in the then prevailing conditions would not give him an automatic pro-clergy majority.

Opting for the second method, on the other hand, would compel him to appoint representatives of secular groups many of which had supported the idea of an Islamic republic as a symbolic notion and not as a mandate to set up a Shia theocracy. Additionally, a smaller elected assembly of experts could claim to be representative and even democratic without the risk of deviating from Khomeini's perception of a Shia theocracy.

Once the assembly had drafted the new constitution it would then be put to a second referendum. It was already decided that the presidential election would be the third step preceding the election of the Majlis, after which the fifth and final step of forming the government would be taken.

The Drafting of the Constitution

The Revolutionary Council, whose membership had not been fully revealed, appointed a sub-committee under Beheshti to draft a law for the formation of an assembly of experts. On 30 June the electoral law governing the proposed Assembly of Experts was released. The preamble of the law read 'For the purpose of passing final judgment on the Constitution of the Islamic Republic which has been drafted in stages, the Assembly for the final consideration of the Constitution will be convened.'[11] Its total membership was set at 75, with 3 representatives for the official minorities. The voting age was reduced to 16, and among the qualifications of nominees was loyalty to and acceptance of the Islamic Republican system. During 3 and 4 August elections were held throughout the country. Except in two constituencies in Kurdistan where an insurgency was under way, most districts succeeded in certifying the election of 73 members. The Assembly began its deliberations in the chamber of the former Senate on 19 August and completed its work on 15 November, just in time for the referendum held on 2 and 3 December, the second since the revolution.

It was in the course of the Assembly's elections that the Islamic Republican Party (IRP) recognized the value of organizational and grass-roots work. Through two networks, one consisting of Islamic societies in schools, factories, government offices and military bases, and the other composed of young students in seminaries in Qom and Mashad, the IRP could mobilize voters in support of its candidates. It also saw to it that the young theology students from Qom were appointed as 'Friday-prayer' Imams in remote towns and hamlets. The party was particularly eager to counteract the influence of such prominent Grand Ayatollahs as Shariatmadari of Azarbayjan and Qomi of Khorassan, both of whom had begun to show strong reservations about the proposed Assembly of Experts as opposed to a nationally elected constituent assembly. These young Friday Imams were destined to play an extremely critical role in retaining the IRP in power as it began to lose the support of the various groups that had joined Khomeini's anti-Shah coalition. An analysis of the composition of the Assembly indicates their success, from which they profited greatly in the next round of elections for the Majlis and the presidency.

The Ministry of the Interior published data on the election indicating that roughly 11 million, or slightly more than one half of the voters for the referendum, had participated in the election. About 50 per cent of the assembly's members were clerics supporting Beheshti, while 10 per cent were better-known clerics such as the late Ayattolah Mahmud Taleghani, whose position was much closer to the secular groups affiliated with Banisadr and Bazargan's followers. Of the remaining non-clerics 40 per cent, or nearly half, owed their election to Beheshti, and were considered even more extreme in their acceptance of a genuinely theocratic state. The other 20 per cent elected to the Assembly were either independent popular personalities, or followers of Banisadr, or of Bazargan, who as head of the Provisional Government was not a member of the assembly.

On controversial issues like that of *Velayate Faghih* (supreme theologian-jurist), the Beheshti group could usually muster a majority of around 65 per cent. This majority worked in close co-ordination with the Beheshti faction of the Revolutionary Council. Its subcommittee for constitutional affairs, consisting of Beheshti, Rafsanjani and Montazari, literally dictated the draft to the assembly. To facilitate the drafting of a theocratic constitution, such a renowned Ayatollah as Taleghani was bypassed in favour of Montazari as President of the Assembly.

Numerous well-known political groups such as the National Front, the Mojahedin and Fedayeen guerrilla organizations were either totally absent, or represented by their lesser-known supporters, who were expected to show no reservations about the Islamic substance of the new constitution. A number of secular personalities like Banisadr and Dr Yaddolah Sahabi, a close associate of Bazargan, joined Taleghani to insist on the inclusion in the document of liberal provisions related to democratic freedoms and rights. They were also instrumental in incorporating in the constitution some features of the French Fifth Republic's fundamental law, some of which generated many difficulties, as will be noted later.

Even a casual examination of the new constitution makes it evident that Khomeini's perception of a Shia theocracy for Iran is fully reflected in it.[12]

A Textual Analysis

The most crucial of its fourteen general principles is the first, which after defining the Iranian political system as an Islamic Republic, recognizes Khomeini's leadership of the revolution and identifies him as the glorious Marjae Taghlid. By so doing, the constitution seems to grant him what could not be achieved through consensus among the five Grand Ayattolahs.[13]

Principle 5 defines the Velayate Faghih, theologian-jurist regency, in a manner dovetailed to Khomeini's qualifications. More significantly, this principle states that in the absence of the Hidden Imam, all rights and authority of the Imamate will be exercised by the *Faghih*. If such a person is not recognized by the majority of the people, then a single leader or a leadership council composed of three to five theologians chosen by an assembly of popularly elected experts will assume his functions.

Another general principle which has alarmed some of the neighbouring Islamic states is number 11, which makes the new Islamic Republic duty-bound to pursue a pan-Islamic objective for the political, economic and cultural integration of Islamic nations. This principle, along with the first, is the main bone of contention between revolutionary Iran and Iraq and the other smaller Persian Gulf states, some with large Shiite minorities.

As to the concept of popular sovereignty, Chapter Five of the constitution grants absolute sovereignty to God, but recognizes that God has made man self-sovereign and that this divine right cannot be wrested from him or be put at the service of any particular group or individual. Functionally separate, legislative-executive-judicial powers are derived from the state's sovereignty and 'will be exercised under the aegis of the Regent of Faith and the People's Imamate.'

To bolster Khomeini's power and fidelity to Islamic concepts, the constitution imposes a further check on a popularly elected unicameral parliament. This is done under Article 91, which requires the formation of a 12-man Council of Custodians in order to 'safeguard Islamic injunctions and the constitution *vis-à-vis* parliamentary enactments.' Half of the council will be elected by the leader or leadership council from amongst 'just and well-informed' theologians. The other half is to be nominated by the supreme judicial council and approved by the parliament, from amongst Islamic jurists.

A fascinating device which assures this council's superiority over parliament is that the latter will not be legal unless it has elected the second half of the former's membership. The absence of either half of the membership of this council would virtually paralyse the National Consultative Assembly, or Majlis, as the embodiment of the legislative authority stemming from popular sovereignty. Further, the council has ten days in which to ascertain the compatibility of legislation with Islamic principles and the constitution. If they are found unacceptable, they will be returned to the Majlis for revision. Judicial review is given to the majority of theologians of the council concerning parliamentary legislation, and to the majority of the entire council concerning its constitutionality. Thus, in two ways popular sovereignty is denied the Majlis. One, through the refusal of the council to constitute itself and the other by vetoing its legislation as either anti-Islamic or anti-constitutional.

The constitutional provision concerning the supreme leadership of the country is contained in Chapter Eight of the constitution and expands on the concept of Velayate Faghih enumerated in Chapter Five. It also lists the prerogatives and duties of the leadership, which include the appointment of theologians of the Council of Custodians, appointment of the highest judicial authority, assumption of the supreme command of the armed forces, presiding over the supreme council of national defence, declarations of war and peace, approval of the presidential candidates and the President's official appointment once elected, and dismissal of the President with the approval of the supreme court and the Majlis.

Articles on the executive power place the President below the supreme leadership as responsible for the implementation of the constitution and the co-ordination of the tripartite powers and presiding over the executive power, except when it is assigned to the supreme leader. A cause of contention among non-Shiite Iranians is that the President should be of the Twelfth Imam Jaafari sect of Shiadom. In the wake of serious clashes between Sunni Baluchies and Shia Sistanies at the end of December, Khomeini promised a modification of the constitutional provision regarding Iran's state religion so as to legalize Sunni judicial and religious practices in areas with dominant Sunni populations.

A further innovation relates to the armed forces. The revolutionary guards replace the old gendarmerie as a counterweight to the army, whose loyalty continues to be suspect. In foreign policy, non-alignment is recognized as the main characteristic, but it also provides for the defence of the rights of all Moslem people.

Chapter Three relates to the rights of citizens and contains many liberal-sounding principles. Equality of rights for men and women irrespective of race and colour is recognized. Principle 20 provides for guarantees of all human, political, economic, and social and cultural rights for men and women, 'in accordance with Islamic standards.'

Principle 24 provides that the Press will be free to express opinions, unless they are contrary to Islamic tenets or public rights. Parties, political groups, professional and trade associations, and Islamic and recognized minority religious associations are allowed on the condition that 'they will not violate independence, freedom, national unity, Islamic standards and Islamic Republic's foundation.'

It is evident that the above rights are seriously restricted by the provision that they should not contravene Islamic principles or public rights. Thus, not only are such religious minorities as the Bahais not so recognized, but literally interpreted, these provisions do not allow for parties and groups opposed to or different from the prevailing single Islamic ideology.

Concerning the organization of the state institution, Principle 57 recognizes the separation of the three powers, legislative, executive and judicial, but puts them under the auspices of Velayate Faghih and charges the President with the task of regulating their relationships. The legislature is a uni-cameral, consultative assembly of 270 members elected for four-year terms. Additional representatives will be elected for each 150,000 of the population after a census to be conducted every ten years.

Principle 73 prohibits the Majlis from enacting legislation contrary to the tenets and injunctions of the official religion in the constitution. The Council of Custodians would enforce this provision. The Cabinet is made accountable to the Majlis under the provisions of Principles 87, 88 and 89. Thus, the Cabinet will become official when it receives a vote of confidence from the Majlis. Members of the Majlis can impeach the Cabinet as a whole or its individual members, who will be dismissed upon a vote of no-confidence. No Cabinet, or members thereof, can be re-appointed immediately after dismissal by such a vote.

As mentioned earlier, the Council of Custodians is in effect an appointed upper house with a great deal of power in the affairs of state. Principles 91–99 elaborate its authority and its composition, but its most important power remains the power of original judicial review, as noted earlier in this chapter. Finally, the leader or members of the Council of Custodians could be dismissed by the Assembly of Experts when they are found to have violated their duty or lost their qualifications for that office. The details of the election and composition of the Assembly of Experts, which is to function as a kind of continuous constitutional convention, will be decided by the majority of theologians of the first Council of Custodians with the approval of the leaders of the revolution. Thereafter the Assembly itself will determine any changes in these provisions.

A comparison of this constitution with that of the first constitution of 1906 shows that while the latter was patterned after the Belgian or British democratic monarchical system, the former represents a peculiar mixture of the French Fifth Republic and fundamental Islamic concepts, many of which are contained in Khomeini's writing, notably his *Islamic Governance*.

In terms of the scope of power given the Faghih and *Rahbar*, which maybe one and the same as it is now, there is no doubt that his power exceeds those of the Shah, if the 1906 Constitution and its supplements are literally interpreted. The difference is that the Faghih does not hold a hereditary office, but is elected by an assembly whose composition is determined by Khomeini as the first leader of the Islamic Republic.

As to the relations amongst the judicial, executive and legislative powers; while separation of power is recognized, the ability of the legislature to overthrow the Cabinet is acknowledged, while no such power of dissolving the Majlis is granted the Cabinet. None the less, the emergence of political parties within the Majlis is not prohibited. In reality it is known that the IRP, which controls the Majlis, also controls the Cabinet, an issue on which the crisis of Banisadr's presidency hinged.

Next to Khomeini himself the constitution entrusts tremendous powers to the Council of Custodians which could effectively paralyze the Majlis, veto its legislations, approve and disapprove presidential candidates and their election. So Khomeini literally rules the country as an elected monarch, with the help of an appointed Council of Custodians, and with a great deal of control over every branch of government.

Of course every constitution must be tested in practice so that the adequacy of its original provisions or need for revisions and amendments can be determined. In future sections of this study some of the critical tests to which the new republic was subjected barely a few months after its inauguration will be considered.

As indicated above, the constitution in its present form has been opposed by secular, religious, ethnic and national minority groups for a variety of reasons. Without a doubt, its provisions concerning the *Rahbar* (supreme leader) and/or Velayate Faghih are its most controversial features. As far as the secular democratic opposition groups are concerned, the grant of these specific powers to Khomeini, or a collective group which might succeed him, contravenes the cherished principle of popular sovereignty. They believe it entrusts to the leadership constitutional powers far beyond those embodied in the original 1906 Constitution and its four supplements enacted since.

The Shia opposition leaders who share this misgiving find another basic flaw in the document. They firmly believe that to put the highest Shia leader at the apex of this hierarchy of power, and to do so in the name of Divine Qoranic law, would expose him and Islam to political errors for which no secular or divine remedies are provided. That is to say, every other authority under the constitution is made somehow accountable to the supreme leader or to several collective bodies. It is

the supreme leader whose scope of authority recognizes no institutionalized limitations. This, they believe, may prove in the long run
much more detrimental to the status and prestige of Islam than any
formal denial of substantive political power to the Shia clergy.[14]

A third main criticism relates to the imposition of various limitations on the rights of ethnic religious national minorities. To confuse
the issue further, such non-Shia groups as the Kurds feel a sort of
double jeopardy by being excluded from certain positions by virtue
of their Sunni religion, and by being denied the right of self-govern-
ment or limited autonomy.

Towards the end of October the completed draft of the Constitution
aggravated relations between the provisional government and Khomeini,
with the Revolutionary Council split between a majority siding with
Beheshti and a minority identified with Prime Minister Bazargan. As
political parties and groups were jockeying for position in the conflict
of principles and personalities, a major crisis in US–Iran relations
diverted all attention from the process of institutionalizing the new
regime. The crisis soon proved to be of decisive significance, not only
for the resumption of that process, but also for the consolidation of
the theocratic groups which had become progressively identified with
Khomeini.

Notes

1. *Inter alia* see the author's, *Iran's Revolutionary Upheaval* (Alchemy Books,
San Francisco, 1979), pp. 39–45.

2. Interview with Parviz Raeen, Tehran correspondent for the Associated
Press, 15 January 1981.

3. Interview with Dr Shahpour Bakhtiar and Dr Ali Amini in Paris, 14 April
1981. The latter was at one point recommended to the Shah by Shariatmadari as
an interim premier, but the Shah refused to accept him because of the experience
of 1961 when President Kennedy's pressure for internal reform led to the
appointment of Dr Amini. Some of the close associates of the Shah were opposed
to Amini's reappointment because of his conclusion of the 1954 oil agreement
with the Western Oil Consortium, which had evoked fierce opposition from
nationalist and leftist groups.

4. Data collected from *Keyhan, Ayandegan* and *Ettelaat* between 25 February
and 31 May 1979 indicate that at the end of February there were 237 such
committees in Tehran and over 1600 in provincial towns with a total membership of 22,000. By the end of the spring these committees were consolidated by
separating their membership from the Pasdaran and from the armed agents of
committees. In the process supporters of the secular groups and the main
guerrilla organizations were purged and at present these committees, which
number 20 in Tehran, are for all practical purposes neighbourhood branches of
the Islamic Republican Party.

5. Bazargan also testified to the accidental and unplanned nature of the

clergy's ascendancy as a result of the disorganization and incoherence of the secular forces in the anti-royalist coalition. Interview with Oriana Fallaci reported in *Iran Post*, Los Angeles, 5 November 1979, p. 12.

6. Data collected from pro-government newspapers such as *Keyhan* and *Bamdad* and later *Jomhuriye Islami*, the organ of the IRP, as well as from publications representing exiled army officers like *ARA* (Iran Liberation Army), indicate that between 485 and 600 army officers were executed between 13 February 1979 and 5 June 1980. In July the discovery of an attempted coup resulted in the execution of 140 air force and army officers, some of whom expressed allegiance to Dr Bakhtiar in the course of the trials. (Interview with Dr Bakhtiar, 14 April 1981, Paris.)

7. Principle 1 of the new Constitution states that 98.2% of all eligible voters, estimated to number some 20 million people, voted affirmatively. The *Full Text of Iran's Constitution*, published in Farsi by the Embassy of the Islamic Republic of Iran, 20 November 1979. Direct quotations hereafter are the author's translation.

8. For a perceptive analysis of some aspects of this issue see Joseph Eliash, 'Misconceptions Regarding the Judicial Status of the Iranian "Ulama",' *International Journal of Middle East Studies*, Vol. 10, No. 1, February 1979, pp. 9–25.

9. A prominent example with views akin to those of Shariatmadari was the late Ayattolah Mahmud Taleghani, whose relations with Khomeini from the outset were extremely tenuous. As an impeccable foe of the Shah he represented the philosophy of the late Ayattolah Naini, the author of a famous treatise on Shia Islam in which he warned the faithful against two types of despotism, the monarchical and the theocratic. *Omide Iran*, Tehran weekly, 21 April 1979.

10. Quoted from an open letter to Khomeini written by Dr Hossein Miriyan, professor of Shia theology and a recognized authority on Qoranic interpretation. *Bamdad*, Iranian daily, Tehran, 15 October 1979.

11. The summary of the law appeared in *Shahed*, a weekly publication of the Embassy of the Islamic Republic in Washington, DC, 23 July 1979.

12. Apart from the concept of Velayate Faghih, the provisions of the constitution giving the Council of Custodians the right to veto Majlis legislation, most accurately reflect Khomeini's views on the Shia theocracy as expounded in his book, *Islamic Governance*.

13. These in order of prominence are Shariatmadari of Azarbayjan, Khoi of Nejaf, Golpaygani and Marashi of Qom and Hassan Qomi of Khorassan. It should be noted that the prominence of the senior ayattolahs is reputational. The only measurable criterion is the amount of contribution to them known as *Sahme Imam*, or the Imam's share, which pays for religious schools and mosque-related charity organizations.

14. Shariatmadari, before the Tabriz uprising at the end of November 1979, was quite outspoken in his criticism of the Constitution, but shortly after the referendum, under pressure from pro-Khomeini groups, he chose to remain silent on this and other political questions. Excerpts from his statements in *Enghelabe Islami*, Tehran, 14 November 1979.

3 THE HOSTAGE CRISIS

Because the state of the revolution prior to 4 November 1979 is as significant to the understanding of the reasons for the assault on the US embassy as are the composition and the leadership of the assailants, its chief characteristics should be reviewed. This should be done in reference to events since June, when the draft of the controversial constitution was completed.

(1) The proposed constitution at once became a divisive factor which finally broke up the broad coalition of the revolutionary forces responsible for the Shah's overthrow. It did so because it sought to institutionalize the monopolization of power by that faction of the Shia clergy which enjoyed Khomeini's unconditional support and was represented by the Islamic Republican Party.

(2) In the process of the gradual disintegration of that coalition, the following groups either completely defected from the regime or assumed an attitude of 'wait-and-see', pending further evidence of Khomeini's determination to realize his vision of a purely Shia theocracy:

(a) The People's Fedayeen, which had an impeccable record of struggle against the Shah. It had waged urban guerrilla warfare, at least since the early 1970s and most significantly, had played a critical role in the transformation of a non-violent power seizure into a bloody insurrection between 20 January and 11 February 1979;

(b) The People's Mojahedin, whose revolutionary credentials were equally impressive and who represent, even to date, a political orientation best described as non-communist Marxist–Islamic. The chief reason for the defection of these guerrilla groups, apart from forcible exclusion from power, was their different perceptions of the new political system;

(c) secular groups such as the National Front, the National Democratic Front, the Pan-Iranist Party, and the Radical Party representing the Western-educated middle and lower middle classes. Their desertion from the pro-Khomeini forces during the summer stemmed from similar reasons to the above;

(d) perhaps the most critical defection from Khomeini occurred when several prominent Shia leaders, to some of whom Khomeini owed his life, turned against him. Notable among these was Mohammad

Kazem Shariatmadari, who almost single-handedly elevated Khomeini to the highest of Shia ranks so that the Shah would spare his life after the unsuccessful religious uprising of June 1963. Shariatmadari's part in mobilizing public opinion, particularly in his native Azarbayjan, against the Shah, beginning in January 1978 was paramount. To many Iranians he, rather than Khomeini, was the revolution's initial driving force.

Apart from Shariatmadari, Hassan Qomi of Mashad, Khoi, now residing in Nejaf, Iraq and Marashi of Qom also expressed varying degrees of opposition and reservation about the new constitution. It was thus evident that the Islamic Republic, on the eve of its constitutional consolidation — which was to be ascertained by yet another plebiscite — faced an extremely uncertain future.

Memories of 1953 Revived

Adding confusion to the internal crisis over the new constitution was a series of events between September and 4 November 1979.

On the occasion of the anniversary of Algerian independence, Prime Minister Mehdi Bazargan and his Foreign Minister, Dr Ibrahim Yazdi, visited Algiers, where confidential talks took place between them and President Carter's National Security Adviser, Zbigniew Brzezinski. Even before their return to Tehran, press reports reflecting the views of leftists and fanatic members of the government and the Revolutionary Council expressed concern and even severe criticism of the reported meeting with the American officials. As a matter of fact, the Prime Minister's position, which had been already weakened as a result of his general moderation and largely secular viewpoints about the constitution, was further jeopardized.[1]

Throughout the summer he had become progressively identified with the secular and moderate Shia leaders as described earlier in this chapter. His relations with Khomeini from the outset had been plagued by fundamental differences in perception, policy and direction of the revolution. Having failed to secure Khomeini's consent to his numerous offers of resignation, he left an open-dated letter to that effect with the Imam shortly before visiting Algiers.

The arena in which these fundamental differences clashed was the Revolutionary Council, which ever since February had acted as the real centre of power of the new regime. With this background of events, it became obvious that the Prime Minister's visit to Algiers would be utilized by his many opponents to dislodge him from power. Clearly the event which culminated in the assault on the embassy was the US decision to admit the former Shah into the USA for medical reasons. It has been documented now that the State Department did indeed consult the Iranian Government about the risks of admitting the Shah. The Prime Minister, through his Foreign Minister, informed the Americans of serious potential reactions, but simultaneously assured Washington of his capability and determination to protect the safety of the embassy's personnel.[2]

On 24 October, the former Shah's birthday, events were set into motion which appeared at the time to be totally unplanned and haphazard. It is known now that, far from being so, the occupation of the embassy had been carefully planned at least since the first assault on the embassy in mid-February.

To understand the logic of the radical groups which either plotted the embassy takeover or insisted on the prolongation of the crisis, it is imperative to note the excessive fear of Iran's new regime about its own viability *vis-à-vis* the USA. This fear, bordering on paranoia, stemmed from memories of the 1953 coup. It was in turn aggravated by the reports of the involvement of Henry Kissinger and David Rockefeller in the Shah's admittance to the USA. Put differently, the radical forces sensed that the USA, the repeated assurances of President Carter notwithstanding, was co-ordinating events in and outside Iran for the purpose of destroying the revolutionary regime.

The significant differences between 1953 and 1978-9 were either deliberately ignored or failed to persuade even the moderate forces of their relevance. Thus, the assault on the embassy at once became a unifying factor similar to the early opposition to the former Shah. In both cases President Carter became the symbol of alleged US oppression and/or its design to reinstate the pre-revolutionary regime. Because of the unifying role of anti-American radicalism, it is possible to assume that even had the Shah not been admitted to the USA the radical supporters of the regime would have most likely taken this or similar measures.

But why did eleven days elapse between the admission of the Shah and the assault on the embassy? Why had the Mexican embassy not been attacked months earlier? All indications point to the fact that the planners needed the time to refine and finalize their design. It is now known that one issue which had to be resolved before the assault related to the Provisional Government and its tenure. The leadership of the assault on the embassy tried to ascertain the reaction of the Prime Minister and his relatively moderate Foreign Minister to the likely occupation of the embassy. Cognizant of fundamental ideological and policy differences between Khomeini and the Prime Minister, the leadership of the assailants took its time in considering its response to the government's reaction. Since some of the Cabinet members and, more significantly, close to half of the members of the Revolutionary Council were in open opposition to the Provisional Government, it was logical that the assailants of the embassy had to make sure that the Imam would this time accept the Prime Minister's resignation. Regarding an assault on the Mexican embassy because its government had let the Shah into Mexico, the obvious response was that Mexico was nowhere as important as the USA and such a move would not have had the desirable results sought by the radical groups.

The Fateful Sunday

Sunday 4 November 1979 was a bleak and cold day. On the previous Friday and Saturday the state-controlled media had announced the holding of a major meeting in the campus of Tehran University, about a mile and a half from the US embassy compound. Eleven rallying points were announced for political groups of all shades. One of these was at Pole Chubi, a quarter of a mile from the embassy on the corner of Roosevelt Avenue (since the revolution renamed the Avenue of the Combatants) and Takhte Jamshid (renamed Taleghani, after a prominent nationalist Ayattollah).

This particular place was reserved for a small political group known by its Farsi acronym JAMA (the Movement of Moslem Combatants). Around 11 o'clock in the morning approximately 400 members of JAMA assembled at that place. The group included roughly 120 well-armed young men and women. As they moved down Roosevelt Avenue toward Tehran University, they decided to pass by the embassy.

At this time the embassy was 'protected' by a small contingent of Revolutionary Guards and regular police. When the group assaulted the embassy, the guards, led by 'Mashallah Khan the Butcher' put up a token resistance, because they had not been informed by their immediate commanding officers, or for that matter anyone else in the government or the Revolutionary Council, of the intention to occupy the embassy. The American marines guarding the embassy similarly resisted the assailants. Simultaneously, a small group of the assailants reached the embassy's compound from Kuchehe Ardalan, by breaking into several houses adjacent to the embassy. Together they succeeded in gaining full control of the embassy within two hours.

Flashback to 1976 and 1978

The plot for the occupation of the embassy was in the making at least three months prior to 4 November. Indeed, it is possible to reveal that such a plot had had its genesis in the last few years of the reign of the Shah, within the Evin prison, involving several personalities who were destined to rise to power with the triumph of the revolution.

The principal actors in this drama, at least in its planning phase, were Dr Habibollah Peyman and a radical cleric, Mussavi Khoeini. Dr Peyman, who actually master-minded the successful assault on the embassy, had been in and out of the Shah's prisons three times, to be finally released in the early autumn of 1978. He had joined the pro-Mossadegh Nehzate Moghavemate Melli (National Resistance Movement) after the 1953 coup. In 1960 he was elected to the leadership committee of the Second National Front. His first arrest was in 1957 when several leaders of National Resistance Movement were arrested by the recently organized SAVAK. It is then that he became a cellmate of Dr Ali Shariati and began to accept his views about the political potentials of Shia religion. After the unsuccessful religious uprising of June 1963 he helped to organize Jonbesh Azadi Mellat Iran (Movement of Iranian National Liberation) which had an Islamic ideology and a belief in the indispensability of armed struggle.[3] Among his celebrated prison mates, apart from Dr Ali Shariati the renowned ideologue and theorist of Shia political philosophy, were Mohammadali Rajai, the first Premier and the second President of the IRI, and Dr Kazem Sami of the radical wing of the National Front. While in prison Dr Peyman had organized a secret committee to penalize and intimidate those political prisoners who tended to co-operate with SAVAK in order to gain freedom. The committee, known as Tufan (Hurricane), was quite successful in radicalizing some of the political prisoners whose ideological reliability was suspect. From this common and at times dramatic experience had emerged bonds of friendship and ideological conformity which had well served Dr Peyman's purpose since the triumph of the revolution.[4]

All the evidence indicates that his armed followers had accurate knowledge about the embassy's floor plan. This was so because during the short-lived occupation of the embassy on 14 February several of his followers had made the necessary reconnaissance of sensitive areas such as code rooms, communications centre, guard houses, etc.

As a result, Dr Peyman's followers gained quick access to these areas and indeed were able to prevent the complete destruction of critical documents and records. It should be noted that very few knew either the identity of the master mind of this operation or the exact number and composition of the original armed assailants. A contributing reason to the confusion was that as soon as other political groups learned about it, they either left the rally at Tehran University or diverted their routes to reach the embassy in a hurry.

The two next immediate problems were: (a) access to the state-controlled media, and (b) determination of a proper name for the embassy occupiers. The first problem was resolved by selecting as the spokesman and the spiritual leader of the group Mussavi Khoeini. He established himself on the 9th floor of the state TV and radio head-quarters next to Sadegh Ghotbzadeh, the then Director-General of the Agency. The second problem was resolved by choosing the term 'Students Following the Imam's Line' (DAPKHA, its Farsi acronym). The captors of the American hostages were thereafter known as the Militant Students.

Through their access to the state-controlled media, as well as to the foreign and in particular American media, they were able to stage a frenzy of anti-American radicalism surpassing in intensity and organization any similar efforts in the region since World War II. Their skill in staging 'events' and mobilizing huge rallies outside the occupied embassy, and their highly sophicated methods of interrogation of hostages have led some observers to conclude that non-Iranians were involved in these events from the very first day to the very end.

The most commonly mentioned group is the leftist affiliate of the Palestine Liberation Organization (PLO) led by George Habash. Others mentioned in this connection are Iranians trained in such communist countries as Cuba and East Germany, or in radical Arab states including PLO-controlled camps in Syria and Lebanon. Evidence available to foreign and Iranian newsmen and observers is rather inconclusive about the identity of these groups. What is known, however, is:

(1) several hundreds of well-trained guerrillas and young militants returned to Iran in the last phase of the 1979 revolution;
(2) the ability of those who received their training in the PLO camps or

other radical Arab states to speak fluent Arabic;
(3) the early participation of Yasser Arafat, the PLO Chairman, in celebrating the triumph of the Iranian Revolution and in later disputes with the Provisional Government on such issues as the rebellion in Khuzistan province or the question of the three Persian Gulf islands. Pro-government newspapers disclosed that the more radical elements within the PLO had actively agitated amongst Arab–Iranians in that oil-rich province in favour of autonomy and even self-determination for that province, which they deliberately called 'Arabistan'.[5]

Once the uprising was crushed in April of that year, these Palestinian groups joined communist-leftist forces in the Arab world to denounce 'the new militarism' of the Islamic Republic. In point of fact the Nationalist and anti-royalist Governor of the province, Admiral Ahmad Madani, was singled out for systematic criticism by the pro-Soviet groups in Iran. These groups, while paying lip service to Iran's territorial integrity, attempted to frighten Khomeini about the inherent dangers of the re-emergence of the military. This latter point was well taken when several months later the Admiral was forced into exile along with other Nationalist-secular politicians, even though he had been elected as a Majlis deputy from his native Kirman with a landslide victory at the poll.

Organizational Set-up

Within a week the captors had set up a tightly disciplined organization for managing the different aspects of their activities. Five committees were named to take care of security, public relations, maintenance, interrogation and liaison. These committees, ranging from three to five members, were represented in a council (*Shora*) which was the highest authority in overall control of the occupied embassy and the hostages. It was through the council that Dr Peyman exercised *de facto* leadership of the Militant Students, at least in the initial phase of the hostage crisis.

All accounts, including those relayed by some of the more harshly treated former hostages, indicate that the security and interrogation committees consisted of the most radical and well-trained captors. Next in significance were the public relations and liaison committees. Their functions as the official spokesmen of the captors were the publishing of countless daily communiqués as well as 'revealing' allegedly captured and compromising documents. One purpose was to destroy the credibility of the moderate secular personalities; another was to utilize the media to mobilize public support for their cause.

An example of their success with regard to the first purpose was the disclosure of documents implicating Dr Abbas Amir Entezam, the faithful deputy to former Prime Minister Mehdi Bazargan, and later ambassador to Sweden. Despite his impeccable revolutionary credentials, the man was imprisoned for what appeared to be a routine diplomatic contact with the American envoy in Stockholm. It should be noted that the most sensitive documents had already been removed from the occupied embassy. The best guess is that Dr Peyman and a selected few of his foreign-trained militants were in possession of these documents. Some radical Arab newspapers closely affiliated with the PLO used them throughout the crisis, proving the reported liaison between Dr Peyman and Arab radical forces.

Be that as it may, soon after setting up the organizational network the Militants began using the term 'Nest of Spies' in reference to the occupied embassy as a further means of justifying a blatant act of international terrorism. Once Khomeini had finally accepted Bazargan's resignation, the Revolutionary Council became the unchallenged ruling body and functioned as such until 25 January 1980 and the election of Abolhassan Banisadr as President. It was in this period that the Imam cautiously, but assuredly, espoused the Militants' actions and policies. On several occasions such as Ashura, the anniversary of Imam Hossein's death and 11 February, the anniversary of the revolution, the Imam quoted, almost verbatim, from the Militants' statements and thereby legitimized their illegal action.

Consequently, the hostage crisis assumed an important distinction from the other '2700 precedents since World War II'. (US State Department data.) That is to say, the Islamic Republic, recognized as Iran's legitimate government by the international community, identified itself with the captors of diplomatic, military and civilian personnel of a foreign embassy. This critical distinction complicated the difficulties of negotiating a settlement of the crisis. Additionally, in the interim between 5 November and 25 January it was virtually impossible to regard the Iranian ruling authorities as a government in the conventional sense. While Khomeini's espousal of the cause of DAPKHA came after the fact, Dr Peyman's role was critical from the outset of the crisis. What were his politics and what motivated his actions? As noted earlier, he had started in politics like many other young Iranians as a supporter of the National Front. By the early 1960s he had become convinced that the Shia religion had a paramount political role. Shortly after the takeover of the US embassy Dr Peyman discussed his political views in a number of articles and interviews in leading Iranian publications.[6]

He believed that the Iranian revolution should pursue a Pan-Islamic or even an international course, because any revolution which was forcibly confined to its territorial context would be defeated. 'Our Constitution requires us to export our revolution, or else like Russian and Chinese revolutions ours will be obliged to compromise with American imperialism.'

He felt Iran's foreign policy should be determined by relations between the masses of the people and not by those of governments. The masses should establish direct relations with oppressed masses everywhere, the Palestinians, the Black Americans and the Africans. The Islamic political system should be one of total decentralization, with the affairs of each community in the hands of a people's council. This regime of people's councils would be the best guarantee against the emergence of bureaucracy and fascism. Similarly, the army must be an Islamic people's army consisting of volunteers and managed by people's councils.

As to relations with the United States, he expressed doubts that America would ever accommodate the Islamic revolution, and therefore advocated a policy of total enmity toward the United States. 'Imperialism will compromise with us only if we lose the revolutionary contents of our movement.'

As for his ties with the Militant Student captors of the American hostages, Peyman denied that the group was under his leadership. He attacked liberal groups for trying to attribute the action of the Militant Students to any one individual or ideology. 'It was a mass action which liberal elements, as well as the reactionary clergy and opportunists, cannot comprehend.'

His organization, the Movement of Moslem Combatants, would see to it that the momentum of the revolution was maintained and that the masses of the people were mobilized against any deviation by the less committed individuals who supported Khomeini, not out of conviction but because of political opportunism. Many of his views to the end of the hostage crisis were echoed by his followers, but once the hostages were released Dr Peyman did not insist on accusing the Rajai government of accommodating the United States. Indeed, the harshness of his criticism of the liberal clergy and secular personalities like Banisadr put him in a dilemma over the final settlement of the crisis.

If he joined in criticizing the settlement, he would be echoing the line of Banisadr and those very liberals whom he had so harshly attacked. If he supported the Rajai government, he would have to support the settlement which resulted from a compromise with the United States.

For several months his organization remained silent until the crisis of the Presidency pitted Rajai, Beheshti and Rafsanjani against Banisadr. Ever since that crisis Dr Peyman had shown no hesitation in supporting the fundamentalist hardliners, for the primary reason that they continued to be anti-imperialistic, i.e. anti-American as well as anti-liberal. A survey of Peyman's writing would certainly indicate that while he was not a pro-Soviet communist, his views on Iran's economic political structure were akin to Marxism. His anti-Americanism was his main bond of affinity with Khomeini even though he had long used Islamic concepts and terms of reference to propagate his radical views.[7]

His behaviour during the various phases of the crisis revealed a degree of flexibility which distinguished him from other prominent Islamic Marxists.

Phases of the Crisis

With the espousal of the cause of the Militant Students by Khomeini, the hostage crisis proceeded through several stages. During each of these phases numerous internal factions exercised a different degree of control over the crisis.

Most Western accounts of the resolution of the crisis identify the nature of the complex negotiations leading to the Algiers agreement of 19 January 1981.[8] What is lacking in them is the internal Iranian dimension of these negotiations, in particular as far as the Militant Students themselves were concerned. In what follows an attempt will be made to fill the gap. To do this the prolonged crisis will be examined in a chronological order determined primarily by the internal political developments, and only secondarily by the secret diplomatic negotiations between the two governments and their intermediaries.

The Initial Phase

The ease with which the embassy was taken over and the speed by which the government-controlled media became a mouthpiece for the Militant Students surprised many people, among them the students themselves.

A number of them who were quite close to Dr Peyman later acknowledged that their initial intention was a brief sit-in and that the enthusiastic support given them by the government and the intense attention paid them by the foreign media, notably the American, were all totally unexpected.[9] The initial aims of the leadership of the Militant Sudents, now joined by Dr Hassan Ayat, a leading supporter of Beheshti and his Islamic Republican Party, may be summarized in the following way:

(1) The Provisional Government should be overthrown and Khomeini be persuaded not to reappoint a new Prime Minister. This was achieved on 5 November. The Revolutionary Council, which included some members of the Bazargan Cabinet, became the exclusive authority. Banisadr was named acting Foreign Minister for a brief time. His many enemies in and outside the Revolutionary Council prevailed upon Khomeini to prevent his trip to the United Nations despite an earlier announcement that he would do so 'in order to use the UN forum to publicize Iran's grievances against the US'. Shortly afterwards Sadegh Ghotbzadeh replaced him. Despite serious misgivings about keeping the US hostages, Banisadr chose not to antagonize his radical rivals publicly pending the presidential elections, on which he had fixed all his attention.

(2) The other aim of the leadership was to assure the prompt departure of the Shah from the United States. Though officially they clamoured for the Shah's extradition, they knew full well that this was most unlikely. So instead, they sought to persist in their maximum demand, hoping that their minimum request of the early removal of the Shah from the United States would be granted.

(3) A third objective of the leadership was to maximize public mobilization in favour of the adoption of the controversial constitution. The controlled media equated support for the Militant Students with support for the new constitution. Those who opposed the 'Great Satan' could demonstrate their good faith by supporting the constitution, which was to be put to referendum on 2 and 3 December, a day after Ashura, the most sacred Shia religious holiday. This goal was also achieved. Opponents of the new constitution were intimidated, and the overwhelming vote in the referendum was interpreted as a double confidence in both Khomeini's proposed political system and his intense anti-American radicalism demonstrated by the continuing detention of the US hostages.

Indeed, once the value of massive mobilization in favour of the constitution became evident, Khomeini was determined that as long as various institutions of the Islamic Republic were not yet constituted, the hostage crisis should not be resolved. Some time at the end of the week 10-17 December, Khomeini made the critical decision of putting off the resolution of that crisis until the presidential and parliamentary elections were completed and the first government of the Islamic Republic was installed. This decision, which was announced much later, had the additional advantage of giving the United States a vested interest in a peaceful and smooth completion of these institutional procedures.[10]

(4) The safeguarding and selective revelation of embassy documents was the other goal of the Militant Students and their supporters within the Revolutionary Council. Some of these documents related to the negotiations with the Shah's Army leaders in which such notable Khomeini associates as Beheshti and Taleghani had participated. Others related to the contacts that the US embassy had established with the leaders of secular opposition such as the National Front in the autumn of 1978. Reliable reports indicated that Peyman and Khoeini had the first pick of these documents and used the incriminating ones to pressure Beheshti and other Revolutionary Council members into an uncompromising posture *vis-à-vis* the United States. In June 1981 several Mojahedin members who either had seen or made copies of these documents threatened to publicize them if the IRP persisted in opposing the Mojahedin.[11]

It should be noted that Beheshti on several occasions had acknowledged these contacts, including those with Ambassador Sullivan and US General Robert Huyser. Even though Beheshti could be credited with wanting to avoid additional bloodshed and to safeguard the transfer of several hundred US advisers to the relative safety of the capital, the mere fact of his having dealt with US officials could have had devastating effects on his image.

With the appointment of Ghotbzadeh as Foreign Minister, he became the central figure in finding a solution to the crisis. In co-operation with a leftist French lawyer, Christian Bourquet, the Iranian Foreign Minister began secret contacts with the USA once he had become persuaded that the Revolutionary Council had no authority over the Militant Students, and that the Ayattolah himself was the only one who could order them to release the hostages or at least set the conditions for their release.

Since internal sources could not influence Khomeini, the idea of using outside sources with reputations of both opposition to the Shah and anti-Americanism became attractive. The Iranian government could request a UN investigation of the Shah's and the United States's crimes. This would be granted over American objection and hailed in Iran as a victory. However, Kurt Waldheim announced this prematurely, denying the Iranians the opportunity to claim a victory.

It should be noted that neither Khoeini nor Dr Peyman were in agreement with Ghotbzadeh's plan, but once the presidential election was completed they concentrated their efforts on using the hostage crisis to influence the Majlis elections. They achieved a major victory when on 23 February Khomeini finally accepted their viewpoint and ruled that the fate of the hostages should be determined by the as yet unelected Majlis. With that decision the first phase of the crisis came to an end. What had appeared initially as a student protest against the admission of the Shah to the USA, later became a critical factor in Iran's internal politics. The impotence of the USA during the affair simply convinced Khomeini that as long as the holding of the hostages served the purpose of his regime, he should not be in a hurry to resolve the matter.[12]

The net gains of the first phase were quite impressive. A secular moderate premier had been forced out of office. Renewed mobilization efforts had brought some of the defecting political groups, particularly on the left, back to the fold. Any US plan for reinstating the Shah had been nipped in the bud. A controversial constitution had been ratified. Above all, the impotence of the United States, which by the way had still maintained its diplomatic relations with Iran, had been publicly revealed. Radicalism at home and abroad had received such a powerful momentum that the assault on the US embassy was now marked as the second Iranian revolution in one year.

The Second Phase

With Khomeini entrusting the resolution of the crisis to the forthcoming Majlis, the issue of the custody of the hostages continued to be debated in the Revolutionary Council.[13] The Council was the scene of bitter in-fighting, with Beheshti supporting the Militant Students and Banisadr and Ghotbzadeh representing a more moderate posture.

On many occasions the Council would be split 7 to 6 in favour of Beheshti, but the secular group once in a while could also prevail, but only on peripheral matters. One such occasion was when in June an international conference on 'the crimes of the US and the Shah' was held in Tehran. Scores of liberation movements from Third World countries attended. Ramsey Clark, a former US Attorney General, addressed the conference and appealed for the release of the hostages although, he thought, 'God knows the Iranians were justified in seeking vengeance against the Shah's American backers.'

Since February a number of other developments had also occurred. In April the United States finally broke off diplomatic relations with Iran and tightened the sanctions imposed earlier. On 25 April an unsuccessful military mission to rescue the hostages was launched.[14] Even though the mission failed dismally, it brought home to the militants and the Islamic government several significant facts:

(1) It showed that even an indecisive and demonstrably weak US President could launch a military operation against Iran, and that the Iranian military was incapable of guarding the country's airspace or detecting the dispatch of helicopters and transport planes into its territory.

(2) The mission also proved the emptiness of the threat of the Militant Students that the slightest military action by the US would result in the blowing up of the embassy compound and the killing of all the hostages and their captors.

(3) The unsuccessful rescue mission necessitated the dispersal of the hostages throughout Iran, which could have made the task of the government of taking over their custody easier — if such were its intentions.

(4) It showed that the hostages would not be physically harmed, despite the repeated threats which seemed to be taken seriously only by the intimidated American President.

Together these developments also affected the leadership of the Militant Students. For the reasons explored earlier, the possibility that incriminating US documents might have fallen into the hands of Dr Peyman and his radical leftist colleagues, had made his relations with Beheshti quite uneasy. To ensure that Peyman and his followers would not defy his order, Beheshti put Khoeini in charge of liaison with the Revolutionary Council and the state radio-television. Additionally, in the election for Majlis Beheshti saw to it that Khoeini would be assured of a seat in the Majlis and that he would be elected to the Deputy Speakership of the Majlis.

These measures gradually eroded the authority of the secular leadership of the Militant Students. Peyman and others had long advocated the trial of at least some of the hostages. Beheshti, who behind the scenes had several times supported such an action, argued that the hostage crisis could be used as a leverage to secure additional concessions from the United States. Having worked closely with American officials in the last phase of the revolutionary upheaval, Beheshti argued that with the departure of the Shah from the Western hemisphere the tactical nature of the crisis had changed. As a realistic politician he had also underlined Iran's military weakness to withstand a renewed and determined US military operation.

The death of the Shah in Cairo on 27 July 1980 and the appointment of Mohammadali Rajai as Prime Minister on 9 August reinforced Beheshti's position in the crisis and pushed to the background the more radical groups within the militant leadership. Scores of Mojahedin, who had witnessed the gradual exclusion of their organization from power, left the embassy. Dr Peyman's access to the compound and the students was restricted because his followers were either assigned to hostages outside the capital or had left for their home towns.

With the election of the Majlis and the inauguration of Rajai's Cabinet, the Revolutionary Council was disbanded. Banisadr and Ghotbzadeh were for all practical purposes removed from any direct involvement in the hostage crisis. The former had in effect become a figurehead President because of the imposition of Rajai by the IRP-dominated Majlis. The latter had lost his Cabinet post without gaining a Majlis seat because of the opposition of the IRP.

All in all, in mid-September it had become obvious that the critical domestic role of the hostage crisis had been satisfactorily performed. As Khomeini had wanted, the institutions of the new Republic had now been almost fully established and the secular-liberal wings of the revolutionary front had been effectively reduced to insignificance.

In early September the hostage crisis became the chief responsibility of the Rajai government and the Majlis.[15] It is now known that parallel with the initial steps of the Majlis to set up a committee to investigate the matter and formulate conditions for the release of the hostages, secret negotiations had also begun.

Sadegh Tabatabi, a brother-in-law of Khomeini's younger surviving son Ahmad, through the good offices of Gerhardt Ritzel, the West German Ambassador to Iran, let the United States learn about the four conditions that Khomeini would soon announce for releasing the hostages. Obviously, with the Shah's death the demand for his extradiction had become moot. Instead Khomeini wanted: (1) the return of the people's wealth plundered by the Shah; (2) the lifting of the sanctions imposed by the USA; (3) a pledge of non-intervention in Iran's internal affairs; (4) the approval of the Majlis of the above conditions.

Simultaneously Beheshti's man Khoeini was elected chairman of the parliamentary committee, composed of Moslem hardliners put in charge of the hostage crisis. When Iraq invaded Iran on 22 September the urgency of the resolution of the crisis was enhanced. The US-armed Iranian military was in dire need of spare parts, especially for its Air Force. Banisadr, who as Commander-in-Chief was in charge of Iran's military efforts, insisted that the lifting of sanctions should openly include the resumption of shipments of military hardware to the tune of some $500 million, already paid for by the previous regime.

Radical elements in the Majlis commission vehemently opposed it. It was inconceivable to acknowledge any indebtedness to the United States in fighting a war which they believed the United States had urged Iraq to unleash against Iran. As noted elsewhere, this issue became a new bone of contention between Banisadr and the Beheshti-dominated Majlis and government when the crisis was finally resolved on 20 January 1981.

Another interesting by-product of Iraq's attack on Iran was a further thinning down of the ranks of the Militant Students. Close to fifty of them, including those initial followers of Dr Peyman, left for the front and joined the guerrilla resistance force led by Mostafa Chamran, the Palestinian-trained former Minister of Defence and Khomeini's representative in the High Defence Council.[16]

This phase ended with the hostage crisis having fulfilled its internal political function, now beginning to show signs of becoming a liability. In a sense one could surmize that with the war against Iraq, the clergy-dominated government and Majlis became the hostage of their own anti-American rhetoric. Herein lies the reason for the lengthy and tortuous negotiations that during the final phase of the crisis succeeded in resolving it.

The Third Phase

In the final phase of the crisis a new revolutionary leader assumed the ultimate role of negotiating an agreement through the Algerian government. This was Behzad Nabavi, an ardent opponent of the Shah who had spent eight years in prison. He was appointed Minister in Charge of Executive Affairs. Fully supported by Beheshti, he was an arch enemy of Banisadr and in league with the emerging triumvirate of Beheshti, Rafsanjani and Rajai.

His aim from the outset was to assure that whatever form the final settlement took, it would not be sabotaged by the secular leftist elements among the Militant Sudents. In this he found support among influential IRP members in the Majlis. Not only did the Speaker, Rafsanjani, pledge support for a complete takeover of the negotiations about the hostages by the Rajai government, but he also made sure that secular leftists like Dr Peyman would virtually lose all contact with the Militant Students. The party's ideologue Dr Hassan Ayat was given the task of neutralizing any possible opposition to a settlement over the hostages inside the Majlis and among secular radical groups. Since the dispersal of the hostages in late April, the Pasdaran acquired a role in the protection of the embassy compound as well as the hotels and military bases in provincial towns to which some of the hostages had been moved. Evidently the government was now ready, if need be, to use the Pasdaran to take over custody of the hostages. Such a measure could not have been taken under Banisadr's leadership when on 31 March the Revolutionary Council had voted for their transfer to the Council and the Militant Students had successfully defied that order.

In the meantime, secret negotiations to find a common ground between Khomeini's four conditions and the USA continued. On 9 September the German embassy in Washington DC arranged a meeting in Bonn between Sadegh Tabatabai and Warren Christopher, Assistant Secretary of State for the Middle East. In mid-September a meeting took place, with Tabatabai assuring Christopher that the US position appeared reasonable to him and that he would convey his own constructive recommendations when he returned to Tehran shortly.

Although the war with Iraq interrupted the sequence of events temporarily, Tabatabai gave a favourable report to Khomeini, who shortly thereafter authorized Rajai to visit United Nations Headquarters in New York, something that he had denied Banisadr early in the first phase. The reason given was that Rajai was to plead Iran's case against Iraq before the Security Council. However, Nabavi who accompanied Rajai, entered into substantive talks with representatives of Algeria, Pakistan, Syria and Indonesia. The Algerian government offered to mediate, and all four countries urged the Iranian officials to end the crisis while there was time lest the forthcoming presidential election brought to power a tougher, Republican President in the USA.

On his way back to Tehran Rajai listened to similar warnings in Algiers, where he stopped briefly. In a top-level meeting between

Beheshti, Rajai, Nabavi and Rafsanjani held on 31 October, a decision was made to hasten the parliamentary debate prior to 4 November, the date of the US elections. Beheshti and Rafsanjani made sure that the Majlis would substantially approve Khomeini's four conditions. Nabavi took charge of neutralizing leftist opposition within the Militant Students as well as among secular political parties, and of course from Banisadr.

On 2 November the Majlis finally adopted the resolution on the hostages. Two days later the landslide victory of Reagan showed that the impact of the announcement was negligible in terms of President Carter's fortune. The huge anti-American mass rally in front of the US embassy on the anniversary of the hostage-taking, was watched by millions of US voters just as they left home for work and the polling stations, and if anything reawakened a sense of bitterness against the US government's impotence to resolve the crisis.

At this stage the Iranians involved in the crisis were divided into several groups. On the one hand Nabavi and Beheshti pressed for a quick solution, for they were convinced that the longer hostages were held the more difficult it would be to secure more favourable terms. Several pronouncements by President-elect Reagan convinced them that if they waited until his inauguration they might be forced, at the least, to re-negotiate from scratch.

Opposed to them were Banisadr and such secular leftist groups as the Mojahedin, who believed the final terms which had begun to leak into the still relatively free Iranian press were much worse than those Banisadr could have secured a year earlier.[17] This was particularly so because the United States had not agreed even in principle to resume shipment of the military spare parts so direly needed in the war against Iraq. However, Banisadr was hard put to it to maintain his long-held opposition to the release of the hostages. The Beheshti–Rafsanjani–Rajai triumvirate was quite sanguine about trouble from that quarter. What worried them was that some of the Militant Students had reportedly demanded special conditions for releasing their captives. While there was no indication that Dr Peyman had re-established contact with his followers, amongst them the truth was that these very students had expressed reservations about the settlement and insisted on a particular timetable for the release of the hostages.

As to Khomeini himself, by then he was convinced that an impressive victory over the 'Great Satan' had been achieved. But at the end it was he who conceded to the Militant Students the condition that under no circumstances should the release come before the official departure of Carter from office. Either out of naiveté or because of his personal animosity toward Carter, Khomeini accepted the Militant Students' argument, conveyed to him by Nabavi, that to expedite the release would mean that the people of Iran were afraid of the Republican President. As an act of defiance, they insisted Carter should not be given the satisfaction of having the hostages released while he was still in power.

At any rate, the interval between Election Day and Inauguration Day was spent in laborious negotiations at every step of which the Iranians were forced to tone down their demands. Thus, they first requested $24 billion[18] to cover their frozen assets and the property taken by the late Shah and his family. In early January this was cut to $9.5 billion, enabling Warren Christopher to fly into Algiers where after thirteen days of day and night negotiations, the ultimate agreement was reached in the form of a declaration by the Algerian government signed by the USA and Iran.

On 16 January Iran paid off the entire $3.67 billion in outstanding loans with Western Banks. Under the agreement the USA released about $8 billion worth of frozen Iranian assets, but about $5.1 billion of these were set aside to pay off Iran's debts to American and European banks.

The prolonged hostage crisis temporarily interrupted the process of the institutionalization of the Islamic Republic. But by the end of January not only was the process resumed, but the legislative branch of the government and its appointed Prime Minister, as has been noted, became intimately involved in that crisis. To understand the institutional evolution of the Republic, the presidential and parliamentary elections and the formation of the first Cabinet must be considered next.

Notes

1. Interview with Oriana Fallaci, *New York Times* as well as in *Mizan*, Tehran, 12 October 1979.

2. Testimony of Abbas Amirentezam during his trial before a revolutionary tribunal, April 1981. *Enghelabe Islami*, 14 April 1981.

3. From his own paper, *Ummat* (Islamic term for community) and *Ettelaat*, 12 December 1979.

4. Interview with Parviz Raeen, the Associated Press correspondent in Iran, New York, 11 January 1980.

5. *Jomhuriye Islami* and *Keyhan*, 17 October 1979.

6. *Ettelaat*, 21 December 1979.

7. Two of his widely distributed works are: *Osule Sosyalizme Mardome*

Iran (Principle of Iranian People's Socialism), Tehran, 1979, n.p. and *Kar*, *Malekiyat va Sarmaye dar Islam* (Labour, Ownership, and Capital in Islam), n.d.

8. One of the best available accounts is 'America in Captivity', *New York Times Magazine*, 14 May 1981.

9. Interview with Mohammad Zanganeh and Abbas Radmehr in Paris, 22 April 1981. (The above were the second fictitious names which had to be used as condition of the interview, the first being those that they assumed when they captured the embassy.)

10. Banisadr, the deposed first President, has so testified in his press conference in Paris, *Le Monde*, 28 July 1981.

11. *Mojahed*, the underground Farsi organ of the Mojahedin, 12 April 1981.

12. Some Iranian specialists had cautioned against giving Khomeini an appearance of helplessness because he would regard it as a sign of his own weakness, just as he had interpreted the Shah's helplessness during the struggle with him. *Time*, New York, 12 December 1979.

13. Khomeini's statement read in part,

The occupation of the Nest of Espionage was one of the manifestations of popular demand for the return of the Shah and the plundered property of the people. Since in the near future the people's representatives will assemble at the Islamic Consultative Assembly, it will be up to the people's representatives to decide about the release of the hostages and the concessions and conditions that they want in return.

Keyhan, Tehran, 24 February 1980.

14. On the rescue operation see Drew Middleton, 'Going the Military Route', *New York Times Magazine*, 14 May 1981.

15. On 2 July 1980, 185 Congressmen wrote to the Speaker of the Majlis requesting the release of the hostages. In response the Speaker wrote a lengthy indictment of US errors and abuses in Iran and elsewhere in the Middle East, demanding that the Congress should urgently investigate these so that the road toward a solution be paved. *Islamic Revolution*, Falls Church, Virginia, September, 1980.

16. In early June Chamran was killed in Kurdistan under mysterious circumstance. Exiled groups in France in close touch with the Kurdish Democratic Party claimed that he had been liaising between Banisadr and the Army, and that his death was planned by the operatives of IRP in preparation for the final showdown with Banisadr, *Iran Post*, Los Angeles, 28 June 1981.

17. Mehdi Bazargan's newspaper, *Mizan*, published a series of lengthy analyses of the agreement which angered the ruling party and caused the paper's closure some weeks later, 21 February–12 March 1981. Bazargan had earlier reflected the views of the National Front which not only opposed the Assembly of Experts but also demanded the postponement of the constitutional referendum at the height of the hostage crisis. *Ettelaat*, Tehran, 21 November 1980.

18. US billions are used throughout.

4 THE PRESIDENCY AND THE MAJLIS

Once the Constitution had been ratified the next step in laying the foundation of the Islamic Republic was to conduct an election for the Presidency.

At the end of December Khomeini had not yet decided whether the parliamentary or presidential election should be the first order of business. What is clear is that the Revolutionary Council was hopelessly divided on the issue. Not knowing whether Khomeini would approve of a cleric as President, Beheshti, Bahonar and Rafsanjani all clamoured for the holding of the presidential election, which each thought he could win. On the other hand if Khomeini preferred a non-cleric as President, these clerics believed the Majlis election should precede the presidential one. They were fearful that a non-clerical, popularly elected President might influence the upcoming Majlis election by organizing his supporters in the various electoral districts.

An analysis of the Revolutionary Council deliberation and the composition of its membership indicate that several positions were taken by members concerning this matter. First, the supporters of former Prime Minister Mehdi Bazargan were of the opinion that Iran needed a secular head of the executive just as soon as it was possible. The hostage crisis and the Soviet invasion of Afghanistan, they believed, had necessitated the prompt establishment of the new executive. They had even suggested that if elections could not be held immediately the Revolutionary Council should itself appoint the Cabinet and its Secretary Beheshti be accepted as Prime Minister.[1]

It should be noted that since the resignation of the Provisional Government on 5 November, Iran had had a Cabinet but no Prime Minister. About 40 per cent of its members were simultaneously members of the Revolutionary Council including, oddly enough, the recently resigned provisional Prime Minister Mehdi Bazargan.

This group, which had the support of 3 or 4 other members of the 15-member Revolutionary Council, did not mind which election took place first.

A second position was that of Beheshti and his 5 or 6 supporters in the Revolutionary Council. While nothing would perhaps have pleased him more than becoming Chief Executive, he shrewdly rejected the idea and instead favoured the early election of the Majlis. Additionally, he did not as yet know whether Khomeini would agree to a clerical President. At any rate, as the Secretary of the Revolutionary Council, and soon after the approval of the constitution the Chief Justice of the Supreme Court, he was already exercising considerable power. Rather than expressing clearly his preference for the precedence of one election over the other, Beheshti refused to give any advice on that matter to Khomeini.

A third position was attributed to Banisadr and three more members of the Council, including Dr Hassan Habibi, who in the post-hostage era had acted as the spokesman for the Council. As was the case in a number of critical decisions concering the hostage crisis, these three vacillated in supporting either the Beheshti or Bazargan faction, but more often than not they would end up supporting the Beheshti faction. As for which election should be conducted first, this group agreed with Banisadr that the presidential election should come first. Not only would it be easier to elect from one national constituency one single President, but it would be also more conducive to the national mood of unity so conclusively demonstrated in the course of the constitutional referendum.

All accounts indicate that Banisadr played his cards extremely carefully. At the end of December Ahmad, Khomeini's son, assured Banisadr that his father did not want all institutional powers to be monopolized by the clerical leaders, but that he was reluctant to order anyone not to run for office. Khomeini, who preferred at that point to be 'above politics', routinely insisted that the Revolutionary Council should decide the matter and then seek his consent. Once it learned that Khomeini preferred a non-cleric for the job, the Beheshti faction urged that the presidential election should precede that of the Majlis. If no cleric could be nominated for President, Beheshti was confident that enough secular personalities, affiliated with and completely trusted by the fundamentalist clerics, could be found to run. The moment the announcement that the presidential election was to be held on 25 January was made the IRP ruled out its support for anyone who did not belong to the party. The various political factions at the outset of the electoral campaign adopted the following attitudes.

The IRP first nominated one of the leading members of its leadership council, Jalaleddin Farsi, but withdrew his nomination when it became known that his father was of Afghan origin. In his place the party nominated Dr Hassan Habibi, who had served as a member and later as spokesman of the Revolutionary Council. Secondly, the supporters of Bazargan, including the National Front and a considerable segment of the Bazaar leadership, nominated the former Admiral Ahmad Madani, who had served in a number of important positions in Bazargan's government.

Thirdly, the clerical leaders who did not support Beheshti and the IRP, the secular forces who were critical of Bazargan, and a number of close associates of Khomeini such as his son, Ahmad, and his son-in-law Ayattolah Eshraghi, joined forces to nominate Banisadr. The Mojahedin nominated their leader Massud Rajavi, but were forced to withdraw his name when the IRP and the fundamentalist clerics successfully argued that since the organization had boycotted the referendum for the constitution, its leader could not possibly serve in the highest executive office created by that constitution.[2] Scores of other candidates were also nominated, creating the impression that the presidential election would require a run-off, for no candidate seemed likely to secure the required 50 per cent of the votes in the first round.

The Ministry of the Interior indicated that 65 per cent of all eligible voters had participated in the election and that, except for Kurdistan where a partial boycott was in force, participation across the country had been fairly even. The total votes cast were put at over 14 million, of which 10.7 million went to Banisadr and over 2 million to Admiral Madani. IRP candidate Dr Hassan Habibi was said to have received close to 700,000 votes.[3]

With Banisadr elected, the IRP concentrated all its efforts on the elections for the Majlis. In the interim between the elections IRP clerical leaders like Beheshti, Ardabili and Mahdavi Kani gained important positions within the Judiciary and the *de facto* government. Beheshti was appointed Chief Justice of the Supreme Court, Ardabili became the Prosecutor-General. Others were appointed to the all powerful Council of Custodians. These appointments more than compensated for the victory of a non-IRP presidential candidate, because for all practical purposes they put the judicial and constitutional control of the country in the hands of the IRP. Mahdavi Kani and Rafsanjani literally took control of the elections for the Majlis, through which the IRP planned to control the government, thus rendering the new President merely the symbolic Head of State, as in such European political systems as Italy and West Germany.

The Majlis Election

The Revolutionary Council in March approved the double-ballot majority system for the Majlis. The law provides that:

Members of the National Consultative Assembly will be elected by an absolute majority (50% +) of votes. If in the first round in single or multiple districts such a majority is not obtained, there will be a second round. Thus from among those candidates who do not receive an absolute majority twice as many as the number of representatives in each district will run in the second round, in which a relative majority will suffice.[4]

The law encountered vehement opposition from political groups which had been excluded from the Assembly of Experts and/or had boycotted the constitutional referendum. These groups preferred the proportional representation system under which they could aspire at least to some representation. They rightly feared that under the double-ballot majority system none of their candidates, assuming they could be nominated, was likely to win an absolute majority in the first round. In the second round the IRP would make electoral coalitions with smaller parties and against their candidates. The Mojahedin, the Progressive Radical Party, and National Front personalities such as Dr Aliasghar Hajseydjavadi and Abdolkarim Lahiji, all joined in criticizing the action of the Revolutionary Council.[5]

Noted Shia leaders like Shariatmadari and Qomi did not bother to protest against the electoral law for they had strongly objected in the first place to some of the provisions of the Islamic constitution which provided for the election of the Majlis.

In addition to an electoral system which was designed to help the pro-regime groups, an elaborate process of screening candidates was also announced. During the four weeks that candidates throughout the country were screened, the IRP waged a decisive campaign to discredit nominees whose local support was sufficiently strong to threaten the success of IRP candidates.

Full advantage was also taken of the so-called revelations of the Students following the Imam's Line, that is to say the captors of the American hostages. These students exposed a number of pro-National Front personalities as having been in touch with the United States embassy, even if the contact had been confined to securing information about student visas or American academic institutions.

If these efforts did not succeed in forcing the withdrawal of a candidate, the Majlis majority would use its power of approving, or otherwise, the credentials of elected members so as to reject 'undesirable individuals'. As will be seen later, this power was used in a number of vital elections.

A third method of achieving IRP hegemony was simply to suspend elections in districts where the opposition was likely to win, on the grounds of 'lack of security'. Acting Interior Minister and a powerful member of the Revolutionary Council Hashemi Rafsanjani, who was in charge of these elections and was rewarded by being elected as the first Speaker of the Majlis, saw to it that these methods brought the desired results.

In March the first stage of the elections was held for 228 deputies out of the constitutionally sanctioned 270. Not more than 40 per cent of these deputies received the required 50 per cent or more of the votes. The Interior Ministry declared that a total of 6.1 million people had voted in these elections. Instead of holding the second round two weeks later, the Ministry appealed to the Revolutionary Council for a delay of a couple of months. It was not until July that the second rounds were completed, and the other 60 per cent of the 228 deputies were elected.[6]

Needless to say, this opportunity was used to form electoral coalitions with the smaller pro-IRP parties so that IRP candidates would be assured of victory in the second round.

Thus the Majlis which met in early August represented the following line-up:

(1) About 131 seats belonged to the IRP, consisting of about 60 per cent of clerics ranging in rank from Hojatolislam to Ayattolah, and 40 per cent of non-clerics drawn from the lower middle class and the Bazaar. This group was instrumental in electing Rafsanjani to the Speakership of the Majlis, despite the protest of other deputies who charged that as Minister of Interior he had had a major role in assuring an IRP majority in the Majlis.

(2) A second group was the so-called *Monfaredin* or independents, some of whom represented the more progressive clergy who had supported the National Front in the past and had expressed at least moderate opposition to some aspects of the new constitution. At the outset they numbered between 68 and 74 members, but their solidarity was severely tested in a number of the critical issues that the Majlis faced almost as soon as it was inaugurated.

(3) A third group was affiliated with Bazargan's Iran Liberation Movement and had between 15 and 23 members, half of whom had served in Bazargan's provisional government as ministers and deputy ministers. The group represented the secular and moderate forces in the Majlis and proudly asserted its affiliation with Dr Mossadegh's National Front of the early 1950s. Even though Bazargan had many grievances against Banisadr, his group in the Majlis became increasingly identified with the President as he became entangled in battle after battle with Beheshti's IRP. It is important to note two other facts about the Majlis. One is that the last two groups did not form even a tactical coalition on important issues before the legislature, and the second is that for a variety of reasons their numerical strength changed quite dramatically almost immediately after the Majlis had begun to function. Some of these reasons had to do with the practice of deputies joining the government as ministers without their successors being elected in by-elections, as provided for by the constitution.

The other factor was the rejection of the credentials of deputies, often on dubious grounds, by the IRP majority. Three important deputies had their credentials rejected in this way, one of them being Khosrow Qashqai, a leader of the Qashqai tribe and a long-time foe of the Shah. He was accused of being a feudal landlord and of having co-operated with the United States government. The Militant Students and pro-Soviet leftist groups joined in a bitter campaign to discredit him and urged the Majlis to reject him. The second important deputy to be rejected was the former Admiral Ahmad Madani, a foe of the deposed Shah who had served as Commander of the Navy and Governor of Khuzistan, crushing the rebellion of the Arab Iranians of that province in the early months of Khomeini's regime. He had run second to Banisadr in the presidential election and had a reputation of honesty, integrity and having had administrative experience. His home town of Kirman had given him a landslide victory, but the IRP managed to reject his credentials on the grounds of his involvement in vote-peddling and vote-buying in his district. Shortly thereafter he turned against Khomeini and is presently in West Germany working with other exiles to overthrow the Islamic Government.

Abolfazl Ghassemi, representing the Executive Council of the National Front, was the third prominent deputy to have his credentials rejected. The IRP seemed to single out those members who had either a large following in their districts or had the reputation of supporting secularism and being non-committal about Islamic fundamentalism. Ghassemi was later given a life sentence for alleged pro-American activities.

The war with Iraq made the pretext of not holding by-elections a more plausible one. But even if these had all been held at the prescribed times, the bombing of the IRP headquarters in June which killed 20 of its deputies, plus the individual assassinations of another four IRP members, reduced the Majlis membership to under 200. But defection from the Monfaredin group as well as from Bazargan's has resulted in the IRP's continuing domination of the Majlis.

The IRP in the Majlis

Although it is a majority faction in the Majlis, the party is not well known in Iran. It was organized by nine clerical and non-clerical supporters of Khomeini in the wake of the approval of the referendum to establish an Islamic Republic on 1 April 1979. Apart from Beheshti, its other leaders were Ayattolah Mohammadreza Mahdavi Kani, serving as interim Prime Minister after the assassination of Bahonar in August, Aliakbar Hashemi Rafsanjani the Majlis Speaker, the late Hojatolislam Ali Ghoddusi, Prosecutor-General of Revolutionary Courts and the late Hojatolislam Mohammadjavad Bahonar, second Prime Minister of the Islamic Republic.

The IRP had won its first major victory with the election of the Assembly of Experts, which was to draft the constitution. It had suffered a slight setback when Banisadr was elected President. That setback had been more than compensated for when the party imposed Mohammadali Rajai as Prime Minister on a reluctant Banisadr.

As far as it can be ascertained, the party is not a hierarchically centralized political organization. Instead, it is a coalition of Islamic societies organized throughout Iran and led by a Central Council which, as of last spring, had 30 members. The campaign of bombing and assassination waged by anti-government guerrillas killed ten of those in June and July alone. None the less, under Beheshti the party had managed to spread into all institutions including the civil service, the Army, the universities, factories and schools by engaging in massive purges of its opponents.

At the beginning of the tenure of the present Majlis three factions could be recognized within the IRP parliamentary party. First, the supporters of Beheshti; secondly, the supporters of Hassan Ayat, the ideologue of the party; and lastly the followers of Ayattolah Mussavi Ardabili, the former Prosecutor-General who later replaced Beheshti as Head of the Supreme Court after his death in the bomb blast at IRP headquarters at the end of June.[7]

These factions have displayed varying degrees of disagreement on several issues. First, on the question of co-operation with secular nationalist personalities such as Bazargan, Beheshti's position has been consistently anti-co-operation, whereas Ayattolah Ardabili's group has sought to co-operate with all Islamic groups — even those who wish to emphasize nationalistic tendencies. Dr Ayat's faction, on the other hand, was dedicated to working covertly for the ousting of Banisadr, and was not concerned about the Bazargan faction as long as it remained a minority in the Majlis.

Secondly, on the issue of the Islamic Republic's economic policy the Ayat faction is in favour of the total nationalization of all industries and services, and opposes even small-scale free enterprise and limited private investment. Not so the other two factions, which are concerned that total state ownership and control of all the means of production would destroy Iran's middle-level, skilled and independent national bourgeoisie. The issue of a correct economic policy, however, is not given the highest priority at the present time, when the issues of the consolidation of power, relations with the USA and the war with Iraq are more pressing.

A third issue which divides the different factions of the ruling IRP concerns foreign policy. Beheshti and his allies adhered strictly to the slogan of 'neither East nor West.' Others were concerned that blind militancy and indiscriminate hostility toward the West would sink Iran deeper into international isolation. To convince everyone of Iran's sincere non-alignment posture, the pro-Ardabili faction now feel that opposition to the Soviet action in Afghanistan and Moscow's dubious posture in the Iraq–Iran war must be more pronounced and consistent.

Some of the divisive issues having been outlined, it is worth noting that the party is united around the three goals of common opposition to US imperialism, struggle against Shah-introduced Westernization and loyalty to the person and principles of Ayattolah Khomeini.

Although with the Majlis election the IRP acquired institutional legitimacy, the party could by no means be regarded as merely a parliamentary party. It has striven to sustain its mass basis of support by several methods. First, it relies on the Revolutionary Guards, whose leadership remains loyal to the party as long as the party represents Khomeini. Secondly, it relies on the mobs of *Hizbollahi* or Followers of the Party of God, which consist of the urban poor, the homeless and the unemployed. Repeatedly, the two have combined to suppress brutally any demonstration of opposition to the IRP. The usual pattern has always been that the club-wielders of Hizbollah will disrupt a rally or a march of the opposition and then the Pasdaran will be called in to restore order. In so doing, they actively support the Hizbollahis and forcibly disperse the opposition groups. The third instrument of IRP control are the village Mullahs who work as grass-root agitators for the party and co-ordinate their activities with those of local revolutionary committees, a remnant of the early revolutionary period which has survived the efforts of institutionalization by the new government.

So far the IRP has won all its battles in and outside parliament. Its basic strength is that it appeals to the lower classes by virtue of its close identification with Khomeini. Its chief weakness is that it suffers from several inherent liabilities: (1) its authority is so exclusively dependent on Khomeini that it is inconceivable it could survive the disappearance of the Imam; (2) as the ruling party it suffers from accusations of corruption and artificiality just as in other attempts to impose political parties from above in recent Iranian history; (3) the party tries to ignore other nationalist and secular political groups whose contribution to the success of revolution cannot simply be wiped out. In doing so the party has become susceptible to the charge of monopolistic and exclusive tendencies.

Whether these liabilities are likely to render the party ineffective outside the Majlis remains to be seen. What is beyond any doubt is that its control of the Majlis, and through it the government, has been so far firmly established.

At any rate, on Sunday 19 July the Majlis opened its session with 206 deputies, while about 40 deputies from Kurdistan, Fars and Khuzistan did not show up, either in protest against the central government or because of the refusal of the Interior Ministry to certify their election.[8]

The first victory of the IRP was demonstrated by the election of Rafsanjani as Speaker with 146 votes of a total of 196. The second victory was gained when the same majority a few days later voted to change its name from National Consultative Assembly to Islamic Assembly. This change of name, which was vehemently opposed by the Bazargan faction and some of the independent deputies, was supported on the grounds that it represented a complete break with the past. Even though the new constitution had retained the traditional name for the parliament, the IRP succeeded in striking out the term 'National' as it was 'rather secular and, after all, had originated from the West.'

The Opposition and the Majlis

The completion of the Majlis elections and the victory of the IRP further alienated the opposition groups. The most outspoken opposition came from the Mojahedin, which, in a detailed analysis, declared its non-recognition of the results, in particular those in Tehran. An analysis of the results showed that the IRP had won a total of 25 seats in the less-populated districts with a total vote of 506,000, whereas the Mojahedin had won no representation even though their leader, Massud Rajavi, had gained 530,000 votes in the first round of the election in Tehran and had therefore qualified for the second round.

Other data cited by the Mojahedin showed that in the first round, which more accurately reflected the relative strengths of the candidates, the IRP had won 41 seats with a total of 1,617,000 votes. The Mojahedin with a total of 906,000 votes could win no seats, even though two independent candidates supported by the Mojahedin managed to be elected. According to Rajavi himself his party, which despite all the alleged riggings, received 13 per cent of the total ballot and should have received a total of 25 seats, or the same percentage of the total deputies elected in the two rounds.[9]

The argument of the Mojahedin and other groups, including the Fedayeen and the pro-Soviet Tudeh Party, was a familiar one. Nearly all the parties who had opposed the system of double-ballot majority knew that their ability to translate their votes into parliamentary seats would be radically undermined. They, therefore, as noted earlier, had opted for a proportional representation system. Once the elections were over they calculated their share of the seats in proportion to their share of the votes and accused the IRP of electoral fraud.

This complaint was not uncommon in countries such as France during the Fifth Republic. The IRP had formed a 'grand coalition' with the so-called 'Activist Clergy' and the 'Hamnam Group' consisting of the supporters of Bazargan's Liberation Movement. This coalition had succeeded in dominating the second rounds of the ballot just as in the Fifth Republic the French centrist and non-communist leftist parties had done.

This is not to cast doubts on the complaints of the opposition parties about electoral malpractices in the Islamic Republic. The point is that the double-ballot majority system gives some inherent advantages to the pro-government and anti-leftist parties by enabling them to reduce radically or deny totally the opposition representation in proportion to their relative public support.[10]

The Mojahedin had used the same argument in the presidential election in January 1980. Although their leader Massud Rajavi had been forced out as a candidate, the movement did not actively agitate to disturb the elections. Instead, it tried to show that the decline in the voting turn-out marked a clear alienation of secular and leftist groups from the Islamic Republic.

The organization put out a statement claiming that the difference between the 20.4 million votes cast in the referendum for the Islamic Republic and the 14 million votes for the election of the President indicated the growing apathy towards the regime.

Other opposition groups used similar arguments against the elections. However, the Mojahedin protest was much more significant because not only had they proved to be numerically the strongest organized opposition, but unlike other groups such as the Tudeh they had refused to accept the legitimacy of the Majlis.[11]

The First Cabinet

Even the most optimistic supporters of the IRP knew that the first battle with the President had to be waged on the question of the formation of the first Cabinet.

In Chapter 7, in dealing with the demise of Banisadr some of the relevant constitutional and ideological issues underlying the conflict between the Majlis and the Presidency are discussed.

What must be noted here is that the struggle at the outset did not seem too serious. Even when the hint of Admiral Madani's candidacy had aroused a chorus of clerical opposition in and outside the Majlis, Banisadr learned that he should find a *Maktabi* or fundamentalist non-cleric for the job. After some soul-searching he nominated Aliakbar Mirsalim, the head of the civil service organization. His nomination was rejected both by a coalition of the Beheshti group who thought he was not sufficiently Maktabi, and by secular and progressive deputies who thought he was inexperienced and incompetent.

It was after that failure that Mohammadali Rajai was recommended to the President by the IRP, which assured him that as a popular member of the Majlis from the capital he would have no difficulty in gaining a vote of confidence.

Before his nomination by the Majlis Rajai was Minister of Education in Bazargan's Provisional Government. His appointment was seriously opposed by Banisadr, who as President had the constitutional right to refuse his support, Banisadr described Rajai as headstrong, ill-informed and incompetent for the job.[12] But Rajai was a protégé of Beheshti, and since the IRP controlled the Majlis and had earlier rejected two of his nominees, the President had accepted Rajai hoping that at least a competent Cabinet could be put together.

Rajai's record as an opponent of the Shah was not very impressive. He was twice arrested, once in the 1960s and imprisoned for several months, and again in 1974. During his second imprisonment he had become acquainted with a number of clerical opponents of the Shah such as Ayattolah Mahmud Taleghani.

A self-taught high school maths teacher, he embraced a fundamentalist line after the revolution. Even though he had served in the Bazargan Cabinet, he had criticized the Provisional Government when he finally became Prime Minister in August 1980. Ideologically he was both anti-American and anti-capitalist. In presenting his Cabinet to the Majlis he set the redistribution of wealth as the principal goal of his government. In the intensive struggle for power between Banisadr and Beheshti, Rajai had acted subserviently to the latter.

A major issue of conflict between the President and Prime Minister concerned the rejection of 7 out of the original 21 nominees for the Cabinet. Until he was forced out of office on 24 June several of these positions had been left vacant including that of Foreign Minister. The Majlis, unable to force the President constitutionally to accept its nominees, voted to authorize Rajai to take over those posts as a further rebuttal to Banisadr.

Those who served in his Cabinet until he was nominated for President after Banisadr's ousting in June represented a mixed bag. Some, like Ayattolah Mahdavi Kani, Minister of the Interior, were experienced administrators. Others like Tondguyan, the Minister for Oil, who was captured by Iraqi forces near Abadan in October 1980, was inexperienced and unqualified. Sixty per cent were members of the IRP and the rest were former associates of Beheshti and Rafsanjani. They had all had some experience in active opposition to the Shah. Indeed, the longer that opposition had been, particularly if it had entailed imprisonment, the more prominent was their position as Cabinet members.

None the less, two of its members, Kani, and Minister of State Behzad Nabavi, succeeded in distinguishing themselves as shrewd administrators and capable politicians. Kani took charge of security and the election of various offices of the Republic. Nabavi, who almost single-handedly concluded the hostage negotiations, has served Rajai's successors as a kind of troubleshooter since June 1981 in charge of coordinating security operations against armed resistance to the regime.

Needless to say, on repeated occasions Banisadr tried to convince Khomeini to change the government by offering concrete cases of mismanagement and even of some financial corruption. With the outbreak of the war with Iraq the President felt it was even more imperative to install an experienced and qualified government. Khomeini turned this argument around to argue that precisely because of the war it was not prudent to change the government lest the 'heathen Baathist enemy construe it as sign of weakness.'[13]

Notes

1. Shortly after his ouster Bazargan vehemently attacked this suggestion, arguing that the Council did not accurately represent all the forces in the revolutionary coalition. Beheshti's people believed this was a plot to undermine him by making sure that he would become a sort of second provisional Prime Minister unable to devote his full energy to the forthcoming Majlis election. *Mizan*, Tehran, 28 November 1980 and *Jomhuriye Islami*, 11 December 1980.

2. The Mojahedin pointed to the fallacy of this argument by referring to the French Constitution of the Fifth Republic, which though opposed by the powerful Communist Party did not prevent communist candidates running for either parliamentary or presidential elections, *Mojahed*, Tehran, 3 January 1980.

3. *Keyhan*, 26 January 1980. It is noteworthy that the US media vastly exaggerated Banisadr's electoral victory, believing that as a moderate politician he would expedite the resolution of the hostage crisis. This author cautioned the American public against such an illusion, pointing out that the election was a contest amongst several close associates of Khomeini, rather than a free party election which could measure the relative strengths of the various political groups and personalities. *Transcript of MacNeil-Lehrer Report* (Public Broadcasting System), Washington, DC, 25 January 1980.

4. The text in *Jomhuriye Islami*, Tehran, 5 February 1980.

5. *Mojahed, Jebhe Melli, Ranjbar* published lengthy communiqués of their respective organizations and argued forcefully in favour of proportional representations 21–28 March 1980.

6. At the end of June the Ministry of Interior announced the election of 242 deputies of the constitutionally authorized 270. Of these 97 were elected in the first round and 145 in the second round. Due to internal difficulties elections in 24 districts, which together choose 28 deputies, had been postponed. In some the result of the first round had been invalidated because of massive protest against violation of electoral codes. Most of these districts were located in Kurdistan or Western Azarbayjan, where government authority had not been fully established in the wake of the Kurdish rebellion in progress since the summer of 1979. Most of these districts had given the required 50% majority in the first round to the KDP or the Kumeleh, the major and minor political parties respectively of the Kurdish people.

7. Younes Parsa Benab, 'Iran in Transition: The Present Struggle for Power', *Review of Iran's Politics, Economy and History*, Washington, DC, No. 1, Spring 1981, pp. 122–31.

8. The session began by a recitation from the Qoran and a message from Khomeini exhorting the Majlis to enact only laws which were fully compatible

with Islam. *Ettelaat*, 19 July 1981.

9. *People's Mojahedin Organization of Iran*. (The English-language monthly published until June 1981 in Europe). See No. 5, May 1980.

10. An analysis of nearly every parliamentary election since the birth of the Fifth Republic in France in 1958 shows how parties of the radical left and right suffer under this type of electoral system.

11. 'The Content of the Islamic Republic,' PMOI's Organization, *Mojahed*, Vol. 1, Nos. 4–5, April–May 1980 is a detailed analysis indicating the gradual widening of the gap between the Mojahedin's expectations in the new Iran and what has actually been achieved in the Islamic Republic.

12. *Mizan*, 5 August 1980.

13. On 31 October Banisadr went to Khomeini and asked for the dismissal of Rajai's Cabinet for 'his incompetence was a serious threat to Iran at the time of Iraqi invasion'. As was his habit, Khomeini offered no response. A few weeks later, without acknowledging Banisadr's request, he decreed that as long as the war continued there would be no Cabinet changes. *Iran Post*, No. 6, 13 December 1980.

THE RESURGENCE OF OPPOSITION

The resolution of the hostage problem did not signal the return of normalcy to the country. If anything, the removal of an international crisis allowed domestic issues to shift to the centre of politics. The constraint of refraining from opposing the government when it was entangled in a major external crisis no longer inhibited the political groups. Nor did the protracted war with Iraq restrain domestic political forces from continuing their struggle for power and influence, and at times, for mere survival.

By the time that the revolution was about to celebrate its second anniversary, the Islamic Republic faced countless difficulties in its efforts to consolidate its legitimacy. On the occasion of the Iranian New Year, 20 March 1981, Khomeini declared the New Year as one of 'order and normalcy'. Halfway into the year the Islamic Republic was as far from these objectives as the former regime had been in the second half of 1978. The intensity and the scope of the activities of the various opposition groups are both the causes and effects of Iran's continuing turmoil.

In previous chapters the grievances of the various opposition groups against policies and programmes of the Islamic Republic were noted. It is now incumbent to discuss the progressively more volatile opposition to the regime, beginning with a review of the religious groups and personalities, and continuing with the secular, ethnic and intellectual dissidents.

Shariatmadari's Dissent

It should be noted that the policies and activities of the various subgroups frequently overlap. Thus the ethnic Kurds have both political and religious grievances against the regime. Similarly, the Azarbayjanis who generally follow Ayattolah Shariatmadari may simultaneously oppose the regime for political and ethnic reasons.

Without a doubt the opposition of Shariatmadari to Khomeini's Islamic Republic has been both the most consistent and, precisely because of his religious prominence, the most troublesome for Iran's supreme theocrat. Above all, despite an extremely active role in mobilizing the opposition to the Shah, he held the firm belief that the clergy should not be involved in politics once the supreme danger to the faith had been removed with the ousting of the Shah.

Bluntly and boldly he had often admonished the clerics, 'return to your mosques and seminaries and leave politics to professional statesmen.'[1] He was one of the Grand Ayattolahs who had criticized the regime for the hostage crisis, saying that the matter should not have been permitted to become a major international crisis.

In mid-December, when his followers in and outside Moslem People's Republican Party staged a mass protest movement and twice occupied the local television station in Tabriz, Shariatmadari came close to openly breaking with Khomeini. What had appeared as a spontaneous protest against the Pasdaran's shooting of one of Shariatmadari's personal guards in Qom soon got out of hand. Close to half a million of his followers rose up against the Tehran government, expelled the Governor-General and other city officials. More ominously, the Air Force declared its solidarity with the civilian population.[2] The Tabriz uprising so alarmed Khomeini that he sent a delegation to Qom led by acting Interior Minister Hashemi Rafsanjani with three other members of the Revolutionary Council, to plead with Shariatmadari. The Azarbayjanis' senior Ayattolah was given a pledge that in future only Azarbayjanis approved by their religious leader would be appointed to government positions in that province. The government in return secured a pledge from Shariatmadari that he would ask his followers to desist from further demonstrations.

A delegation of government and Khomeini representatives led by Banisadr flew to Tabriz and managed to stage a counter-rally in which all leftist groups such as the Tudeh, the Fedayeen and the Mojahedin participated. The Pasdaran re-occupied the television station and government buildings, and since Shariatmadari had ordered them to disperse, his followers allowed the pro-Khomeini forces to regain control of Tabriz.

In a characteristic about-face, as soon as the immediate danger had dissipated, Khomeini ordered strong retaliatory measures against Shariatmadari's supporters. Ayattolah Assadollah Madani, a close associate of Khomeini and himself an Azarbayjani, was given overall control of the province. The leaders of the MPRP were forced to dissolve the party. Its offices in Tabriz and other towns were occupied by the Pasdaran and leftist armed groups on the grounds that they had served as headquarters of an insurrection against the Islamic Republic. In two months 54 members of the leadership cadre of the MPRP were executed and several hundred banished to either Tehran or to remote provincial towns. In desperation and in order to spare the lives of his followers, Shariatmadari requested the dissolution of the party. By January a large political party supported by the Bazaaris and the middle classes in the province, as well as the Azarbayjani communities elsewhere and representing close to 9 million people, almost totally vanished.

Having lost the legitimate means of exercising his political influence, Shariatmadari confined himself to issuing occasional communiqués which his supporters would circulate both in Qom and his native Azarbayjan. In one of his statements after the referendum on the constitution, he echoed the views of such secular groups as the National Front when he said it was necessary to revise those articles of the constitution which abrogate the sovereign rights of the people.[3] Specifically, he thought granting the Council of Custodians the right to veto Majlis legislation was against popular sovereignty because it was the Majlis representatives who were elected precisely to exercise such sovereign authority.

It is significant to note that some of the leftist groups which in December and January 1979-80 had joined Khomeini to crush the protest of Shariatmadari's followers, shortly thereafter became themselves victims of Khomeini's vengeance. Both the Mojahedin and the Minority Fedayeen have since tried to enlist Shariatmadari's public support. However, the aged Ayattolah has so far refused to give it. Quite apart from earlier political opposition, these groups had once joined in a vicious campaign to depict him as a collaborator of the Shah, by the selective publication of some SAVAK documents many of which had indicated Shariatmadari's untiring efforts to intercede with the authorities on behalf of his fellow Azarbayjanis.[4]

In the spring and summer when the secular forces one by one joined the opposition, Shariatmadari refused to make public statements. Exile sources close to him believe that he does not wish to contradict himself by active political participation on the side of the opposition, believing that the Islamic regime will sooner or later succumb to its own grave errors. It is further believed that the Pasdaran maintain the tightest control on him and that the check on religious contributions to his seminary by Qom's custodian, Ayattolah Montazari, has caused students loyal to him to dwindle in number. Since traditionally these students have functioned as couriers for the Ayattolahs who have fallen out with the governing authorities, communication with his native Azarbayjan has become difficult.

Be that as it may, other voices from Shia clergy opposed to Khomeini have been raised against his regime with considerable regularity and bluntless.

It seems that as the Islamic regime has become more repressive in its effort to retain power, the gap between the ruling Mullahs and their adversaries within the clergy has widened. Frequent manifestos, public sermons and other statements by his clerical opponents so alarmed Khomeini that in April 1981 he broke the unwritten law of not attacking fellow Ayattolahs and issued a serious warning against their continuing opposition. Singling out the Qom and the Mashad theological centres, he warned that these centres were engaged in subversive activities and that he would urge the people to identify those responsible so that they could be turned over to the revolutionary Islamic courts for prosecution. Though mentioning no names, his targets were the two Grand Ayattolahs: Shariatmadari residing in Qom and Qomi residing in Mashad.[5]

The Clergy of Mashad

Unlike Shariatmadari, who was forced into silence, the irrepressible Qomi joined, in March 1981, the second highest ranking cleric of Mashad, Ayattolah Shirazi, to deliver a blistering attack on their fellow fundamentalist clerics.

A month later, when charges of torture were aired against the Islamic Republic, the two venerable clerical leaders of Mashad issued another proclamation, this time directly attacking Khomeini. They accused government leaders of deviating from the path of Islam. 'Torture, arbitrary trials, confiscation of private property are all against Islam's precepts. Islamic courts are staffed by corrupt and cruel individuals,' read their joint statement.[6]

Qomi, who had spent fourteen years in banishment under the Shah, urged the clergy not to concentrate political power in their hands, for with power came responsibility and accountability. To him the fundamental role of Shia clergy was the moral and spiritual leadership of the Islamic community. Shirazi told the representative of the French News Agency that a huge explosion was awaiting the country as a result of the continuing trend of the ruling circles to monopolize power and reject all dissension as treason.

It should be noted that prior to the revolution Mashad, as the burial place of the Eighth Shia Imam Reza, had more religious significance than Qom. Between 3 and 4 million pilgrims visited the holy shrine annually. With the revolution Khomeini did everything to make Qom superior to Mashad by, among other things, ignoring the advice of its two senior Ayattolahs and appointing a junior cleric as the Friday Imam of the city. Khomeini was evidently aware of the great role that the clergy in that city had played in mobilizing anti-Shah resistance. The issue of the clearance of the area around Imam Reza's shrine by the mayor in 1978 had irreversibly alienated the Mashad clergy, which for a long time had been the target of co-optation efforts by the Shah. Khomeini's tactic towards religious opposition from Mashad, as elsewhere, was guided by his total unwillingness to allow the emergence of competing centres of power.

Other Dissident Clerics

Those considered previously are merely the better-known clerics residing in the two holiest Shia centres in Iran. Scores of other leaders have taken the regime to task for many of its actions, which they view as non-Islamic if not totally contrary to the true principles of the faith. One notable example is Ayattolah Zanjani, the elderly nationalistic cleric who had supported Dr Mossadegh's National Front to the very end. In January 1981 he issued a detailed condemnation of the regime, accusing it of pursuing policies patently contradictory to Islam's teachings.[7] Much of his criticism is shared by the anti-regime clerics and generally reflects the viewpoints of the religious opposition.

Reviewing political events since 1979, Zanjani accused the regime of excluding from political participation many long-time crusaders against the dictatorship of the Shah. Instead, he remarked, deviationists and monopolists had tried to put the concept of *Fatva* and *Marjaiyat* in a limited context and determine exclusively the ranks of the religious hierarchy in the name of the leader.

Unlike the Catholic hierarchy, he warned, in *true* Islam there was no place for a Shia leader to play the role of a pope or for the present Council of Custodians to function as a Council of Cardinals.

Accusing the fundamentalists of emulating Russia's October Revolution, he urged that the Islamic Revolution should take inspiration from such genuine historical precedents as the Mohammadan revolution. Bluntly attacking the regime's retribution against former government officials, the aged Ayattolah demanded that the example of the Prophet

Mohammad and the Shia Imam Ali, both of whom had shown mercy, compassion and humane treatment toward the misguided and vanquished, be followed.

Reviewing the more than two-year record of the new regime, Zanjani cited the following as gross misdeeds discrediting Shia Islam and endangering the Moslem nation:

(1) the general condemnation of all employees of the former government – even though many of them had served the true interests of the country;

(2) the appointment of scores of young students of various divinity schools as religious judges, and the designation of an ignorant and incompetent individual as the revolutionary prosecutor. Together they had denied the accused the right to a defence attorney and to appeal against the verdict, in disregard for the two most basic principles of justice. Many sentences for prostitution, homosexuality and theft had been carried out arbitrarily and without the due process of the law;

(3) the violation of property rights. Zanjani asked where in Islam confiscation of all the property of the accused as well as of his relatives was sanctioned? Islamic law authorized the return of misused or stolen property to its rightful owner and not to the public treasury as had been done by the regime.

Ayattolah Zanjani listed further social and political misdeeds, but his sharpest criticism was reserved for the process of drafting the constitution and for the document itself. Acknowledging that he had not voted for the assembly and that he had serious doubts about Velayate Faghih, he raised two fundamental objections. One was the atmosphere of fear and intimidation created by the clubwielders of the 'Party of God' and the other was the claim that Velayate Faghih should be given the ultimate authority to interpret constitutional and legislative laws.

Furthermore, this right, according to Islamic teaching and tradition, could be exercised by any qualified theologian-jurist rather than exclusively by one individual as Khomeini's fundamentalist supporters believed. In a broad sense the concept meant the ability and the right of competent jurists of the Shia clergy to issue Fatva, or judgment and guidance, on matters of the faith which are brought to them by believers. Zanjani and his followers believed this in no way meant the exercise of full political authority as incorporated in the new constitution.

A further criticism was directed at the suppression of opposition to this interpretation, by the supporters of Khomeini. Supposing we could accept the claim of Velayate Faghih as just as legitimate as the Kaliphate of Imam Ali, was it right to denounce the opposition? Had Ali excluded his opponents from their rightful share in the Islamic community? Zanjani and other Ayattolahs like him saw no difference between the emerging dictatorship of fundamentalist Mullahs and that of the deposed Shah. Under the old regime, he wrote, people had been forced to give allegiance to the White Revolution, the monarchical system and the Rastakhiz Party, whereas now allegiance to the Islamic Revolution, to the Assembly of Experts and the so-called Imam's Line was required. The slogan of 'God, Shah and the Motherland' was being replaced by that of 'God, Qoran and Khomeini'.

A distinctive feature of the grievances of Shia leaders like Zanjani was concern for the general well-being of the people rather than for theological issues.

The deteriorating economic conditions and the chaos prevailing in the educational system of the country alarmed them equally gravely. The economic crisis was attributed to such excessive anti-Islamic measures as taxes on inheritance and the expropriation of lands, and to the flight of the managerial class. The promise of free housing and utilities to the rural poor had encouraged hundreds of thousands of farmers to move to the cities and become consumers rather than producers.

Similarly, instead of reforming worker-employer relations, industries had been nationalized and Marxist concepts of exploitation used as the excuse to drive out even the second-level managers running the nation's industries, with a resulting decline of 50 to 60 per cent in industrial output.

The emergence of multiple-power centres, which perhaps had been unavoidable in the early days of revolution, had been allowed to continue. Even with a constitution in place, the intense power-struggle with the Militants Following the Imam's Line as a new claimant to power, had created several states within the Islamic Republic.

Had the new regime performed any better in foreign policy? Two of its fundamental mistakes had been the decision to export the revolution and the active pursuance of an isolationist policy. The net result was that Iran's disgruntled neighbours had reacted by agitating amongst the ethnic minorities in the outlying regions of the country, thus seriously threatening Iran's territorial integrity.

Another senior Ayattolah who, by the second anniversary of the revolution. had openly attacked the fledgling Islamic Republic was Bahaeddin Mahallati, who felt that by then the regime had completely deviated from the revolution's original goal.[8] The grave danger, he wrote, was that while the oppressive Pahlavi regime had not carried the label of Islam, today in the name of Islam they were witnessing the emergence of oppression and a repetition of the misdeeds of the former regime. He too voiced the strongest protest against the dubious revolutionary Islamic justice meted out to the enemies of the regime, and the confiscation of their property in the name of Sharia-sanctioned laws. These mistakes had portrayed an ugly picture of an Islam traditionally known for its humanistic precepts and its love, justice, logic and mercy. In a thinly veiled appeal he asked his compatriots to regain control of their destiny through unity of action and purpose so that genuine Islamic teachings might again be observed and the homeland saved from the brinks of deviation and collapse.

The above clerics are examples of those who refused to become politically active, but deemed it a religious duty to warn their followers of what they perceived to be the anti-Islamic actions of Khomeini's regime. A number of less senior clerics chose instead to participate fully in the political process, but soon found themselves outnumbered and outmanoeuvred by the IRP. Ayattolah Lahouti of the Caspian province of Gilan and Sheikh Ali Tehrani, who is from Khorassan, are amongst this second group, whose alienation from Khomeini became finalized in the conflict between Banisadr and the IRP.

In a revealing interview with the French journal *Libération*, Tehrani blasted the IRP as another SAVAK, the Shah's secret police, and claimed that the majority of senior Ayatollahs, who were conservative and extremely popular, considered the present regime corrupt and totalitarian.[9] He thought that the Shia clergy as a whole were not satisfied with the present situation. For them the regime was not Islamic, and those who led it had sullied the face of Islam throughout the world. As to why the regime nevertheless appeared to enjoy the support of some of the clerics, Tehrani indicated that the IRP leader represented a small minority of Shia clergy under Beheshti. They were not learned men in the true sense of the word. They had joined the revolution in the name of Islam in order to seize power. Most senior ulama, or Shia learned men, were now critical of the, but except for a few they had kept quiet out of respect for Khomeini.

As to his personal relationship with Khomeini, Tehrani stated, 'I have told the Imam that IRP is like another SAVAK. Its budget is larger than the SAVAK. The crimes it commits are more numerous than those perpetrated by SAVAK. The IRP has its private prisons where torture is practised and has resulted in the death of several persons. Party leaders monopolize all power and are placed at the head of all organizations of the country. They use repression to impose their control on schools and universities and the Bazaars just as the deposed Shah did.'

Concerning the clergy and the IRP, Tehrani asserted that neither in Qom nor in Mashad did the clergy support the party. Only a group of about 14 theology students in Qom did so. But most of them were neither real students nor real Islamic experts. The real students of Qom, nearly 300, were against the party and when he had asked some of them why they did not protest they said the party would use its clubwielders against them. Even some among the 14 student supporters of the party in Qom have shown signs of disaffection recently when a group of them rejoined Grand Ayattolah Golpaygani, known for his conservatism and opposition to the IRP.

Before his death Beheshti exercised complete control over the pro-regime Mullahs organized in the so-called Combatant Circles, the Majlis and the Qom theology students. Now that role seems to have been acquired by Khamenei, who survived an attempt on his life to become the third Secretary-General of the IRP after Beheshti and Bahonar had been assassinated in June and August 1981 respectively. In early October he was elected as the third President of the Islamic Republic and as such is as powerful as Rafsanjani, the Speaker of the Majlis.

Not all opposition has been confined to verbal attacks. The Kurds, beginning in the summer of 1979 and some of the guerrilla organizations by the early summer of 1981, rose up in armed struggle against the Islamic Republic.

The Kurdish Opposition

As noted earlier, with the collapse of the former regime and the demonstrable inability of the central government to extend its control across the country, ethnic minorities began to challenge the new regime. When the Assembly of Experts began to draft the constitution it became clear that neither the Sunni religious affinity nor the demands of ethnic minorities for a substantial degree of autonomy would be considered. The Islamic Republic would be as centralized as the Pahlavi system had been.

Of all the ethnic Iranians, the Kurds have displayed the most tenacious resistance to the central government and perseverance in pursuing their goal of autonomy. Shortly after the revolution the city of Sanandaj in Central Kurdistan became the scene of minor clashes with security forces. Dr Abdolrahman Ghassemlou, leader of the largest and best-organized party, the Kurdish Democratic Party, rushed to Qom to convey the demands of the Kurds to Khomeini. The Ayattolah sought to invoke the unity of Islam, and while acknowledging the sufferings of the Kurds under the Shah refused to commit himself on the question of autonomy. Dr Ghassemlou, who had met Khomeini in France before the revolution, pinned his hopes on the secular associates of Khomeini such as Banisadr and Bazargan.[10]

In August 1979 the government felt strong enough to order Army units and the recently organized Revolutionary Guards to restore government control to Kurdish towns and hamlets. The combined forces, one of which had no stomach for new fighting, while the other was poorly trained, suffered at the hands of the Kurds. When they withdrew, negotiations for a peaceful settlement started. The setback caused Khomeini considerable embarrassment, particularly as he had boldly declared a holy war, *Jehad*, against the Kurds. Once he realized that no military solution was possible, Khomeini sounded a conciliatory note towards a peaceful settlement.

Many secular and clerical leaders tried to mediate in the dispute. Chief amongst them were the late Ayattolah Taleghani, Sheikh Ali Tehrani and Banisadr — both before and after his election to the Presidency. In every instance when a reasonable settlement appeared imminent, Khomeini would procrastinate in the hope that the armed forces would regain their strength and impose a military solution. Sheikh Tehrani has accused the IRP of sabotaging his own mediation efforts begun shortly before the August 1979 offensive. According to him the IRP had urged the Imam to reject the six-point plan for autonomy and instead use the pretext of an impending Iraqi offensive to send the Army through Kurdistan to the Iraq–Iran frontiers.

The Kurds, who were in virtual control of nearly 80 per cent of their region, believed this to be a ruse. This led to serious fighting as a result of which the KDP decided to evacuate the major towns and pull back to the mountain hamlets and fortifications. Banisadr thought the issue of autonomy should be put to a referendum, while Taleghani and Sheikh Tehrani thought the central government should offer to end the war and then put either self-rule or autonomy to a referendum. The views of the latter were communicated to Khomeini via his son

Ahmad, who reported back that the Imam did not believe the Kurds themselves would accept such a solution. Khomeini seemed convinced that if the Kurds were granted autonomy the United States would create a second Israel in the region to strike at Iran and other Moslem countries. To allay such fears the Kurdish leaders made several gestures.

The KDP Congress of April 1980

At the end of April 1980 the KDP held its 4th Congress in Mahabad. In a conciliatory resolution it confirmed its support for the Islamic Revolution under Khomeini's leadership and asked all its members to protect Iran's territorial integrity. It also appealed to the President to prevent anti-Kurdish elements in the Army and the Pasdaran from inciting bloodshed and fratricide.

It went on record in endorsing Banisadr's views on 'the autonomy of the masses in their internal affairs, the freedom of expression and the right to utilize the mass media, the need for restricting centralization of administrative and economic institutions.'

The six demands which had been accepted in principle by a number of mediators, and even Banisadr as President included:

(1) the inclusion of the right of autonomy of all ethnic groups in the constitution;
(2) Kurdistan must include all Kurdish inhabitants of the region;
(3) apart from foreign relations, defence, long-range planning, the Kurds should be able to resolve their own problems;
(4) an elected Kurdish Executive Committee should administer the region as an autonomous unit;
(5) the Kurds would be entrusted with maintenance of internal security;
(6) the Kurdish language would be recognized on a par with Farsi in all official correspondence.[11]

The resolutions of the Congress did not satisfy Khomeini's close associates. Sheikh Tehrani, who had tried to mediate in the dispute, became convinced that 'as long as IRP remains in power the Islamic regime will not reconcile its differences with the Kurds. The Army could pursue the war, the Kurdish guerrillas will pull back to the mountains in accordance to the classical doctrine of this type of warfare. The massacre of innocents and the non-combatants will continue as long as the government fails to see that in the existing condition no military solution is possible.'[12]

In April 1981 Ghassemlou gave a candid account of the more recent events in Kurdistan. According to him the military had resumed the war against his people in March 1980. The Army had concentrated four of its nine divisions against the Kurds and only three to counter Iraqi forces since September 1980. Additionally, the 40,000 Pasdaran assigned to the Kurdish region had committed unspeakable atrocities against the Kurds. Just before the Iraqi invasion the Air Force had begun a month-long bombing and strafing of Mahabad, which the Kurds had refused to evacuate even though they had pulled out of every other major town. The KDP estimated its own casualties since March 1980 at over 10,000, but asserted that most of these were civilians and that its guerrilla forces had not yet suffered a military defeat.

According to the party's Secretary-General, the four Kurdish towns of Oshnuyeh and Bukan in the north, and Nowsud and Nowdousheh in the south plus 100,000 square kilometres of Kurdistan, an area over ten times the area of the territory of Lebanon, were under its control. Government forces controlled major cities like Sanandaj, Kirmanshah, Saghez and Mahabad, but in the latter their control was tenuous. All strategic roads leading to these cities were additionally either threatened or controlled by the Kurds. The winter campaign had not changed the military situation drastically, but the KDP had acknowledged suffering from fuel shortages and scarcity of medical supplies and services.

Autonomy, Not Independence

With the protracted war between Iran and Iraq, the KDP once again in April 1981 sought to clarify its position. Dr Ghassemlou denied that his party and people were secessionist.[13] Refuting that charge, he said he and his people considered themselves Iranian and wished to remain so.

We are not seeking independence from Iran. Our own party is called the Kurdish Democratic Party of Iran. The most fundamental principle of our party is democracy for Iran and autonomy for the Kurds. By democracy, we mean full political participation of masses of Iranians and freedom of political parties and press and culture so that the people within the framework of the democratic constitution be guaranteed equal opportunities and feel a sense of belonging to the country. Democracy, the way we understand, relies on two fundamental principles of public freedoms and social justice.

As to the autonomy which they were seeking for Kurdistan, added Ghassemlou, in no way did it mean independence from Iran. Its purpose

was that Kurdistan should have its own administrative system; the
school system should enable Kurdish children to learn their own language and culture; and internal security should be in the hands of the
Kurds. This autonomy would allow them to develop their deprived
land. These areas had been victims of the central government's racial
discrimination policy – one which had fully ignored 6 million Kurds.

The Army, national currency and foreign policy would all be under
the control of central government and its representatives. 'It is thus
clear that we are not seeking independence. Thirty-six years ago our
party enumerated these principles in its programme and has remained
faithful to them ever since.'

On another issue, namely alienation from the Islamic regime, the
KDP leader said, 'Having struggled against the Shah, who neither
granted Iran democracy nor Kurdistan autonomy, we find Khomeini
doing the same. We are therefore as opposed to his regime as we were
to the Shah's.'

When the revolution triumphed the KDP believed Iran had entered
a new epoch of public freedom and social justice. But religious leaders,
the Kurds felt, had monopolized political power and the poorer classes
were becoming more impoverished. 'The wealthy class which was
becoming richer is replaced by a new authority exploiting the resources
of the country.'

Just as the secular political parties, which were left out with the
victory of the revolution, the ethnic minorities too had played a critical
role in overthrowing the Shah's regime. These Kurds, Arabs, Azarbayjanis. Baluchies and others form 60 per cent of Iran's population.
Khomeini himself had acknowledged their role in the revolution.

> At the critical stage of revolutionary struggle, from his French exile,
> he praised the Kurds for their struggle against the Shah. None the
> less, as soon as the revolution was over the fundamentalist clerics
> began to monopolize the credit for what the masses of people had
> accomplished in deposing the Shah. These religious men joined the
> struggle against the Shah rather late whereas we the Kurds had been
> doing so for many long years,

declared Ghassemlou. A further grievance of the KDP concerned the
preferential treatment of the Shia Moslems, which according to the
party was unfair and unjust toward Iran's non-Shia Moslems.

Only Shias can become President and Prime Minister and several other high officials of government. Sunnis are second class citizens. We opposed the Shah because of his despotism and dictatorship. Khomeini is the same. His Council of Custodians is superior to the constitution and he himself is superior to the Council. What happened to the government of popularly based Islamic units?

The KDP also insists that it has been quite flexible in negotiating with the regime. When in late March 1980 Ayattolah Nouri, one of the more progressive clerics, had urged the Kurds to cease using 'Khodmokhtari,' Farsi for autonomy, they had agreed to do so. They had also agreed to the term 'Islamic Autonomy' so long as the government recognized the concepts of decentralization for itself and home rule for the Kurds and other ethnic minorities.

Mindful of the accusation of being leftist or in league with the Soviet Union, the KDP has frequently insisted that it is opposed to both the super-powers and wishes to work for a truly non-aligned Iran. Dr Ghassemlou insists that allegations about an understanding with the Soviet Union are absolutely inaccurate.

We have 50 kilometres of common border with Soviet Union where 200,000 Kurds live, mostly in Armanistan. We have natural mutual concern and sympathy with all Kurds anywhere but we are an Iranian Party. The Soviets are our friends and we need their political support, but only political. No foreign government gives us any aid.

With the outbreak of the Iraq–Iran war the Kurds faced another dilemma, i.e. how not to become a pawn for either side.

We are opposed to it. It should stop because it is in neither side's interest. As Iranian Kurds, we cannot support Iraq's invasion and occupation of Iranian soil. But we also believe Iran shares some of the responsibility for the war. We all know how Khomeini has threatened to export his revolution abroad especially to Iraq.

From the start of the war the KDP declared its readiness to defend Iran's territorial integrity provided the government would stop bombing their towns and villages.

As I said, four army divisions are fighting us whereas only three are fighting Iraq. Khomeini himself has said that the war against Iraq is a new one, whereas the war against the Kurds has gone on for many years.

In the circumstances, the KDP had not asked for the Iraqis for support.

Our basic condition for accepting any foreign aid is that it should not commit us to the donor as happened in the case of Mostafa Barzani several times. Foreign aid is a positive factor, but helping our own people is even more important, and that is why we will not accept foreign support from countries which subjugate their own Kurdish minority.

Relations with other Anti-Khomeini Forces

Almost immediately after the outbreak of hostilities in August the KDP found support amongst secular leftist and centrist groups. Above all the Mojahedin and later the minority faction of Fedayeen declared their solidarity with KDP. They were already in a *de facto* alignment over the course that the Islamic Republic was taking. Like the Mojahedin they had boycotted the referendum on the Islamic Republic. The KDP was particularly keen to accept the support of the Mojahedin for it was a Shia Islamic progressive group with impressive credentials in fighting the Shah. The KDP joined the Mojahedin in issuing a common declaration embodying many of their common viewpoints against theocracy and for a decentralized and popularly based republic. After the demise of Banisadr and his flight to France accompanied by the Mojahedin leader, Massud Rajavi, the KDP was one of the first to accept their call for the forming of a National Resistance Council. It also subscribed to the political covenant that Banisadr and Rajavi had signed as the embodiment of their aspiration for post-Khomeini Iran.

Among other secular groups which rushed to the support of KDP, the National Democratic Front as well as the Trotskyite Peykar group should be mentioned. Not all the left, however, could be counted on for support. The Tudeh Party, which supports the Islamic Republic either out of conviction or cowardice, is totally opposed to KDP. The majority faction of the Fedayeen also opposes KDP, and in the more recent past has even contributed to anti-guerrilla warfare against the insurgent Kurds.

The KDP does not take the opposition of pro-government leftist groups too seriously. On numerous occasions since the revolution it has been able to show that it has a broad popular base of support in Kurdistan. Thus, in the elections for the Majlis in the spring of 1980, the KDP received 100 per cent support in Mahabad, 95 per cent in Piranshahr. In Bukan, which was penetrated by the Maoist Ranjbaran (Toilers) Party activists, the KDP received 57 per cent of the votes.[14] Clearly the Kurds are Kurds first, and only secondarily identified with any given ideology. Their survival depends above all on their correct assessment of the relative strengths of prevailing political forces in the country. In Khomeini's Iran they face both opportunities stemming from the weakness of the central government and dilemmas stemming from such factors as the Iraqi invasion and dormant, but none the less powerful, Iranian nationalism.

Directly related to the viability of the central government is the attitude of other parties and political groups. Aspects of their words and deeds regarding the institutionalization of the Republic have been touched upon earlier. One group which has broken with Khomeini consists of secular intellectuals who are particularly dismayed at Khomeini's so-called cultural revolution.

The Intellectuals and Khomeini's Cultural Revolution

With the consolidation of the power of the fundamentalists by the time the Majlis election was completed in June 1980, secular political parties and personalities were one after another denounced by the regime. However, as long as Banisadr remained President secular forces hoped that while in office he would protect Iranian secular and basically Western-educated groups. The closure of the universities and the launching of a so-called Islamic cultural revolution in the autumn of 1979 marked the opening of Khomeini's concerted campaign against 'Western intellectualism'. Characteristically, he attacked the universities as nothing but centres of Western moral decadence. 'If all they do is to train either communist or Western-oriented youth, let them remain closed. We do not need them.'[15] Like the Shah before him, he shows a strong bias against intellectualism for he knows that the universities everywhere are hotbeds of radicalism and political activism. But unlike the Shah he does not appreciate the technological services that the universities have rendered to Iran's modernization and industrialization.

Furthermore, the universities were basically secular and not amenable to accepting Shia Islam as a panacea the way that Khomeini viewed it. Thus, as soon as he felt sufficiently secure, he turned against them. Ignoring his own early glorification of the students' role in overthrowing the Shah, he publicly minimized that role and ridiculed their ideal of a free and democratic Iran. 'We waged the revolution for Islam not for nationalism or democracy. Our martyrs died for Islam and nothing else.'

It took the anti-Shah intellectuals about two years to lose all hope of a possible co-existence with Khomeini. On the occasion of the second anniversary of the revolution thirty-eight writers, poets, playwrights, teachers and jurists, representing the very best of their own profession and having fought courageously against the Shah, issued a statement of principles.[16] Since it may be considered as the basic position of all the secular forces in Iran, it deserves closer scrutiny.

It begins by lamenting the loss of the two years which could have witnessed the fulfilment of the anti-despotic and anti-imperialist goals of the revolution and the mobilization of the masses in support of a free and independent society. Instead, violations of human and social rights of the people are so rampant that a casual glance at contemporary Iran would convince everyone of the failure of the fundamental goals of the revolution. Power is monopolized by those authorities which deny that the masses are capable of exercising popular sovereignty. The popular demand for a constituent assembly was rejected in favour of an Assembly of Experts which represented the clique already in power. Likewise, the National Assembly has become a private association by forcing out nominees whose only fault lies in not completely accepting the domination of the new ruling classes. Worse yet, all individual and public freedom and that of speech and assembly have been totally and brutally suppressed and the offices of opposition groups and newspapers occupied by armed supporters of the regime.

To achieve this all editorial staffs have been purged and total censorship imposed, first in the name of Islam and then of the war with Iraq. Simultaneously, workers and employees have been assaulted on the slightest provocation, and Islamic associations have become the arms of the government security organizations. More importantly, tens of thousands of teachers, professors, civil servants and workers have been sacked in the name of an ideological purge. Women's social and human rights have been revoked, and thus one half of the people have become the subject of accelerated exploitation. 'The Shah's old prisons are now filled with the brave crusaders of liberty and justice, some of whom have been tortured.'

In foreign policy the regime has not been any more successful. Unable to resolve Iran's foreign problems, it has allowed the country to be dragged into an imposed war, resulting in the destruction of vital oil refineries, the occupation of parts of the land, the creation of over two million homeless, and the deaths of thousands of innocent compatriots.

The intellectuals end their gloomy analysis of the first two years of the revolutionary regime by alerting their fellow countrymen 'to the grave danger threatening our country' and by asking 'all progressive forces to unite their actions so that the democratic and anti-imperialist goals of our revolutionary movement may be achieved.'

The signatories of the declaration represented the centre and the left-of-centre of Iran's political spectrum. They made sure to criticize the USA and the Soviet Union equally harshly. However, their earnest appeal for unified action did not seem to make a noticeable impact. Several months later, during the crisis of Banisadr's Presidency, some of them joined the beleaguered President. When Khomeini showed an iron fist in dealing with Banisadr, these intellectuals became convinced that the traditional methods of issuing declarations and pamphleteering against the new dictatorship were in consequential. Many fled from Iran fearing for their lives, while others appealed to the Mojahedin for protection when the first wave of the new reign of terror overwhelmed the dissidents who had taken to the streets in protest against Banisadr's dismissal. The celebrated poet Saeed Sultanpoor executed at the end of June, has so far been the only one of the signatories of the declaration of the thirty-eight to suffer this fate. When the records of this phase of the Iranian turmoil are fully disclosed, undoubtedly others will be found to have become victims of Khomeini's anti-intellectualism.[17]

It should be noted that Khomeini's anti-Westernism had more practical reasons. In the spring of 1980 his regime was witnessing the gradual emergence of the universities as bastions of resistance to his Islamic fundamentalism. Since he had already decided that no independent centre of power should be allowed to compete for the allegiance of the people, it was obvious that the universities would soon join the secular groups on the list of anti-Islamic and therefore anti-revolutionary organizations.

In April there were serious clashes between the fundamentalist groups and secular student organizations including the Mojahedin, the Peykar and the National Democratic Front. Instead of carrying pro-Khomeini or anti-American slogans, tens of thousands of students carried the banners, 'Death or Freedom', 'Revolution Back on its Course.'

In the meantime new text books are being published. Those dealing with history and literature are particularly under revision and being rewritten to present recent Iranian history in a manner that glorifies everything Islamic, and ignoring or discrediting everything non-Islamic. An example of the new Islamic text is a 6th-grade Iranian literature textbook. It begins with revolutionary songs and poems which raise Khomeini to the level of deity. One poem is entitled 'O Khomeini, you are the light of God', another addresses him as the 'Saviour of all Oppressed People' and a third is entitled 'The American Shah should be Executed'. The text totally ignores the recent contributions of secular personalities to Iran's literature and poetry. Indeed, such epic poets as Ferdowsi and Farrokhi are blasted as adulators of kings. The name Ferdowsi was removed from the title of the university in Mashad, which now bears merely the city's name, just as the Pahlavi University in Shiraz had been instructed to drop 'Pahlavi' from its title.

The so-called Cultural Revolution, however, has not been a glorious success. In the spring of 1981 many thousands of idle students joined the protest movement against the fundamentalists. Purged university teachers and staff either left Iran or became active in a variety of opposition groups. What was particularly disturbing for the idle students in the country was that Iranian students studying abroad continued to receive government support for their education. Since most of these belonged to better-off families, students at universities at home began to protest against this apparent discrimination as a denial of the equal rights of the oppressed, whose cause the Khomeini regime had claimed to champion. By the late summer of 1981 there was no sign of any intention of reopening the universities. Except for medical schools which were allowed to complete the designated six-year curriculum, no university planned to reopen.

If anything, the start of the armed struggle against the regime late in June made the fundamentalist authorities even more suspicious of the wisdom of reopening the universities. The activities of pro-Mojahedin student groups abroad, together with those affiliated to the veteran anti-Shah Confederation of Iranian Students in Europe and American further antagonized the regime. In July and August, when pro-Mojahedin students occupied at least fifteen consulates and embassies across the world including the special Iranian department of the Algerian Embassy in Washington, the Tehran government ordered the identification of those students and reprisals were taken against their families. They all risked losing their remittances in local currency, which even at the height of the hostage crisis had continued to be sent. Khomeini's attitude toward the universities and the dissident students was marked by the same dogged determination which he had displayed towards other dissidents. On the occasion of the start of the new school year in Iran, on 22 September, he issued a new order to Iranian schoolchildren openly instructing them to purge their schools from non-Islamic political elements.

> Your sacred duty is to protect the sanctity of schools against the inroads which anti-Islamic and anti-revolutionary forces may make into your hearts and your minds. Leftist and dissident teachers and pupils alike should be forcibly ejected from amongst you.

So far, however, the Islamic cultural revolution has been more destructive than constructive. The seven-man committee, which was appointed in the summer of 1980 to revise and revamp university curricula, has not been able to attract sufficient support among the non-purged faculties for genuine co-operation on this matter. The fundamental reason is that not even the IRP can make up its own mind concerning the substance of the curricula, apart from such subjects as history, literature, theology and the Arabic language, which under the constitution must be taught throughout primary and secondary schools.

Undoubtedly the main beneficiaries of Khomeini's anti-intellectualism have been the parties of the left. Denied the continuation of their education, and suffering from an extremely high rate of unemployment, many of the idle students have become susceptible to the recruiting campaigns of these parties. Those intellectuals who did not support any of the leftist parties could only ally themselves with such personalities as Bazargan, who used his newspaper *Mizan* to sound the alarm at the rapidly disappearing democratic freedoms.[18] Which parties represent the left, and why are some opposed to and others supportive of Khomeini? These questions will be considered in the next chapter.

Notes

1. *Elamiyeh*, 12 December 1979, quoted in *Faryade Azadi*, No. 8, 19 December, London.

2. Transcript, *MacNeil–Lehrer Report* PBS, Washington, DC, 15 December 1979. Also *Faryade Azadi*, No. 8.

3. Quoted in *Shahed*, Washington, DC, 20 December 1979.

4. Some examples could be found in *Mardom* (Tudeh Party organ, 28 April 1979) and *KAR* (People's Fedayeen Guerrillas, 12 May 1979). These documents were supplied to these publications by SAVAMA (Farsi acronym for the new security and intelligence organization which retained some of the cadres of its forerunner, the SAVAK).

5. *Jomhuriye Islami* (organ of the IRP) Tehran, 21 April 1981.

6. Their joint declaration, which was widely circulated by Iranian exiled groups in Europe, was dated 12 April 1981.

7. Ayattolah Zanjani, 'On anti-Islamic characteristics of the Islamic regime,' *Payam*, London, No. 3, 29 January 1981.

8. *Elamiyeh* 11 February 1981 distributed in Paris by *ARA* (Iran Liberation Army).

9. *Libération*, Paris, 26 June 1981.

10. *Enghelabe Islami* (Banisadr's newspaper) Tehran, 12 May 1979.

11. Report of the Congress in *Keyhan*, 18 April 1980.

12. *Libération*, 26 June 1981.

13. Reports on fighting in Kurdistan from *Iran Times*, Washington, DC, 17 April 1981 and *Iran Post*, Los Angeles, 21 April 1981. Ghassemlou's interview from Iranian sources in Paris, dated 25 April 1981.

14. Figures quoted by Dr. Ghassemlou, *Iran Post*, 25 April 1981.

15. Highlights of Imam Khomeini's Speeches (Pars Agency: reproduced by Moslem Student Association in US) No. 3, 19 January 1980, *Iran Post*, Los Angeles, 20 February 1981.

16. Fifty per cent of the signatories were writers and poets, the rest university professors from a variety of disciplines.

17. The revolutionary court accused him of leading the Peykar guerrillas in insurrection against the Islamic Republic, *Keyhan*, Tehran, 30 June 1981.

18. On 3 March *Mizan* published a telegram to the Khomeini-appointed committee to inquire into allegations of torture from the Society for Monitoring the Enforcement and Perfection of the Constitution (known by its Farsi acronym EGHAME). Two days earlier Bazargan had sharply criticized the 'Freedom of Activities of Parties and Associations' bill presented to the Majlis as incompatible with basic freedoms. 'Those who are in authority do not believe genuinely in freedom and instead maintain that dissenting viewpoints are harmful and contrary to Islam.' *Enghelabe Islami*, Tehran, 1 March 1981.

6 THE LEFT AND THE ISLAMIC REPUBLIC

Both in the course of the year-long revolutionary turmoil and immediately after the downfall of the Shah, the parties of the left played a significant part in Iran's political development. Some, like the Tudeh Party, resumed political activity after a hiatus of about twenty-five years. Others, like the two guerrilla movements, surfacing from an underground existence since the mid-sixties, openly vied for a share of political power in revolutionary Iran. But the disintegration of the revolutionary coalition several months after the triumph of the revolution soon caused a considerable disarray amongst the parties of the left. Some were quick to adjust to the emergence of Khomeini's theocracy, while others were forced to oppose it, at first moderately and later vehemently. In terms of political clout and organizational experience the two guerrilla movements stand out.

Mojahedine Khalgh

This organization has been the subject of considerable controversy since it initiated the armed struggle against Khomeini's regime in June 1981. The critical controversy, whether during the Shah's regime or under Khomeini, has centred on its exact ideological orientation and the contents of its political programme. During the Shah's time the SAVAK characterized it as 'Islamic–Marxist'. At the present time Khomeini brands it as 'Monfeghin' — literally hypocrites — but denoting the Shia term for those who betrayed the prophet in early Islam. One way of understanding the Mojahedin is to examine their literature of both before and after the revolution. Another is to examine the records of the trials of some of its leading members during the Shah's reign.

On 4 January 1979, during the final days of the Shah's regime, the organization issued an 18-point declaration entitled the Minimum Expectation Programme.[1] The declaration was an all-inclusive statement about economic, social and political issues. Though since its publication many modifications and revisions have been made, it is evident that at the outset of the revolutionary regime the Mojahedin did their best to integrate fundamental Marxist concepts with Shia doctrines and tenets. This declaration of the Minimum Programme

97

reveals much of their ideological orientation. A comparison of the Mojahedin's later statements with this programme is also instructive because it shows a gradual de-Islamization of the organization, stemming from the enmity of Khomeini and his fundamentalist associates toward the Mojahedin. That comparison also shows that, once war was declared on Khomeini in June 1981, the Mojahedin have steadily de-emphasized the Marxist components of their action programme. This is so because they wish to appeal to the better-educated Moslem Iranians as well as to the non-leftist and nationalist groups whose support they need for staging a massive popular uprising against the Islamic Republic.

The Minimum Expectation Programme first addresses itself to economic policies, demanding three specific measures:

(1) All comprador investments must be appropriated. This capital has been the cause of the greatest misery and oppression for our workers, not to speak of the untold strife it has created for our national enterprise.

(a) Foreign-owned, colonialist banks, which have plundered this nation, must be closed down.

(b) Foreign-owned and comprador businesses, plants and affiliated agricultural enterprises must be expropriated and handed over to the people, and the management of these operations handled by a staff council (comprising workers, clerical personnel and a representative of the government). The aim is to reconstruct, to build anew, on the shards of colonialist enterprise, an equitable system based on Islam and moving towards *Towhid* (Divine Integration).

(2) National control must be established over all of the nation's natural resources, not the least of which being petroleum. All shameful colonialist agreements in this field must be irrevocably terminated.

As the Qoran expresses it: natural resources and public wealth are included in the concept of *anfaal* 'the spoils of war' or, by extension, the commonweal. The utilization of resources in the way of God and His Prophet means employing these benefits for the commonweal, whereby no single individual has an interest and all are freed from the bonds that inhibit virtue.

(3) Massive, large-scale investment enterprises must be avoided, whereby costly, luxury industrial conglomerates are allowed to expand at the expense of moderately scaled and small industries. Preference should naturally be given to agriculture over industry, or a healthy economic

development and the ideological channelling of the technocrats and bureaucrats will be impossible.[2]

It is evident that disregard of this latter point will result in an unbalanced capitalist growth, where certain disposition is made on a *class*, rather than a *need*, basis. Besides the unhealthy effect this would have on the economy itself, this kind of situation militates necessarily towards a renewed dependence on the capitalist bloc.

Ali's Sermon No. 15 in the *Nahjol-balagheh* provides a cogent statement of the situation of balanced economic growth, which must be based on a mobilization of the people, not the cultivation of the economy as a parasitic growth of the capitalist world. A balanced and just economic growth situation obtains when society moves towards the total negation of all class distinctions, such as the isolation of workers and peasants through exploitive conditions. As the Qoranic surah *Al-Qesas*, verse 3, puts it, there will eventually remain no way to 'stratify society.'

Next the Mojahedin programme makes a significant pronouncement about the military.

A popular army must be established. A just and popular economic development, where the welfare of the downtrodden is given priority, has no place for the fostering of a paper-tiger army, top-heavy with the latest in fancy and costly weaponry. The devotion of resources to the building up of an unwieldy façade of an army shares the same unbalanced character as the haphazard growth situation in other economic and social areas.

A political system which lacks popular support, by its very nature, is forced to develop and maintain an army which must be equipped with complex weapons and cultivates a phoney 'professionalism' which divorces it from the masses in its preoccupation with standing up to foreign threats and putting down domestic 'insurrection'.

Such an army has no alternative but to build up the external appurtenance of its weaponry and to play down the human factor of its personnel. Its destiny leads it into becoming absorbed into the imperialist military complex, whereby it is made dependent on imperialist logistics (for the supply of complex weaponry) and imperialist advisory personnel.

Such an army is in direct contact only with the ruling bureaucracy and is dependent on a base which is beyond the frontiers of the land which it purportedly serves. To expect popular reactions and a popular performance from such an army would be the height of absurdity.

Our bitter experience with the Imperial Army over the last 50 years is a clear indication of the truth of this assertion. It is for this reason that we call for the establishment of an army of the people, an army which fights for the things in which the people believe and for the interests of the people as a whole. It is not a hireling army of mercenaries fighting only for money, whose sole motive is the receiving of their wages.

At this point, it should be made clear that the establishment of a popular army in no way implies the deprivation of individual rights or the application of pressure, material or moral, on our brave brothers who make up the Iranian armed forces at the moment. What we are calling for is a foundational transformation of the structure and content of relations in the army, in such a manner that our army brothers may never again be forced into a system which shunts and restricts the expression of their will to participate and develop their talents in the popular way.

This is the place, then, to review the characteristics of what constitutes a popular army:

(a) In the popular army, there is no blind obedience. Ideology and a correct line of policy, blended with political awareness, provide the guiding force for such an army.

(b) The popular army is a national army in the service of the defence of the country and the defender of the interests of the people against foreign aggression.

(c) The popular army is completely integrated in society and completely harmonious, in particular, with the strata of the most oppressed amongst the people.

(d) The popular army is an integrated unity in its own right when it possesses the foregoing characteristics. It permits no undue distinctions of privilege within its ranks, between enlisted man, NCO or officer. All eat the same food and no remarkable differences exist in pay and facilities. Promotions are made through consultations with personnel, and unity is maintained throughout by a common appeal to iron discipline, understood by all.

An army which develops a standard of structural relationships like this will have the closest popular relationship with the masses. Actually the prototype for this kind of army is the model army of the early days of Islam, which was composed of soldiers and officers whose sole motivation was service to God and the people. The internal and external relations of armies under the command of the Prophet and of Imam Ali, amongst the personnel and with the civilians, can provide an instructive case for those who seek to form an army designed to carry out its functions in the name of Islam. In the words of Ali to Malek Ashtar, 'Be kind to your subordinates and hard on arrogant oppressors.'

Other specific points concerning the proposed people's army are:

(e) Service in the popular army is never compulsory.

(f) The popular army can never be dominated by foreign advisors and would never engage the services of imperialist advisors.

(g) The popular army not only does not participate in unjust imperialist wars or in counter-revolutionary conflicts, such as the crushing of the freedom-fighters of Dhofar in Oman, but is at the disposal of all revolutionary movements such as the Palestinian.

On the question of political freedoms and rights of women and ethnic minorities, the Mojahedin sound progressive and secular when they state that complete freedom of the press, the activity of political parties and the holding of political rallies, irrespective of belief or ideological principles, would be guaranteed. In the words of the Qoran, 'Give the good tidings to My devotees who listen to different views then choose the best' (Al Zomar, 17–18).

It is our firm Islamic belief that as long as different ideologies and viewpoints are founded on truth and in direct proportion to their sincerity in seeking justice and equity, they have no fear of their ideologies being the object of debate.

Of course, it should be made crystal clear that there are distinct demarcations between revolutionary freedom and democracy and the approach of liberalism and irresponsible capitalism, distinctions which cannot be ignored in any revolutionary system. As the Qoran expresses it, 'Do not follow that of which you have no knowledge nor penetrating understanding.' (Asraa', 36).

An examination of the lives of the Prophet and of Imam Ali, according to the Mojahedin's statement, reveals no instance of either of them ever suppressing the viewpoints of any of their opponents.

Imam Ali always stressed that he would never be the first to draw his sword or launch a conflict to counter the views of someone else, no matter how hostilely his opponents might present their views. Imam Jaafar Sadeq, the Sixth Imam of the Shiite sect, sat for hours while his ideological and philosophical opponents ranted and harangued him, never losing his patience or dignity or behaving in any way disrespectfully towards them. And, indeed, if we believe that Islam is the highest path, why should we feel threatened by other ideas and opinions?

On women's rights the statement interprets Islam progressively when it vows absolute equality and the total prohibition of exploitation or discrimination.

This position is part and parcel of the uncompromising Towhidi (divinely integrated) world-view of Islam. It is obvious that equal wages for equal work — in addition to special concessions for worker sisters in consideration of their particular needs — is the prime and most fundamental of any underlying principle in the Islamic defence of the rights of our toiling sisters.

Correctly anticipating turmoil among ethnic minorities, the Mojahedin state that the removal of the double injustice imposed on the ethnic and regional peoples is another cardinal principle.

Peoples of different regions must be provided with full political rights to enjoy their own cultural expressions, all within the framework of the overall unity, solidarity and sovereignty of the country. We believe fundamentally that the way the 'nationalities' question is confronted, determines the manner in which we evaluate the extent of genuineness and revolutionary legitimacy of a truly popular Towhidi governmental system.

Looking again at the time of Imam Ali, the Mojahedin observe that there was then 'no aim or action of exploitation or domination or ethnic suppression'. By the same token, when the *Towhidi* point of view is put into practice, any conflict between regional or ethnic groups (the Arabs, the Persians, the Kurds, and so forth) will resolve itself by the momentum gravitating towards unity.

Opposed to this integrative trend is the class-oriented attitude which militates towards a state of antagonism and spiteful conflict. The Mojahedin emphasize the fundamental tie between the revolutionary and progressive national spirit of the Kurds and of the national spirit of the heroic people of Iran as a whole.

If, however, Kurdish ethnic and regional interest is allowed to come in conflict with the national, anti-imperialist struggle of the country as a whole, the imperialists and the enemies of the Revolution will benefit. Therefore, the genuine Kurdish participants in the struggle should be conscious of accompanying their aspirations to assert Kurdish identity with an emphatic condemnation of any tendency towards separatism or secessionism.

Policies towards workers and peasants are also elaborated:

All anti-labour regulations and legislation must be abolished, and new labour laws must be enacted, based on the views of the workers.
— Housing must be provided for all workers.
— The management of the Workers Welfare Bank and other labour banks and funds must be turned over to the workers themselves.
— All governmental wage deductions must be eliminated from workers' salaries. Workers' benefits (health, retirement, casualty, etc.) must be provided from petroleum revenues.
— The administration of factories should be carried out by a council composed of representatives of the councils of the workers and of the clerical personnel and representatives of the employer.
— Contractual labour must be changed to formal employment (with all its attendant wage guarantees and benefit provisions).
— The worker must have a share in the factory profits.
Like the workers, the oppressed peasants of this land must not be forced to bear the debts incurred with governmental agencies of the previous regime.
— The very lands which were usurped from the peasants by the institutions of the previous regime should be returned to the peasant owners.
— Basic technology and interest-free agricultural loans must be provided.
— The working and productive farmer should not be subjected to land or produce tax.
— A concerted effort must be made to encourage and provide the necessary conditions for the establishment of people's co-operatives.
— All foreign interference of any kind, as well as the importation of foreign agricultural products, must be avoided.
— Housing must be provided for farmers through the construction of

suitable complexes, as a deterrent to the motivation of farmers to migrate to the cities.

The Minimum Expectation Programme outlines the following goals in foreign affairs:

(1) A complete political and economic boycott of the racist governments of Israel, the former Rhodesia and the Union of South Africa, should be instituted. By the same token, assistance should be provided to liberation movements around the world, with the adoption of a resolute and decisive political position-taking in support of all freedom causes.

(2) Iran should withdraw from all humiliating imperialist agreements, open or secret, political or military, and join the United Nations bloc of non-aligned nations.

The organization did not succeed in ascertaining the degree of popular support for such a programme because it was denied the opportunity of free participation in election or grassroot activity between April 1979 and April 1981. In previous chapters some of its grievances against the Islamic Republic were reviewed, which as late as March had not yet led to a frontal assault on Khomeini. Instead, the brunt of its attack was on the IRP, whose overthrow the organ of the movement editorialized as the only road to salvation.[3]

However, between April and June the Mojahedin rapidly moved towards open struggle with Khomeini. The high point in that process, as will be noted in a later analysis of the demise of Banisadr, were the bloody street riots of 20 June 1981, in protest against Banisadr's impeachment.

The Mojahedin in Exile

A month later Massud Rajavi, a prominent member of the organization's leadership cadre, masterminded the spectacular flight to Paris of Banisadr, himself, and several Air Force officers. Rajavi, who had survived the SAVAK repression, explained that this had been decided upon when the regime began its reign of terror against their organization with the bloody events of 20 June. It was in the course of this incident that about twenty young girls protecting their fellow Mojahedin marchers were arrested and promptly executed. The Mojahedin had considered that just as during the anti-Shah rallies and demonstrations, the security forces would be reluctant to fire on or otherwise maltreat a protective line of young female fellow Mojaheds. However, the brutal treatment of the Mojahed girls after arrest convinced the Mojahedin that the Pasdaran would show no mercy to Khomeini's opponents. Furthermore, before leaving Iran, Banisadr, who continues to be accepted by the Mojahedin as the popularly elected President, asked Rajavi to organize the National Resistance Council and to form a Cabinet to run the government as soon as the regime was overthrown.

What finally convinced Rajavi that he should leave the country was the execution of Mohammadreza Saadati, a leader of the Mojahedin, already serving a ten-year sentence. His retrial and execution on 27 July convinced the Mojahedin that Rajavi should not risk arrest in Iran. He himself told the foreign press, 'We decided to leave Iran temporarily so that we could expand the activity of the NRC and echo the voice of our innocent people and their just cause in the world at large'.[4]

But would not his absence undermine his personal leadership and reduce the Mojahedin's political effectiveness? Rajavi did not believe this would happen. Their organization was not based on individual leadership. Members of the leadership cadre knew what to do and would accept the necessity of the present move, which was designed to serve the country and safeguard their revolutionary movement. Evidence to support this claim abounds. During the absence of Rajavi the Mojahedin has intensified its war of attrition against the regime, and this was highlighted by the bombing on 30 August of the headquarters of the Prime Minister, killing both Rajai and Bahonar.

In the course of over sixteen years of urban guerrilla warfare against the Shah's regime and now against the Islamic Republic, the Mojahedin have been organized into two distinct networks of cells. The larger organization, now numbering perhaps several hundred thousand followers and sympathizers, is led by publicly known personalities. Apart from that network there is a shadow-structure of secret leaders each allegedly in charge of fifteen-member action committees, whose membership is a highly guarded secret and whose leadership rotates regularly.

It was this shadow organization which made two significant decisions at the beginning of the revolutionary regime. One was to refuse to give up their arms, the quantity of which had increased substantially during the two-day street battle in Tehran, 9-11 February 1979. The other was to keep their shadow structure secret and to acknowledge only their larger organization. The released leaders of this second group such as Rajavi, Saadati, Moghaddam and Khiyabani surfaced as legitimate politicians, and for a while even tried to secure some representation in the new regime's institutions. When in June 1981 war was declared on the Islamic Republic after the Mojahedin had turned down Khomeini's demand that they disarm themselves, the organization returned to the practice it had followed under the Shah — except that this time they had a larger following and certainly more experience in urban guerrilla warfare. Their following, according to Rajavi, extends to every walk of Iranian life, as is demonstrated by the involvement of a number of Air Force officers in preparing the flight of Banisadr and Rajavi from Iran.

How directly and exclusively they were responsible for the two devastating bomb blasts in June and August cannot as yet be ascertained. In the wake of the June bombing of IRP headquarters, Rajavi refused to claim the credit, but asserted that the resistance movement was quite widespread and enjoyed popular support.

After the August blast, the Mojahedin leaders showed the same reticence in claiming responsibility, even though many knowledgeable observers were convinced that Mojahedin infiltrators were responsible. What must be noted is their self-confidence in the justice of their cause and the inevitability of their ultimate success. In early September Banisadr claimed that he had ordered the Mojahedin not to assassinate Khomeini for they did not wish to make a martyr out of him. Indeed, why attempts to eliminate Khomeini have not been undertaken has been a puzzle, even to those who have been duly impressed by the Mojahedin's ability to plant dedicated agents, even into the innermost sanctum of the fundamentalist regime. Some reports have suggested that several such attempts were made during the summer of 1981. The fact that Khomeini, unlike Beheshti, Rajai and Bahonar, never leaves his residence in Jamaran, in north Tehran, makes access to him more difficult.

The Mojahedin have been careful to demonstrate their reluctance to resort to the violence, which according to Rajavi had been imposed on them when Khomeini had denied them every legitimate means of political activity, such as a free press, political meetings and representation in elected institutions. 'Violence, bombing and terror could not resolve Iran's problem, but it is Khomeini's terrorism that has pushed our people to armed resistance.'

What political philosophy do the Mojahedin espouse now that they have joined the armed struggle to overthrow the Islamic Republic? Since the ousting of Banisadr, the Mojahedin have been more forthcoming about their political ideology. In early August Rajavi told the foreign press that the Covenant of Freedom and Independence signed with Banisadr incorporated the fundamental objectives of his organization.[5]

> Firstly we want freedom for all political parties. We reject both political prisoners and political executions. In the true spirit of Islam, we advocate freedom, fraternity and an end to all repression, censorship and injustices.

As to the claim of Khomeini of representing the totality or even a majority of the Shia clergy, the Mojahedin, who had withdrawn their recognition of Khomeini as the deputy of the hidden Imam, seriously questioned that claim.

> The bloodsucking clique following Khomeini is a small minority. The Iranian clergy throughout our history have sided with the masses of deprived people and never turned against them with clubs and bayonets. We have close contact with the genuine clergy many of whose members are in prison or under house arrest.

The Mojahedin have now been concentrating on recruiting army officers. Rajavi seems to be convinced that as long as Khomeini is alive the Pasdaran will remain loyal to him because they owe their very existence to him. The Army, on the other hand, has very few reasons to display irreversible loyalty to the Ayattolah even though after every major act of violence against the government it now issues the familiar declaration of allegiance 'to the Imam of Shia Ummat.' Because the Army reflects the Iranian community as a whole, it is not unlikely that the Mojahedin have gained similar support amongst the military as they have within the community as a whole. It is evident that in the ultimate battle between the Mojahedin and the Pasdaran, the attitude of even some members of the armed forces could tip the balance in favour of the Mojahedin.

Even though the Mojahedin, together with the followers of Banisadr and the secular forces may now constitute a majority of politically articular Iranians, as long as Khomeini remains in power and is backed by the Pasdaran, a peaceful transfer of power to the above coalition seems unlikely. It may be that the Mojahedin are the first to acknowledge this fact, for a concerted effort has been under way to discredit Khomeini as a leader. The Mojahedin are bent on depicting themselves as true martyrs of the new revolution for freedom and independence, and Khomeini's harsh punishments play right into the hands of the Mojahedin's propagandists.

They now picture Khomeini as 'worse than Hitler', with Rajavi claiming that compared with Khomeini the Shah was 'a noble and innocent man'.

Khomeini has killed so far as many people as the Shah did throughout his reign. Nearly 10,000 Mojahedin are in jail. In the worst days of the Shah the number of political prisoners was never more than four to five thousand,

said Rajavi in mid-August.[6]

The Fedayeene Khalgh

The other guerrilla organization, which has a more avowed Marxist tendency, is the Organization of the People's Devoted Guerrillas, commonly known as the Fedayeen. Like their Islamic-oriented counterparts, they had waged a prolonged guerrilla warfare against the Shah's regime and had actively participated in the final insurrectionary assault on the Army and state apparatus in February 1979.

Whereas the Mojahedin systematically and steadily turned against the Islamic Republic, the Fedayeen found the adoption of a correct attitude toward the Shia theocracy difficult and even impossible.

Immediately after the revolution the Fedayeen faced the dilemma of what to do about the Bazargan government. They had labelled that government as a bourgeois-nationalist regime, not sufficiently revolutionary and containing a number of conservative personalities. After some soul-searching they decided to remain neutral towards the government, fearing that their opposition might help the religious groups to monopolize power. However, the Fedayeen, unlike the Tudeh Party, did not support the Islamic Republic in the April referendum. Instead, they concentrated on pressing the Bazargan government for new concessions in favour of the working class. Resistance to their demands, which at one point included the inclusion of a working-class representative in the Revolutionary Council, had turned them against the government by July 1979.

However, important doctrinal issues also plagued the leadership cadre of the movement. In April 1979 the Fedayeen announced the expulsion of Ashraf Dehghani from the organization and its leadership cadre. A week later Dehghani gave an interview in which he detailed the causes of his removal, the most important of which was disagreement over armed struggle. The Fedayeen, since the guerrilla attack on Siyahkal in 1966, had subscribed to the teachings of Massud Ahmadzadeh contained in his well-known book, *Armed Struggle: as Tactic and as Strategy*.[7]

The basic thesis of the book was that under the Shah the imperialist-dependent bourgeois ruling class had established a most despotic political system. This system had made armed struggle, as the highest and ultimate form of political effort, indispensable. Accordingly, the organization had taken a lead in the efforts to make the transfer of power to Khomeini an insurrectional one.

Once the revolution had succeeded, other leftist groups, in particular the Tudeh Party, began to criticize Ahmadzadeh's thesis and brand it as deviationist and anti-Marxist-Leninist. According to Dehghani, in the wake of the severe oppression of the organization in 1976 the original leadership was replaced by new cadres who did not fully appreciate the decisiveness of the 'armed-struggle thesis.'

The truth was that the success of the revolution made the continuing application of that thesis problematic. On the one hand, traditional communist groups like the Tudeh asserted that the thesis was outdated in the post-revolution era. Those who wished to continue armed struggle were accused of what Lenin had described as 'leftist opportunism' after the Bolsheviks had seized power.

Dehghani, on the other hand, accused the new leadership cadre of discriminating against those recently freed prisoners who had not pledged themselves to reject the 'armed-struggle thesis.' According to Dehghani, the Khomeini regime had the same class base as the Shah's, with the difference that under the Shah the bureaucratic bourgeoisie was controlling power whereas now the whole bourgeoisie was in power. The militant protection of land ownership by the new regime suggested that it did not represent the interest of the petty bourgeoisie.

The armed struggle was valid for two reasons. One was to prepare the masses for the protection of the revolution and the other was to prevent the imperialists from military intervention in Iran. As yet Dehghani did not believe that armed struggle should be waged against Khomeini's regime. His sharpest attack was on the leadership of the organization and on the Tudeh Party. His rhetoric convinced a small group to follow suit. Ever since Dehghani's ousting from the Fedayeen this group has claimed to be the sole genuine communist organization.

When the Mojahedin began the armed struggle against the regime in June 1981, as will be shown later, the Dehghani faction became their comrades-in-arms.[8]

Returning to the reaction of the provisional government, even though it could distinguish between the Dehghani faction and the main Fedayeen group, it decided to condemn the whole organization. The Prime Minister accused them of opposing the government. Pro-Khomeini armed groups raided the offices of the Fedayeen in Tehran and provincial university campuses. Shortly thereafter ethnic-minority rebellions broke out in Kurdistan as well as among the Turkomans in Gonbad Ghabus. As shown later, the issue of support for the ethnic minorities caused serious dissension within the Fedayeen. In September and October the Fedayeen were in almost complete disarray as to the correct policy towards the Provisional Government as well as towards Khomeini himself.[9]

However, the occupation of the American embassy in November and the outburst of anti-American radicalism put a temporary halt to internal bickering amongst the competing groups. The Fedayeen, which had no prior knowledge of or actual participation in the taking of the American hostages, resorted to the extreme demand of a trial of the hostages and the rejection of any idea of a peaceful resolution of the crisis. As the crisis lengthened into the spring and summer, the Fedayeen found themselves as the first target of the so-called cultural revolution. It was at this point that doctrinal disagreement on major internal and foreign-policy issues split the organization into several factions.

The Factional Splits

The first split centred on the 'armed-struggle thesis' which had to be addressed as soon as the ethnic uprisings broke out. Should they be broadened into a national uprising? What about the class foundations of ethnic uprisings? Could a genuine Marxist group back a non-Marxist organization like the Kurdish Democratic Party? Compounding the situation facing the self-professed Marxists was the reality that in parts of Kurdistan landowners, whose properties had been distributed amongst the peasants under the Shah, were now forcibly taking back the land. The exact role of Dehghani himself is rather obscure. What can be ascertained is that at the height of the Kurdish rebellion in the summer of 1980, some 30 per cent of the organization's active and armed cadres affiliated themselves with Ashraf Dehghani and declared their support for the KDP. Reportedly, several hundreds of them joined the party in fighting the Pasdaran and the regular Iranian Army around such

Kurdish outposts as Mahabad, Bukan and Mehran. This minority used the name of 'Sazeman', or organization, to identify itself, and continued to oppose the majority group on the issue of Kurdistan as well as on the general question of the correct attitude towards the regime, and in particular toward the Soviet-supported Tudeh Party.

The majority, on the other hand, opposed the Kurdish and other ethnic revolts against the Islamic regime which 'despite many deficiencies continues to be a bastion of anti-imperialism.' After the assault on the US embassy they were bolstered in their claim that the capture of 'America's den of espionage and its refusal to compromise against the Great Satan' made the regime even more deserving of their support.

In January 1981 the majority group organized a joint plenum with the Tudeh Party in which the conditions for unity of action with that party were laid down. The plenum vehemently rejected the notion that the Soviet Union was imperialistic, and dedicated itself to preserving its separate identity, but being prepared to adopt a joint-action programme, 'the moment it senses the revolution was in danger of accommodation with US imperialism.'

For several reasons the plenum did not sit well with some of the majority faction. Some believed if there were identical goals and policies with the Tudeh, why not join them? Others were opposed to continuing support for the Islamic regime merely because it was anti-American. Still others believed the Soviet Union was at fault on several important international issues and that the majority faction should not blindly support it even though it was by far superior to Western imperialism.

In March this faction issued a statement calling itself the Left Wing of the Majority of Fedayeen and reflecting some of the above reservations. Though no reliable data on the numerical strength of the three factions of the original Fedayeen are available, an analysis of government figures on raids, arrests and executions since the beginning of the armed struggle in June indicates that the majority faction has become a minority. That is to say the second split has given a numerical majority to the Ashraf Dehghani group, plus the left wing of the majority faction.

These two are now almost indistinguishable because they both insist on using the full original name of the organization. Because of harsh retribution against the Mojahedin and the Dehghani faction of the Fedayeen, the majority faction decided in July to drop the term 'guerrillas' from its title so that it would not be mistaken by the security authorities. It has been since known as simply the People's Fedayeen Organization.

How broad the basis of public support is for the various Fedayeen groups is very difficult to ascertain. There is no doubt that at the beginning of the revolutionary era they could muster about 100,000 disciplined marchers. At the height of the hostage crisis they were still capable of rallying that number of active supporters to join the massive demonstrations in front of the occupied US embassy.

Some commentators have speculated that an organization which could muster that many marchers must have at least five times that number of supporters. Further, it has been suggested that the numerical support of each group in the capital city constitutes about 30 per cent of its nationwide backing, and thus the Fedayeen may have over 3 million followers throughout Iran. While these estimates may be exaggerated, all the evidence suggests that up to the first of the successive splits in its leadership cadre, the Fedayeen was second in size to the Mojahedin. Not only has it suffered measurably from the internal splits, but its alliance with the pro-Soviet Tudeh Party and the support of its majority faction for the Khomeini regime have cost it dearly in political support throughout the country.

When other guerrilla organizations joined in the armed struggle at the end of June 1981, the Minority Fedayeen came out in total opposition to the regime, which it denounced as reactionary and oppressive. *KAR*, the official organ of the group, published a series of editorials explaining its ideological position concerning the Islamic Republic.[10] One editorial entitled 'Where is the Islamic Republic heading for?' condemned the regime and accused it of having planned the destruction of the revolutionary forces as early as a few months after the revolution, by its assault on Kurdistan. The editorial put the blame for the savage brutality against the opposition squarely on Khomeini, whom it described as

a criminal traitor who diverted the people's revolution from its course, leading it to the present impasse. A demagogue who issues religious Fatva for the massacre of revolutionary combatants and urges the masses to spy on their fellow citizens.

The more terror was used, the editorial contended, the more convinced the people became of the desperation of the regime. By destroying all the bridges behind itself the regime has denied itself the opportunity of reversing its murderous course. It was engaged in a struggle for life and death of which the outcome will be no different from other brutal and repressive political systems.

In a detailed analysis of the transformation of Khomeini from 'the leader to the butcher of the masses', another article listed the following deviations by the Ayattolah.

(1) Reneguing on the pledge to organize a constituent assembly, which was even included in the decree appointing Mehdi Bazargan as Prime Minister. Instead, he had opted for the made-to-order Assembly of Experts.

(2) At the height of the revolutionary turmoil instead of encouraging the masses to fight the army, he had put out the slogan of 'The Army is our Brother' and prevented the destruction of that pillar of the autocracy.

(3) The moment he took over the reins of power Khomeini had turned away from the masses by ordering the end of strikes even though the social and political demands of the strikers had not been fulfilled. By declaring the Army 'Islamicized' and installing the provisional government, he had saved the bourgeoisie from ultimate collapse.

(4) The Kurdish uprising had revealed the true colour of his regime when it issued the infamous 'Fatva' ordering *Jehad* against the Kurdish masses. He had reorganized the SAVAK by including in it the leaders of the Pasdaran and the club-wielders of Hizbollah.

(5) As Commander-in-Chief he had led the bloody suppression of the revolutionary forces, including high school youth, women, workers and ethnic minorities, thereby becoming the butcher rather than the leader of the masses.

The group did not confine itself to general condemnation of Khomeini's regime. Not only did it support armed struggle against it, but issued an action programme with specific instructions to its followers.

KAR, after reviewing the three months of armed struggle, issued the following programme in mid-September 1981:

(1) Establish the closest link with the toilers and workers and organize them for political and economic struggle and convince them that to achieve revolutionary victory in the forthcoming struggle, they must resort to arms.

(2) Organize resistance cells or combat squads with friends whose revolutionary sincerity and combative spirit may be trusted. Collect accurate intelligence data about the identity and residences of the regime's security, prison and top party officials, who must be eliminated for their crimes against the masses.

(3) Make accurate reconnaisances of the enemy's supply, arsenals, transportation and cash centres so they may be confiscated at the proper moment.

(4) Maximize your efforts to give the widest circulation to the organization's publications amongst workers and toilers.

(5) Because the regime has declared civil war against the opposition, self-defence has become a vital task requiring training and the possession of modern weapons.

(6) Collect and store weapons in safe places.

(7) Study the writings of such famous leaders of guerrilla warfare as Vietnam's General Giap.

(8) Avoid wasting energy and manpower by waging only systematic and well co-ordinated strikes against the enemy.[11]

The majority faction, however, displayed a completely different attitude. Not only did it not join the armed struggle to overthrow the regime, but did its best to discredit both the minority and the Mojahedin. In a statement published at the end of June the organization blamed the United States for conspiring against the Islamic Republic, but also found fault with some of the policies of the ruling regime. The absence of a coherent and consistent socio-economic programme to fight economic dependency and imperialism, and the lack of a correct understanding of the friends and foes of the revolution on national and international scales, according to the majority faction, have left the doors open for renewed attempts by imperialism and the world counter-revolution to conspire against the revolution.

Specifically, the Majority Fedayeen blamed the monopolistic and sectarian actions of the IRP, which had created disunity among the progressive and anti-imperialist forces. These errors also have strengthened the ultra-left elements of the popular forces to the extent that they now regard the Islamic Republic as the main enemy to be overthrown.

The Majority Fedayeen viewed the demise of Banisadr with satisfaction because he had represented the middle-class groups wishing to establish a 'moderate' government. It accused the Mojahedin and the minority faction of Fedayeen of wrongly supporting Banisadr and unleashing the bloody events of 20 June in protest against his impeachment. This in turn had strengthened the hands of the sectarian elements in the Islamic Republic with a campaign of summary executions 'without regard to the Constitution.'

To summarize, the majority depicts its ideological rivals on the left as childishly ultra-left, while it also accuses the IRP leadership of monopolistic and sectarian tendencies. Its solutions are no surprise to students of the pro-Soviet left in Iran. Unity of the progressive forces, struggle against the bourgeoisie class and economic dependency, alliance with the world revolutionary front — meaning the Soviet bloc countries — are all dutifully emphasized.

At the end of August, on the occasion of the assassination of Rajai and Bahonar, the Majority Fedayeen issued another statement expressing regret at the murder of the leaders of the Islamic Republic and issued three specific demands:

(1) The summary executions without regard to the Constitution should be stopped and a policy of guidance towards the supporters of the deviant groups be adopted so that treacherous leaders would be separated from their sincere but misguided followers.
(2) The Islamic Republic should struggle relentlessly against the social base of the counter-revolution, namely the big landlords and the capitalists.
(3) The regime should lay aside its sectarian approach and move promptly towards the formation of a united anti-imperialist front and strengthen the alliance with the world revolutionary front, especially with the socialist countries.[12]

It is noteworthy that these demands were completely ignored by the Islamic Republic and were dismissed by the political groups engaged in armed struggle against the regime. If anything, the Majority Fedayeen found itself increasingly marginal to the main currents of Iranian politics, for neither the government nor the opposition took it seriously. As a matter of fact in June 1980, before the split, two leaders of the Fedayeen, Farrokh Negahdar and Mostafa Madani, had almost succeeded in convincing Beheshti to accept the formation of an anti-imperialist front. But shortly thereafter the IRP gave them the cold shoulder, maintaining that their support was neither desirable nor necessary.

The Tudeh Party

Among the pro-Khomeini political groups the Soviet-sponsored Tudeh Party deserves considerable attention. Not only is it a tightly organized and well-disciplined political party used to underground as well as legitimate existence, but in a critical unforeseeable juncture it might play a role disproportionate to its numerical strength.

As was noted in previous chapters, the party has remained steadfastly in Khomeini's corner. It has supported the regime even though in return it has only been tolerated as a sort of quasi-legal political organization. None of its candidates have won any election, though in all second-round ballots it has joined with the IRP to assure the victory of IRP candidates. Its publications have been outlawed, its headquarters occupied and its members harassed.

The party has been at some pains to justify its persistent backing of the regime. There are two fundamental reasons for doing so: Khomeini's anti-Americanism and the party's identification with the Mostazafin (the destitute or the proletariat). To the faithful these reasons appear convincing, but to sophisticated Iranians the chief reason is the party's preference for Soviet interests.

At no time since 1979 has this become more obvious than in the wake of the Soviet invasion of Afghanistan in December 1979. Though the pro-Khomeini media and political organizations joined in a chorus of anti-Soviet propaganda, the Tudeh Party, along with the Majority Fedayeen, echoed Moscow's line and condemned the Afghan Mojahedin as agents of American imperialism, working from the sanctuary of Pakistan to undermine the progressive, popular Khalgh Party government in Kabul.[13] This event, coming as it did at the height of the American hostage crisis, enabled the Tudeh Party, without much difficulty, to convince its supporters that any general criticism of the Soviet Union might indirectly play into the hands of the Great Satan, the United States.

Once the shock of the Soviet occupation of neighbouring Afghanistan had been absorbed, the Tudeh Party with the help of Marxist elements in the leadership of the Militant Students at the US embassy, began a systematic campaign of discrediting those associates of Khomeini who had advocated a more pronounced anti-Soviet course of action. Men like Ghotbzadeh, Bazargan and later Banisadr were singled out as vehemently anti-Soviet and leaning towards the USA. The Militant Students disclosed captured US documents purporting to show the anti-Sovietism of some of the secular associates of Bazargan and Banisadr.

The fact that all these three had, from the outset, pleaded for a prompt and peaceful solution of the hostage crisis evidently made the Tudeh accusations against them more plausible.

There is no doubt that the party cannot be dismissed as simply a nuisance. Nor should its strength be imagined as being at the level it enjoyed in the immediate post-World War II era. A careful analysis of its performance since late 1978 leads to two significant conclusions. In the first place the party suffers from the continuing liability of being Soviet-created and Moscow-directed. It is true that in the 1941-53 era the party had quite successfully turned that liability into an asset, but clearly the Soviet Union is not in the same position as it was in that era, nor are recent Iranian political developments quite akin to that period.[14] For one thing, the Soviet Union is now challenged by competing communist systems from Yugoslavia to China; for another, the Soviet Union had not only coexisted with pre-revolutionary Iran, but had fully supported the Shah, sometimes at the price of sacrificing the lives of some of the hapless Tudeh Party officials who had sought sanctuary in Soviet territory. The indisputable fact is that the Soviet Union joined the anti-Shah opposition only after it had become absolutely convinced that the Shah was doomed. As for the Tudeh Party, it is also evident that it had not played any significant role in unleashing the revolutionary turmoil which overthrew the Pahlavi monarchy.

A second liability which plagues the party is that it no longer enjoys the monopoly of representing the ideological left in Iran as it did in that early period. A variety of political groups which have embraced Marxist ideology have been noted; sometimes Marxism has been combined with Islamic teachings, and at other times in association with Trotskyism and Maoism. The loss of that monopoly has been quite costly for the pro-Soviet Tudeh Party, for it has been accompanied by a considerable suffering of the non-Tudeh leftist groups both at the hands of the Shah and of Khomeini's regime. In reality, while the Tudeh Party was almost completely incapable of maintaining an underground organization inside the country between 1963 and 1978, other leftist groups were remarkably successful in forming and maintaining clandestine guerrilla networks. To quote a leader of Mojahedin, 'while Tudeh leaders enjoyed safety as exiles in the Soviet Union or East European countries, the Mojahedin and Fedayeen faced the firing squads and torture chambers of the SAVAK.'

These two liabilities add up to a sense of betrayal that has worked against a successful reformation of the party's organization since 1979. Above all, the young intellectuals who were traditionally susceptible to the appeal of the party find the competing Mojahedin, Peykar and Ranjbaran more attractive as genuine revolutionary organizations. The advanced age of the Tudeh leaders and their long absence from Iran have also made the party less attractive than the competition.

More recently the party has tried to compensate for its lack of broad popular appeal by efforts at tightening its organization and training its cadres in guerrilla warfare. As noted earlier, the party has consistently supported the Soviet-supported Barbak Karmal regime in Afghanistan. When the more radical faction of the Afghan Khalgh, or People's Party, was out of power the Tudeh Party helped it organizationally and financially. When that faction, called Parcham (Farsi for flag), was installed in power by the invading Russian Army, the Tudeh Party found its fellow pro-Soviet communists in power in neighbouring Farsi-speaking Afghanistan. The Tudeh Party has ever since acted as an intelligence service for the Barbak Karmal regime. News of the anti-Soviet plans of political groups as well as the activities of several thousands of Afghan citizens in Iran are systematically passed to the government authorities in Kabul. A common ethnic and linguistic background has facilitated the flow of Tudeh agents across ill-guarded borders to the government-controlled areas of Afghanistan. The party has been also involved in organizing a network of pro-government organizations amongst Afghan refugees in such provinces as Khorassan and Sistan. More ominously, in June the party decided to take up an outstanding invitation from President Karmal to send several hundred Tudeh Party members to Kabul for military training.[15] These cadres will bolster the embattled regime in Kabul, and when the opportune time comes will be sent back to Iran. The outbreak of guerrilla warfare against the Khomeini regime seems to have convinced the party's leaders that at a critical juncture the availability of even a small contingent of guerrillas to the party may radically improve its bargaining power. This will be particularly so if the balance of forces fighting and defending the regime becomes so precarious that the support of the Tudeh Party and its armed cadres is actively enlisted by both sides.

For the time being the Tudeh finds its position quite indefensible among Iranian dissident groups. It insists that Khomeini's government is anti-imperialist, anti-feudal and anti-capitalist, but is at a loss to explain the Pasdaran's forcible expulsion of farmers in Gorgan and Kurdistan from land confiscated from prominent feudal landlords.

It believes there are two Islams: one for the poor and disinherited and the other for the bourgeoisie; but it cannot deny that the Islamic Republic believes in the unity of Islam and that the IRP contains many bourgeois elements among its leadership. The Tudeh is compelled to acknowledge that it has some problems with the Shia fundamentalists, but tries to paper them over by distinguishing between primary contradictions and so-called secondary contradictions. Religious laws imposing restrictions on women are considered a secondary contradiction and not sufficiently grave to cause defection from the regime. The Mojahedin on the other hand, so believes the Tudeh Party, confuse secondary and primary contradictions. They forget the most important thing, which is the revolutionary content of the regime. The party is also ambivalent about such important demands of the Mojahedin and Fedayeen as the dissolution of the Army. A party spokesman recently indicated that while they still believed in the necessity of creating a new army, other factors should be considered. For instance, not everyone in the armed forces is outside the revolution. Soldiers and middle-level officers have changed. In addition, the Pasdaran has been created and with over 300,000 light arms in the hands of the people the Army's capability of staging a coup has been dramatically reduced.[16]

The party makes no apologies for its sympathies for the Soviet Union. While applauding every anti-American measure, it states that it does not agree with the government that the Soviet Union and the United States should be put on the same plane, and hopes that the government leaders will correct their position on that score.

All the groups described in this chapter took up different positions when the crisis of the Presidency intensified at the end of the spring, and the subsequent armed struggle against the regime was unleashed in the wake of Banisadr's dismissal on 24 June 1981.

Notes

1. *Mojahed* (organ of the People's Mojahedin Organization of Iran) London, May 1980, Vol. 1, No. 5, pp. 25–9. Also, *Last Defense of Martyred Mojahed Ali Mihandust*, (PMOI) publication distributed in the USA by the Moslem Student Society, Long Beach, Ca., March 1981. An important statement in Mihandust's defence is that, 'we and the revolutionary Marxists have a common objective, and that is the elimination of exploitation. So for this reason we have undertaken the struggle with a common strategy to deal with a common foe.' pp. 16–17.

2. The fundamentalist Shia publications blame the pro-Marxist orientation of the Mojahedin on the more secular forces who, in 1974, dominated the movement. Government records indicate that in a struggle for the leadership the secular forces succeeded in assassinating two of the more religious members of the leadership cadre in 1974, namely Majid Sharif and Morteza Labaff. In early 1975 two Mojahedin publications, *Recognition* and *Evolution*, used a fundamentally Marxist dialectical materialist approach to its discussion of social and political

issues. Some of the Marxist members who thought they could not convert and recruit the religious elements left the movement to organize a Trotskyite group known as Rahe Kargar (Workers' Path). In the autumn of 1978 they formed a larger organization Peykar Baraye Rahaiye Tabaghehe Kargar (Struggle for the Liberation of the Working Class) with a weekly called *Peykar* as their organ. It is this group that after the revolution opposed the return of confiscated weapons, and urged the street fighters to hide them until safe storage places could be located. See Chapter 8 for the relative parts being played by this and other guerrilla groups in the ongoing armed struggle.

3. *Mojahed* Tehran, 5 March 1981. The same issue published the statement of the Society of Moslem Jurists, a pro-Mojahedin group and attacked Beheshti's TV interview in which he had divided the parties into four groups. The Society said that analysis showed Beheshti's intention to establish the IRP as the single dominant party. Evidence of this is the bill which prohibits political parties from any propaganda activity in favour of anti-Islamic and deviant schools of thought. Their non-belief in Velayate Faghih is prohibited under severe penalty.

4. *Le Monde* Paris, 28 July 1981.

5. Text circulated by the Moslem Student Society, a pro-Mojahed group with branches all over Europe and the USA 12 August 1981.

6. *Mojahed* (clandestine), 17 August 1981.

7. This book combines some of the doctrines of Mao with those of Che Guevara with regards to guerrilla warfare.

8. *Mosahebe be Rafigh Ashraf Dehghani*, (interview with Comrade Ashraf Dehghani) clandestine publication of the Minority Fedayeen.

9. *Keyhan*, 18 May 1979.

10. *KAR*, No. 126, 9 September 1981.

11. *KAR*, No. 127, 17 September 1981.

12. Iranian Student Association in the US (pro-Majority Fedayeen) Berkeley, California, 1 September 1981.

13. *Mardom*, Tehran, 7 January 1981.

14. For background see the author's *The Communist Movement in Iran*, (University of California Press, Berkeley and Los Angeles, 1966).

15. Interview with officials of ARA, (Iran Liberation Army) Paris, 22 April 1981.

16. Interview with Koshroui, a member of Tudeh's central committee, *Newsfront International*, 28 October 1981.

7 THE DEMISE OF BANISADR

As noted earlier, the election of Banisadr as the first President of the IRP was, from the outset, accompanied by tensions and uncertainties. Above all, the peculiarities of the new constitution, which integrated features of the separation of power with those of the fusion of the executive and legislative branches of government, must be mentioned. Leaving aside the institution of Velayate Faghih and the unlimited power granted it by the new constitution, the Islamic Republic's fundamental law indicates heavy borrowing from the French Fifth Republic Constitution in terms of organizing the relationship of executive and legislative power. To a large measure this is attributed to the French educational backgrounds of several influential non-clerical members of the Assembly of Experts, notably Abolhassan Banisadr himself.

Thus, for example, executive power in France is vested in a President who has since 1965 been elected separately and by popular vote in a nationwide election, according to the amendment to the original constitution approved in a referendum three years earlier. Moreover, the election of the President is undertaken by a double-ballot majority system to assure that the occupant of the office represents at least 50 per cent of the voters.

The Presidents in both systems could justly claim a larger constituency than that of parliamentary districts, even more so in Iran where well-organized political parties were not responsible for parliamentary elections. Needless to say, there are significant differences between the time-tested and well-established traditions of democratic freedoms in France and the absence of those in Iran. The purpose of this discussion is merely to underline the major source of ambiguity and uncertainty in so far as the Presidency of the Islamic Republic is concerned.

An analysis of the functions of the office reveals a similar borrowing from the French system. A major area of concern is the sharing of executive power with the Prime Minister, who unlike the President is directly accountable to parliament. From the time that Banisadr was elected he became aware that despite his vast popular majority and his additional designation as Commander-in-Chief, the future of his office depended on the Majlis and its choice of Prime Minister. Though the constitution empowered him to name the Prime Minister and approve the members of his Cabinet, since they required a parliamentary vote of confidence, the power to name was less than definitive and had to be exercised with the consent of the Majlis.

Before the start of the Majlis elections Banisadr had tried to name a caretaker Prime Minister to be submitted to the Majlis for its approval when it had acquired the necessary quorum. Despite Khomeini's initial acceptance of this proposal, opposition from within the Revolutionary Council prevented this from happening. Since Banisadr had not succeeded in organizing his supporters in the course of the two stages of the parliamentary elections, it soon became evident that on the question of the formation of the first government under the constitution, Banisadr would face his first trial of strength with the fundamentalist personalities organized in the Islamic Republican Party.

In the course of these elections some secular personalities affiliated with Bazargan did receive Banisadr's support, and indeed in the crisis eighteen months later these deputies opposed the removal of the President. However, not all the non-clerical Majlis members supported the President from the outset of the struggle. Some, like Rajai and Ayat, were not only closely allied with the IRP, but had never accepted the constitutional powers of the President in good faith. Others, like Moinfar and Bazargan himself, while gradually becoming alarmed at the monopolistic tendencies of the IRP, none the less had a vested interest in enhancing and strengthening the power of the Majlis *vis-à-vis* that of the President. In doing so they evoked the democratic concept of representation and accountability, which meant that the head of government should be primarily the choice of the Majlis and accountable to it.

Banisadr himself has maintained that these institutional issues were mere pretexts, for as early as June 1980 influential members of the IRP leadership council were actively conspiring against the President. His newspaper *Islamic Revolution* had published the text of a taped conversation between Dr Hassan Ayat, the prominent non-clerical ideologue of the party, and a leader of the Militant Students. Dr Ayat had revealed the party's involvement in the impending cultural revolution and closure of universities. He had accused Banisadr of being pro-American or else he would not have tried so hard to secure the release of the hostages. The conversation also revealed the IRP's efforts in the Assembly of Experts to reduce the President's powers to a minimum, making the office that of a symbolic chief executive. Dr Ayat had revealed a step-by-step strategy to force Banisadr out. That strategy had been followed literally with the appointment of Rajai as

Prime Minister and the subsequent quarrels between the Majlis and Prime Minister on the one hand and the President on the other.[1]

On the question of the division of the executive power between the head of state and the head of government, the position of Banisadr was in inherent conflict with that of the Majlis, though not all its members pursued a uniform policy to assure the ascendency of the legislature in this critical area. What is undeniable is the critical role that this constitutional ambiguity played in the tension between the President and the IRP and in the ultimate demise of the former.

In retrospect, many of Banisadr's supporters, who increased dramatically in direct proportion with the IRP's success in the monopolization of power, have attributed his demise to a failure to transform his impressive electoral victory into an organized political party. For several reasons, however, Banisadr could not have undertaken such a task. His election, which Khomeini favoured because he did not wish to put fellow clerical leaders at the head of all-significant state institutions, was backed by an extremely loose and heterogeneous electoral coalition. This coalition collapsed almost immediately after the completion of the electoral process. Moreover, because the first round was decisive, no opportunity to reorganize and realign voter groups, which traditionally occurs in double-ballot majority systems, was offered. Consequently, Banisadr's victory was due to the spontaneous support of vast numbers of Monfaredin (independent) voters who could hardly be expected to enrol in a President-sponsored political party. In some sense he seemed to aspire to stand above parties, and instead to appeal to the largest cross-section of the population.

Political Organizations and the President

Political organizations outside the IRP were in no better position to coalesce around the President, though some of them did so at the very end of his tenure when he was perceived to symbolize all opposition to the emerging fundamentalist absolutism. The most logical groups for joining the President were the Moslem People's Republican Party, the National Front and its offshoot the National Democratic Front, the People's Mojahedin, some factions of the People's Fedayeen, Bazargan's Iran Liberation Movement and the Kurdish Democratic Party.

Except at the very end each of these groups faced practical and ideological obstacles as well as serious misgivings about offering organized and dependable support to Banisadr. Thus, for example, as already noted, the MPRP, with its substantial following in Azarbayjan, was forced to dissolve itself in the wake of the December 1979 uprising in Tabriz.[2] Indeed Banisadr, who was then eager to mobilize all pro-Khomeini elements in his electoral campaign, had played a critical role in crushing the uprising and re-establishing the authority of the central government, then exercised by the Revolutionary Council in Azarbayjan. The charged political atmosphere surrounding the hostage crisis made it easier for Khomeini's supporters to subdue the MPRP by accusing any opposition to the government of playing into the hand of the USA. Thus, this potentially significant mass political organization was so mercilessly suppressed that even if it had wished to regroup and rally around Banisadr it would have been hard put to do so in view of the latter's role in putting down the Tabriz uprising. Moreover, Ayattolah Shariatmadari, who was a guiding force of the MPRP, had retreated to political inactivity and refused to sanction the reactivation of the party, let alone direct its support for the beleaguered President.

Both the National Front and the National Democratic Front had suffered at the hand of Banisadr and the Revolutionary Council of which he was an influential member and, since his election, the chairman. Banisadr's early support for the National Front and his efforts to identify his policies with those of the late Dr Mossadegh, founder of the Front, were viewed with great suspicion by the older leaders of the Front. Because of their acceptance of Khomeini's leadership before the triumph of the revolution, and their ousting from power shortly thereafter, they were predictably reluctant to forgive Banisadr for 'betraying' the trust that he was instrumental in securing from the Front for unqualified support of Khomeini in the autumn of 1978.

The two guerrilla organizations, the Mojahedin and the Fedayeen, as noted earlier, showed strong misgivings toward the Islamic Republic. Not only were they denied a share in power despite their undeniable contribution to the overthrow of the Pahlavi regime, but they found serious ideological fault with the new constitution and with the emergence of the IRP as a new monopolistic one-party system.

These groups were placed under serious constraints when the hostage crisis catapulted the American threat to the forefront of Iranian politics. Either by conviction or for political expediency they re-emerged as vehement advocates of defiance of the United States and therefore as supporters of the Islamic Republic. However, Khomeini's refusal to allow the Mojahedin leader Massud Rajavi to run for the Presidency on the ground that his organization had boycotted the referendum in support of the constitution, gradually turned the Mojahedin into open opposition. Although at the end it did come out in favour of Banisadr, it could not join him in an organized and systematic fashion at the time of the electoral campaign for the Majlis.

As for the Fedayeen, the splits in its rank and file in the summer of 1980 and the spring of 1981 were considered in Chapter 6. Suffice it to reiterate that the majority faction, which like the Soviet-linked Tudeh Party fully supports the Islamic Republic, could not have abandoned Khomeini in favour of the President, who among other things had championed the cause of anti-Sovietism in the Islamic Republic. The minority faction was closer to the Mojahedin than any other political organization with regard to Banisadr. As the IRP intensified its pressure on the President and in the process moved the infant republic closer to a one-party theocratic system, the minority faction of the Fedayeen became more sympathetic toward Banisadr. At the end they joined the Mojahedin in a public show of support for the ousted President, not out of ideological conviction but for tactical necessity.

Finally, the position of Bazargan and the Kurdish Democratic Party in this crisis should be noted. During his tenure Bazargan was repeatedly at odds with Banisadr who, as a fairly radical member of the Revolutionary Council, had frequently attacked the provisional government for lack of revolutionary fervour. Although educationally and politically they shared a common background, it was clear to Bazargan that Banisadr had joined the clerics in the Revolutionary Council to undermine his government. However, once Bazargan had been forced out of office and subsequently elected to the Majlis from Tehran, a natural realignment occurred in which the hostility towards the IRP in and outside the Majlis caused all the secular politicians to come together. Indeed, Bazargan and a handful of his close allies in the Majlis openly opposed the IRP's drive to dislodge the President. Nevertheless, the memories of the Provisional Government were too fresh in the minds of Bazargan and his Iran Liberation Movement to allow for a formal and timely alliance with the President.[3]

Similar obstacles did not prevail with regard to the Kurdish Democratic Party, whose leader Dr Abdolrahman Ghassemlou found Banisadr most amenable to a peaceful settlement of the Kurdish autonomy issue. On several occasions it was Banisadr who had pressed the Revolutionary Council for a cessation of hostilities with the autonomy-seeking KDP. Once he became President, Banisadr found open support for the KDP extremely risky, for it could simply play into the hands of the IRP as indicative of the President's encouragement of separatist ethnic minorities which could threaten Iran's territorial integrity. The issue became more complex with the Iraqi invasion in September 1980. As C-in-C put in charge of defending the country, including those very provinces where the KDP wished to achieve autonomy, Banisadr could ill-afford the slightest manifestation of affinity with that party. So it was that until his dismissal Banisadr walked a tight rope in his relations with the KDP. The latter was not so restrained in its support of the beleaguered President. At the end it was the KDP which joined the minority faction of the Fedayeen and the Mojahedin to hide Banisadr in a series of 'safe houses' in Tehran, and offer him shelter in the mountains of Kurdistan. To distract government security forces, these groups spread the rumour that Banisadr had indeed fled to Kurdistan shortly after his dismissal.

The above analysis shows that the foundation of a well-organized political group either during or after the election for the Majlis was perhaps beyond the President's ability. The causes for his defeat by the IRP must therefore be sought elsewhere. Some of the constitutional provisions related to entrusting executive power to the two institutions have already been examined. The practical ramifications of this difficulty were soon to surface.

The Right to Designate

Once the Majlis was officially opened the President sought to interpret his constitutional mandate of naming the Prime Minister in a fashion similar to his French counterpart in the Fifth Republic. That is to say he would appoint the Prime Minister, who would in turn receive the approval of the Majlis and then present his Cabinet members to the President for approval. The final step would be for the Majlis to give a vote of confidence to the entire Cabinet and its programme.

As noted earlier, his first two choices, Admiral Ahmad Madani, a well-known anti-Shah officer, and Mussa Kalantari, the head of the civil service organization, were not acceptable to the IRP, which controlled a working majority of the Majlis. The IRP's interpretation of the constitutional provisions on these matters was more in tune with the parliamentarism of the Fourth French Republic. They viewed the necessity of a Majlis vote of confidence in the Prime Minister and his Cabinet as tantamount to legislative domination of the executive power, or at least that part of it which was centred in the office of Prime Minister. The IRP leadership, which not only controlled the Speakership of the Majlis in the person of Aliakbar Hashemi Rafsanjani, but also the top position in the judiciary in the person of Mohammad Beheshti, insisted upon its constitutional prerogative. It told the President that the logic of a parliamentary vote of confidence necessitated the prior consent of the Majlis in the choice of the Prime Minister and Cabinet members. Since the IRP controlled the Majlis, this argument meant that it should designate the Prime Minister and give the symbolic choice of issuing the instrument of appointment to the President. Otherwise the Majlis would simply turn down every nominee that Banisadr chose.

This dispute delayed the formation of the government for over two months. The President finally accepted Mohammadali Rajai after publicly questioning his competence and qualifications to be head of the government. The choice of Rajai was thus not only a triumph for the IRP's view of how the relationship of the executive-legislative powers should be organized, but was also a personal victory for Beheshti and Rafsanjani in their feud with Banisadr.

As for Khomeini, it is worth remembering that as yet he aspired only to playing the lofty role of a disinterested and impartial arbiter. Indeed, he had even dismissed the ploy of Banisadr, who had asked permission to nominate Ahmad, the Imam's son, as Prime Minister. Neither for President nor for Prime Minister, had he initially favoured a cleric. For one thing the domination of the Majlis by the clergy was already an accomplished fact. For another, he wished to avoid the concentration of too much power in any one clerical faction lest his own ascendency be threatened. Thus, throughout the crisis Khomeini confined himself to general remarks urging his feuding associates to reconcile their differences and complete the formation of the government, which among other things had to resolve the hostage crisis.[4]

These urgings were inconsequential. To the end of his tenure the President refused to endorse the nomination of several Cabinet members and deputy ministers including the Foreign Minister. This refusal was used against him when finally Khomeini was convinced that Banisadr should be ousted.[5]

The War and the Institutional Crisis

When on 22 September 1980 the Iraqi armies invaded Iran, the position of the President received a considerable initial boost. As C-in-C he was given the task of overseeing the defensive efforts of the armed forces of the Islamic Republic. His presence on the fronts and his own daily account in his newspaper *Enghelabe Islami,* known as the 'President's Report Card', helped to foster the image of a patriotic and nationalistic young President who appeared to enjoy the Imam's full trust.

As the war continued and the repeated counter-offensives of the Iranian forces did not succeed in dislodging the Iraqi forces from all the occupied territories, the President began to face a series of critical problems. In the first place his frequent absences from the capital had left the political arena, particularly the Majlis, to his opponents, who used several intriguing arguments to drive a wedge between Khomeini and Banisadr. If the war had gone well, they warned, the President might have used his close relations with the armed forces to challenge the IRP and the Majlis, with unforeseeable consequences for the position of Khomeini himself. Now that the war had almost reached a stalemate, the President had proved incompetent in fulfilling the one task which the Imam had entrusted to him in good faith.

A further problem for the President, was that if he blamed the lack of spare parts on the ongoing US hostage crisis, he would have been accused of being soft toward the United States, which the government had already blamed for having provoked the Iraqi assault in the first place. The IRP-dominated government and Majlis claimed that they were following Khomeini's exact instructions on the question of the American hostages and that the President should not intervene in this matter by raising the question of spare parts for Iran's largely US-made weapons. Moreover, the pro-Soviet groups, such as the Tudeh Party and the Majority Fedayeen faction, were clamouring loudly for an approach to the Soviet Union and other socialist and revolutionary states for weapon procurement. In fact such efforts, involving North Korea and Libya, and using the airspaces of several East European countries and the Soviet Union itself, did result in the supplying of some spare parts to the beleaguered Iranian armed forces at the height of the war in October 1980.[6]

Whether or not the ineptness of the Iranian Army could be explained away in terms of shortages of spare parts is another matter. The point is that the President's command of the war effort, viewed by many as a strong boost in his feud with the IRP-controlled government, did not enhance his political fortunes because of the inability of the Army to free Iraqi-occupied territories.

The End of the Hostage Crisis

Once the hostage crisis was finally resolved on 20 January 1981, the relations between the President and his adversaries in the Cabinet entered a new phase.

As noted elsewhere, the final agreement for the release of the American hostages was criticized by most of the opponents of the IRP-dominated government and Majlis. The President himself led the attack on the agreement, and blamed the incompetence and inexperience of the Rajai government for a deal 'which fell much shorter than what we could have achieved early in the crisis.'[7] Here again, Banisadr's criticism played into the hands of his enemies in the IRP. They shrewdly pointed out that the Majlis and government had simply carried out the wishes of the Imam. The Majlis, as the elected representatives of the people, had ratified a negotiated settlement within the framework of Khomeini's formula. Opposition to it would either imply that the Imam had been wrong in entrusting to the Majlis the resolution of the crisis, or still worse, that his proposed framework for the resolution of the crisis was not compatible with Iran's interests. Banisadr carefully refuted these allegations and instead showed the financial losses which had occurred to Iran as a result of the prolongation of the crisis, and questioned the negotiating ability of Rajai's government.

Khomeini himself persisted in his enigmatic silence concerning the various dimensions of the Banisadr-IRP dispute, preferring his role as a supreme arbiter in the last resort. On the occasion of the commemoration in March 1981 of Dr Mossadegh's death, a new crisis aggravated this feud. A meeting sponsored by Banisadr and other supporters of the late nationalist leader was disrupted by IRP-hired mobs known as Hizbollahi (members of God's Party). The President ordered the police and his supporters to resist and to counter-attack the Hizbollahis, some of whom were arrested and identified to the crowd as members of various IRP-dominated revolutionary committees. The incident, while benefiting Banisadr's reputation among secular and nationalist groups, supplied his opponents with yet another weapon. Now the President was accused of having incited riotous acts by ordering the crowd to arrest 'innocent' civilians.

The then Prosecutor-General, Ayattolah Mussavi Ardabili Kani, called on the victims of the incident to come forward as evidence of the illegal actions of the President. Some of the more zealous IRP members in the Majlis requested the prosecution of the President. It was shortly after this incident that Khomeini took the one final step designed to protect and preserve his own role as supreme arbiter. Rather than siding in this or other disputes with either of the feuding parties, he ordered the formation of a three-man reconciliation commission, one representing Banisadr, one representing Beheshti and Rafsanjani, and one picked up by himself. The commission was to investigate the complaints and grievances of the three major contestants and report its findings to him, and he would accept the majority decision as a definitive resolution of the dispute.

To dampen the increasingly bitter public utterances of the feuding leaders, he also ordered a ban on public statements concerning all controversies involving the President and his leading adversaries. This move was urged on Khomeini by IRP leaders, notably Beheshti and Rafsanjani, who cautioned Khomeini about Banisadr's close ties with the Army and secular forces, which appeared to be rallying to his side in the developing polarization. The formation of a special presidential guard after the March incident at Dr Mossadegh's commemoration rally was presented to the Imam as yet another ominous sign of a new anti-IRP alignment.

The Reconciliation Commission

The IRP nominated Yazidi, an ardent and anti-secular member of the Majlis, to represent Beheshti and Rafsanjani. Banisadr nominated Ayattolah Eshraghi, Khomeini's son-in-law, with a reputation of relative moderation. His initial preference for Ahmad, Khomeini's son, did not sit well with the Imam, who interpreted the suggestion as yet another attempt by Banisadr to involve his close relatives in the ongoing political and personal dispute.

To represent himself Khomeini chose Ayattolah Mussavi Ardabili, thus giving the clerics complete control of the committee, even though Eshraghi, at least, could not be closely associated with the IRP.

While the commission was trying to get to the roots of the Banisadr-IRP differences, the political atmosphere in the country was becoming more and more charged. The government had begun a policy of repression of dissident groups. Under various pretexts scores of publications were banned. Bazargan's newspaper, *Mizan*, the National Front newspaper and ultimately Banisadr's *Islamic Revolution* were all banned.[8] Hired mobs of Hizbollahis raided the offices of opposition groups or disrupted their peaceful rallies. The IRP appeared to be systematically consolidating its control and achieving its goal of turning Iran into a one-party theocratic state. Faced with the increased oppression and frustrated at the no-win war situation with Iraq, Banisadr defied Khomeini's ban on public criticism by the disputing leaders. In interviews with the foreign press and occasionally in publicly reported addresses to Army garrisons, the President stressed two themes in his remarks on the state of the nation. One was that the fundamentalists were pushing the Islamic Republic towards a new despotism. The other was that the government was incapable of putting Iran's economy back on track, without which the war effort against Iraq would never succeed. Additionally, he complained bitterly about Khomeini's ban while his numerous opponents in the Majlis persisted in their attack on him, the President. Reports of his statements were meticulously compiled by the Commission of Reconciliation, which duly charged the President with two gross violations: defying Khomeini's ban on public criticism of the government, and continuing to refuse to ratify the nomination of the remaining Cabinet members as requested by the Prime Minister.

In several letters exchanged between the commission and the President, Banisadr charged it with bias against himself and failure to give equal consideration to the numerous charges brought against the IRP-controlled organs of government. But, as yet Khomeini appeared reluctant to take sides with the President's leading opponents.

However, a highly critical speech that Banisadr had given in June to the Army garrison in Shiraz, the centre of the Southern Fars province, in addition to the declaration of armed resistance by the Mojahedin against the IRP, may have combined to compel Khomeini to abandon his lofty position as arbiter and join the dispute squarely on the side of the fundamentalists.

Banisadr's address to the Army garrison in Shiraz was particularly contentious to Khomeini because in effect the President had attributed the failure of the army to oust the Iraqis from occupied Iranian territories to the IRP. He had charged that the final resolution of the hostage crisis did not oblige the US to resume the shipment of spare parts already paid for by Iran. This condition was one on which he had insisted prior to the formation of the Rajai government and its assumption of responsibility for resolving the hostage crisis. 'By accepting less favourable terms in January 1981 than those we could have received before April 1980, we simply made it impossible for our armed forces to perform their battlefront duties effectively and conclusively.'[9]

Armed with this latest evidence of Banisadr's 'treachery', Beheshti and Rafsanjani finally convinced Khomeini that the time had come for the Imam to shed his cover as a non-political supreme arbiter. 'If we do not move now the future of the Islamic Republic will be in grave danger,' Beheshti reportedly warned him. His other close associates echoed similar warnings. His son-in-law Eshraghi wrote to him to resign as Banisadr's representative in the Reconciliation Commission, charging that the President was beyond redemption and would not heed his advice to return to the 'fold of the faithful.'

Banisadr's opponents' strategy for his removal consisted of the following:

(1) A majority of Majlis deputies would sign a petition requesting that the President's incompetence for holding that office be put on the agenda.

(2) The Majlis would pass a law setting up the procedure for such investigations.

(3) If a majority at the end of its debate voted to declare him incompetent, then the Imam would be asked to dismiss him from office.[10]

Though the result of the Majlis deliberation was a foregone conclusion, the triumvirate of Beheshti-Rafsanjani-Rajai which had engineered Banisadr's dismissal, insisted that the above procedures be faithfully and meticulously observed. The Majlis voted impeachment procedures which even provided for the President to defend himself against all charges for between 5 and 10 hours, although he could not cross-examine his accusers.

Before these steps were completed Banisadr issued an appeal to the people asking them to resist 'the establishment of a repressive dictatorship.' Without mentioning any names his appeal was interpreted as a call for insurrection against the Islamic regime which inevitably included the Imam himself. Khomeini by then did not need much urging by the anti-Banisadr triumvirate. This appeal to resistance, plus exhortations to the Army against the government, sufficiently alarmed Khomeini into dismissing the President as C-in-C of the armed forces and simultaneously warning the military against partisan politics. Dutifully, the acting Chief of the General Staff Fallahi issued a new proclamation of allegiance to Khomeini. Banisadr himself, seeing the writing on the wall, fled from Tehran even before the formal dismissal order was issued by Khomeini, upon the vote of the Majlis declaring the President incompetent.

The ousting of Banisadr was not entirely violence-free. On 20 June, the day that the Majlis impeachment deliberations began, a major demonstration in his support and against the IRP took place in Tehran. In what proved to be an ominous harbinger of what the future held for organized oppositions to the IRP, the regime, using the Pasdaran and an armed Hizbollahi mob, forcibly dispersed the pro-Banisadr march. Over 100 people were shot and many more arrested. The swift justice of the revolutionary courts was once more set in motion. During a period of two weeks the state-controlled radio reported the summary trial and execution of another 150 for 'anti-state insurrection, corruption on earth and fighting God.' The brunt of the punishment was borne by the Mojahedin, the Trotskyite Peykar and the Minority Fedayeen. However, influential members of the Bazaar who generally supported the National Front and by implication Banisadr, were also subjected to severe repression. Karim Dastmalchi and two of the most prominent Bazaar merchants, with an impeccable record of opposition to the Shah and generous financial support for the clergy when they were fighting the Shah, were executed.[11]

Clearly the IRP-dominated regime sought to demobilize and demoralize the Bazaar as a formidable political force before it could act against the IRP. Cognizant of the vital mobilizing role which the Bazaar had played in the struggle against the Shah, the IRP was quick to nip in the bud one of its potentially most dangerous adversaries.

Banisadr's Departure: the Great Escape

Two days after his dismissal as C-in-C the President went into hiding. On the day of Banisadr's dismissal by Khomeini, Ayattolah Ghoddusi, Prosecutor-General of the revolutionary courts, issued a warrant for his arrest on sight, with an ominous warning to those who were found guilty of aiding and abetting Banisadr's flight.

The flight of the ousted President was aided by the Mojahedin leader Massud Rajavi, and the followers of the KDP leader Dr Ghassemlou. Operatives of the two organizations, well-armed and experienced in clandestine operations, spirited the President out of his Tehran office while the Pasdaran were guarding his presidential headquarters, as well as his personal residence in north Tehran. A day later he was reportedly given shelter in a Kurdish hamlet near Mahabad, where a combined corps of Kurdish and Mojahedin bodyguards took over his security. Since most hamlets in the region were far from the control of the

Army and the Pasdaran, the task of protecting Banisadr by moving him around regularly was made much easier. Because of the chaotic situation prevailing in Western Iran, the Kurdistan region in particular has been frequently used for illegal exits from Iran since the revolution.

Once he felt a sense of security in hiding, Banisadr began to organize the forces of opposition to the regime, which could no longer exclude Khomeini himself. The ousting of Banisadr had finally pushed the Imam into the very centre of the political fray. The three political groups with which Banisadr was willing and eager to co-operate, apart from the Mojahedin, were the minority faction of the Fedayeen, the KDP and other autonomy-seeking Kurdish groups. Beyond that Banisadr hoped to appeal to the Bazaaris and the nationalist forces affiliated with the late Dr Mossadegh. He neither expected nor welcomed support from such exiled Iranian groups as those following Shahpour Bakhtiar, the last pre-revolution Prime Minister, Dr Ali Amini, the elderly statesman and a one-time prime minister of the early 1960s, and the monarchists, who were clamouring for the return of the late Shah's son, Reza, to the throne.

For practical political reasons he was also keen to avoid any affiliation with the numerous monarchist military groups in exile, because above all Banisadr aspired to maintain the image of a true Islamic-nationalist revolutionary. He wished to be seen as a victim of those who had conspired to deviate from the revolution's original course. In a statement from exile, responding to Khomeini's appeal to give himself up and return to the fold, Banisadr requested guaranteed access to several hours of air-time to defend himself and to discredit the IRP leaders, 'who would be put to flight once I document their corruption and treachery.'[12]

While the search for Banisadr continued relentlessly, plans for his flight abroad were being meticulously prepared by the Mojahedin and several of their converts within the Air Force and the Army. Massud Rajavi, leader of the Mojahedin, spent many days with Banisadr reconciling differences between the two and preparing for a new alignment in which Banisadr and Mojahedin would form a coalition of armed resistance against the fundamentalist dictatorship. As the new reign of terror against dissidents intensified and the revolutionary courts showed no concern about executing well-known Mojahedin, many of whom had courageously fought the Shah, both Banisadr and Rajavi became convinced that their safety could no longer be guaranteed within the country.

What in particular worried them was the execution on 27 July of

Mohammadreza Saadati, a member of the leadership cadre of the Mojahedin who was already under a ten-year jail sentence at the notorious Evin prison in Tehran. The revolutionary court had retried him on the charge of complicity in the recent murder of the prison's chief, as well as directing from behind the bars acts of terrorism by the Mojahedin, Saadati's execution, as well as the necessary employment of several hundred Mojahedin in the protection of Banisadr and Rajavi, expedited plans for spiriting the two leading figures of anti-Khomeini resistance out of the country.

Late in the evening of 28 July 1981, a Boeing 707 converted tanker plane of the Iranian Air Force took off from the military runway of Tehran's Mehrabad Airport for a routine flight for which the flight plan had been filed a fortnight earlier. Aboard the plane were smuggled Banisadr and Rajavi, as well as Ahmad Salamatian, a member of the Majlis and a long-time supporter of the deposed President. Ten hours later the plane was permitted to land outside Paris and both Banisadr and Rajavi were granted political asylum on condition of refraining from any anti-Khomeini political activities while on French territory.[13]

Details of this great escape indicate the successful infiltration by the Mojahedin of some elements in the armed forces, in particular the Air Force Colonel Behzad Moezzi who piloted the plane. Once in France Moezzi disclosed his membership of the organization and appealed to his fellow officers to join the recently organized National Resistance Council under Rajavi and Banisadr. Moezzi and two other crew members had personal reasons for risking their lives to fly Banisadr into exile. In the wake of the alleged coup attempt in July 1980 they, along with several hundred pilots, had been arrested. When the war with Iraq broke out on 22 September Banisadr as C-in-C had interceded to secure their freedom so that they could participate in the war effort. Moezzi had distinguished himself by more than one thousand hours of combat-flying time.

The reaction from Tehran was predictable. Crowds were mobilized outside the French embassy compound demanding the extradition of Banisadr and threatening a repeat performance of the November 1979 assault on the US embassy. About two hundred French citizens were finally withdrawn from Iran and one more Western country joined the official list of the Islamic Republic's enemies.

Internally the regime reacted by virtually grounding the Iranian Air Force, the war with Iraq notwithstanding. Colonel Mohammad Fakuri, Air Force Chief and Minister of Defence, was dismissed and a new wave of purges of the armed forces was launched. What caused the deepest anxiety within the highest circles of government was evidence of support in the armed forces for the Mojahedin. In a panicky reaction to this latest setback, Khomeini ordered all Iranians to work as agents of a vast intelligence network. Vigilante committees were set up in every neighbourhood. Rafsanjani attacked the incompetence of the security forces, who seemed utterly at a loss to tone down the escalating guerrilla warfare against the leadership of the Islamic Republic.

Once the French citizens were safely out, the ban on Banisadr's political activities in France was to all intents and purposes lifted. The former President issued a political covenant jointly with Rajavi, inviting all Iranians to join the National Resistance Council and work for the freedom and independence of their homeland.

While the new exiles joined a concerted media blitz to discredit Khomeini's regime, armed resistance to his regime, stemming from the bloody vengeance which had started with the 20 June march, continued unabated. The demise of Banisadr seemed to have finally pushed Iran to the brink of the much-feared civil war.

Notes

1. Text in *Enghelabe Islami*, Tehran, 17 June 1980. Significantly, the IRP did not deny the substance of this report, but merely indicated that the plan was not endorsed by the party and reflected the views of only one of the party's members. Dr Ayat was assassinated in mid-August 1981 at the height of armed struggle against the government.
2. See Chapter 5 for a discussion of the Tabriz uprising and the MPRP.
3. In a blunt attack on the Islamic Republic the former Prime Minister lashed at the revolutionary courts and the Pasdaran, comparing the anarchy and the lawlessness that they had promoted, negatively with the Shah's judicial system. 'Never before have Iranians been so helpless and without access to real justice.' *Mizan*, Tehran, 28 October 1980.
4. *Highlights of Speeches*, op. cit., 12 August 1980.
5. One hundred and ten deputies belonging to the IRP issued a statement listing these 'violations' of the presidential oath of office to request the Majlis to consider declaring Banisadr incompetent. *Jomhuriye Islami*, 29 March 1981.
6. Interview with ARA officials, Paris, 18 February 1981.
7. Excerpts from the address appeared in *Enghelabe Islami*, Tehran, 4 February 1981. Since Banisadr's flight to Paris an underground publication, widely distributed in Europe and America, reflects his views. This publication is called *Khabarnameh* or news-sheet of the Islamic Revolution.
8. Reza Sadr, the editor of *Mizan*, who had served in the Bazargan Cabinet as Commerce Minister, was arrested on a charge of divulging war secrets. Tehran, 11 April 1981.
9. The gist of the address was carried in *Enghelabe Islami*, 12 June 1981.
10. *Keyhan*, Tehran, 14 June 1981.

11. They were affiliated first with Bazargan's Iran Liberation Movement and later formed the Islamic Society of Bazaar Merchants.

12. Banisadr's leaflet dated 26 June 1981 was widely distributed in Tehran and carried by foreign news agencies including the *Agence France Presse*.

13. *Le Monde* and *Le Figaro* of Paris gave extended coverage to this episode between 29 July and 11 August 1981.

8 ARMED STRUGGLE AGAINST THE REGIME

The ousting of Banisadr finally brought into the open the irreconcilable disputes between the regime and its opponents concerning the nature of the Iranian political system. That is not, however, to contend that resort to armed struggle or individual acts of violence reflecting these disputes began only at the end of June 1981. As noted in an earlier chapter, armed insurrections by ethnic minorities were unleashed as early as in the spring of 1979. More limited acts of political assassination began at about the same time. A mysterious group called Forghan, allegedly opposing the Islamic Republic because of the Shia domination of the system, claimed responsibility for a number of political assassinations.

In April 1979 General Mohammadvali Gharani, first Chief of Staff of the Islamic armed forces was gunned down. In May Morteza Mottahari, a leading member of the Revolutionary Council, became the second victim of the group. At the end of the same month Aliakbar Hashemi Rafsanjani miraculously escaped death at the hands of two members of Forghan. Taghi Tarkani, a prosperous pro-Khomeini merchant and founder of a theological seminary in Tehran, did not survive an attempt on his life in July. In December another well known cleric, Mohammad Mofatteh, Dean of the Divinity College of Tehran, was assassinated along with his two bodyguards.[1]

Because not much was known about the group these assassinations led to all sorts of rumours. Some exiled Iranians were certain that Beheshti had had a hand in eliminating his clerical rivals. Others believed that former SAVAK operatives were guilty, while still others claimed that members of the disbanded Imperial Guard known as *Javidan* (Immortals) were the culprits. In January 1980 the government announced the arrests of one Akbar Goudarzi as leader of the Foarghan, along with fifteen of his followers. Several months later eight members of the group who had reportedly confessed to their crimes were executed.

While these individual acts of violence contributed to the tension and uncertainty in the first two years of the Islamic Republic, they did not signify the start of a well-orchestrated armed struggle to overthrow the regime. Such a struggle could be waged only by one or another of the experienced guerrilla movements. It fell to the Mojahedin to do so once Banisadr was ousted. The government, on the other hand, went about its business as if nothing important had happened. As provided under the constitution, the triumvirate of Beheshti-Rafsanjani-Rajai took over the Presidency as the Presidential Council, pending the election of a new president within the constitutionally prescribed 50 days. At the insistence of Khomeini the procedure was expedited and on 25 June, the date for the new election was set as 24 July. The Ministry of the Interior set into motion the machinery of candidate nomination and selection. The twelve-member Council of Custodians was to examine the credentials of all candidates and certify their qualifications for running for office.

For a brief moment it appeared that the ousting of Banisadr would be followed by a smooth transition and that the bloody street disturbance of Saturday 20 June would prove to have been the strongest reaction to Banisadr's dismissal. The party's inner circle was convinced that Khomeini would either permit Beheshti to become the new President or if he insisted upon a non-clerical personality this time round, an IRP candidate would be his choice. The day after Banisadr's dismissal Beheshti declared that if called upon he would be ready to serve. When Khomeini refused to endorse this idea, the party set out to ensure that Rajai would be elected President *and* that the party would have more than one candidate so that, if the first round did not produce a new president, the second round would be a contest between the two IRP candidates receiving the highest number of votes in the first round.

Other pressing problems also preoccupied the IRP leadership now that the battle to oust Banisadr appeared to have been won. At the request of Beheshti, General Secretary of the IRP, an extraordinary meeting of the party's executive committee was summoned to assemble at the party's headquarters in Tehran on 28 June. To this top-secret meeting were invited the Prime Minister, the Majlis Speaker, the governor of the Central Bank, Majlis deputies from provincial towns, Cabinet ministers and deputy ministers.[2]

The Decimation of the IRP Leadership

The meeting was scheduled to consider a number of important issues: (a) to nominate formally its candidates for president as well as those for by-elections in scores of constituencies; (b) to deal with the increased acts of violence which, after the bloody clashes of 20 June, had continued sporadically though on a much smaller scale; (c) to determine the annual budget and resolve other pressing fiscal and economic matters; (d) to draft legislation concerning the activities of political parties.

Ever since the declaration of armed resistance by the Mojahedin against the regime in June, the question of how to counter that organization's challenge had become a matter of serious concern for the IRP and the government. They had good reason to take that challenge much more seriously than the opposition of such moderate groups as the National Front or even the Kurdish and other dissident ethnic groups. For the Mojahedin was a battle-tested national organization which could neither be accused of supporting one of the super-powers nor charged with co-operation with the former regime. Some members of the IRP leadership were fully aware of the critical role that the Mojahedin had played in the years of underground armed struggle against the Shah, and in transforming the revolutionary movement into a systematic armed insurrection against the Army and Dr Bakhtiar's government during the final two days of the revolution. Several of the more experienced members, reportedly including Beheshti, knew that repression alone would not suffice and indeed would in a sense benefit the organization by bestowing on it the aura of martyrdom, from which the anti-Shah forces had benefited so remarkably. Instead, the idea of legalizing a number of non-IRP political groups found favour with the IRP leadership.

Any political group which accepted and respected the constitution and had refused to take up arms against the Islamic Republic could be legitimized. Together, while not necessarily joining the ruling IRP, these groups could form a broad coalition with it and counterweigh the power of the Mojahedin and the other political groups which actively opposed the Islamic Republic. But what were these groups and how credible and effective would their support be for the regime? The extraordinary meeting of the IRP was to consider and decide this question. It had already determined that a group did not necessarily need to be Islamic to acquire the mantle of legitimacy. Both Islamic and non-Islamic groups such as the Tudeh communists, the Majority Fedayeen, and even the Trotskyite Peykar or the Maoist Ranjbaran (Toilers) could join the proposed informal coalition. In a fascinating discussion with Eric Roulleau of *Le Monde*, Hojatolislam Mohammad Montazari, son of the senior Ayattolah and Khomeini's heir-apparent, had remarked that to neutralize the counter-revolutionary plot 'hatched by the US' the IRP had decided to support the creation of an anti-imperialist front, bringing together Moslem and non-Moslem groups, even if the latter included followers of Marxism.[3]

Apart from the lack of a reliable popular base of support some of these groups were ardently pro-Soviet. Since the Islamic Republic had espoused the doctrine of 'neither West nor East' as its main foreign-policy doctrine, the inclusion of groups like the Tudeh Party and the Majority Fedayeen in a new anti-imperialist front could have caused major embarrassment. On this question the party leadership was divided. The more radical individuals such as Hassan Ayat and Jalaleddin Farsi favoured any tactical alliance with these groups as long as they fulfilled the two conditions of respect for the constitution and refusal to engage in armed struggle. The traditionally conservative clerics, reportedly Rafsanjani, the Majlis Speaker and Dr Sheybani, a Majlis deputy with former ties with Bazargan's Iran Liberation Movement, had some misgivings about the value of such a formal alliance. Beheshti, as usual, held his cards close to his chest. He wanted the meeting to form a consensus on this and other pressing matters.

But the meeting never got around to debating and deciding the issue. At 9.15 p.m., while Beheshti was addressing the assembly and going over the agenda, a powerful blast shook the building to its foundations. In a matter of a few minutes seventy-two of the top leadership of the IRP and government were killed under the collapsing roof of the building. The IRP seemed effectively decimated. Absent from the casualty list were Rajai, Rafsanjani and Behzad Nabavi, who had been called away a few minutes before the blast. Also conspicuous for their absence were Hassan Ayat and Jalaleddin Farsi, who were known to be more radical on matters of internal and international policies.

Immediately after the blast the Pasdaran were ordered to surround Army garrisons and Air Force bases in the capital for fear that the blast may have been part of a co-ordinated plan to overthrow the government. The state radio and television did not break the news until the next morning, and speculation about the responsibility for the blast covered every imaginable possibility. The initial government account used the familiar 'lackeys of American imperialism' as the culprits. Two days later, however, it identified a member of the Mojahedin organization who had found employment as a maintenance man in the next-door building, as responsible for the actual placement of a powerful bomb next to the meeting hall. Since by then the opponents of the regime had vastly expanded in number, numerous groups could have been involved in planning the destruction of the IRP headquarters. Thus, the various underground or exile royalist army organizations, former SAVAK operatives, the supporters of the Trotskyite Peykar, the Maoist Ranjbaran, the Minority Fedayeen, the Mojahedin, the KDP and even the more radical faction of Ayat and Farsi within the IRP leadership cadre could all have been implicated.

The magnitude of the blast, the infiltration of the next-door building, the exact knowledge of the time and composition of the party's extraordinary meeting, all point to the involvement of experienced and motivated guerrilla organizations such as the Mojahedin and the minority faction of the Fedayeen. On the other hand, the access of the perpetrators to such a powerful bomb and timing device led some reporters to implicate dissident army officers, and these could have included members of the presidential guard. The day after the blast the prosecutor of Tehran's revolutionary court ordered the guards to disband and surrender all weapons issued them, under threat of the death penalty.[4] It is apparent that the full details of the operation may not be revealed as long as the opposition groups remain underground. Several reasons, however, make the accusation against the Mojahedin fairly plausible.

First, the organization had already declared its intention of waging armed struggle against the regime well before the dismissal of Banisadr. The severe punishment of its members during and after the 20 June street fighting had given the Mojahedin an added reason for hostility towards the IRP. Secondly, the Mojahedin had fully embraced the cause of Banisadr, spirited him out of the President's office and found him a safe refuge either in Tehran or in the Kurdish region. The attempt to decimate the IRP leadership was thus the most effective retribution against the enemies of the deposed President. Thirdly, some of the commanders of the Pasdaran had secured, prior to the blast, documents purportedly of a secret Mojahedin meeting revealing such a plot. Eric Roulleau, who has had first-rate contacts with the leadership of the regime, reported in *Le Monde* that he had been shown a priority hit-list prepared by the Mojahedin, which included the Tehran commander of the Pasdaran, Ali Khamenei, the Tehran Friday Imam, Beheshti, Rafsanjani, Mohammad Montazari and others.

At any rate, the decimation of a large group of IRP and government leaders, while certainly shaking the regime to its foundations, did not bring about the collapse of the Islamic Republic. The government immediately set out to salvage what was left of the IRP and the Majlis leadership. Khomeini was persuaded by the two remaining members of the anti-Banisadr triumvirate, namely Rafsanjani and Rajai, to name replacements for the assassinated leaders and to proceed with the presidential and parliamentary elections in over fifty districts as scheduled. Thus, Ayattolah Mussavi Ardabili, the prosecutor-general, was appointed the Supreme Court Chief Justice to replace Beheshti, whose other crucial role as General Secretary of the IRP was filled by another cleric, Mohammadjavad Bahonar, a founder of the party and a protégé of Beheshti. Deputy ministers became acting ministers in four ministries whose heads had been killed. In short, with remarkable speed party and government vacancies were filled. Rajai became the IRP's official candidate for President.

These measures were accompanied with a severe repression of opposition groups, in particular the Mojahedin, the Peykar and the Minority Fedayeen. Already close to 120 members of these organizations had been summarily tried and executed in the wake of the Saturday street fighting and the ousting of Banisadr.[5] Now that the Mojahedin were officially identified as the perpetrators of the bombing of the IRP headquarters, an intensified reign of terror against the armed opposition was unleashed. Within two weeks of the bombing another hundred members of opposition groups were executed and several hundreds more imprisoned.

The Islamic Republic did not show any qualms about this new reign of terror. The day before his death at IRP headquarters Mohammad Montazari had vowed that the executions of those who had waged armed insurrection against the Republic would continue.

We should be merciless and expeditious regardless of foreign criticism. World public opinion should try to understand us. Iran is in a state of revolution, a country at war, surrounded on all sides by allies of the US seeking our destruction.

Comparing the plight of the Islamic revolution with that of 1789 French revolution, Montazari remarked, 'faced with a similar situation, the French revolutionaries, like us, showed no mercy toward their enemies, otherwise the monarchy would still be in power in France and history would have taken an entirely different course'.[6] Montazari's death in the IRP bomb blast, along with the elimination of another 71 leading government and Majlis members, if anything made the regime more repressive and more determined to consolidate and monopolize its power. It was evident that the Mullahs who had assumed power through violence were willing and able to use violence to retain control of the country.

New Elections

A week after the bombing of IRP headquarters the regime seemed to have overcome the initial shock of its heavy losses. The absence of any follow-up moves such as massive strikes, closure of the Bazaars and similar demonstrations of opposition akin to the final struggle against the Shah in the autumn of 1978, accompanied with harsh punitive measures against the regime's more radical opponents, created a new confidence that the Islamic Republic would survive what had been its severest test up to that time.

Constitutional procedures for filling presidential and parliamentary vacancies were meticulously pursued. The twelve-man clergy-dominated Council of Custodians screened out 71 candidates for the Presidency, including Dr Nureddin Kianouri, the Tudeh Party's General Secretary. Only four, all either formally or informally affiliated with the IRP, were declared qualified ro run for President. Heading the list, to no-one's surprise, was Rajai, who despite lacking in personal popularity and being a non-cleric, was believed to be a 'Maktabi' or a doctrinaire believer in Khomeini's Islamic fundamentalism. The IRP clearly believed that as long as Khomeini wished to avoid placing Mullahs in every position of power, it had found in Rajai an 'unturbaned' fundamentalist who, unlike Banisadr, had no reason to challenge the IRP's total domination of the Islamic Republic.

Every effort was made to maximize the pretence of the election's legitimacy. Four days before balloting the legal age was reduced from 16 to 15. Religious leaders declared participation in the elections as a religious obligation, *Farizeh Shari*. Members of the armed forces were ordered to participate. The vast network of IRP-established Islamic Associations spread throughout the country in schools, hospitals, government offices, the bazaar, factories and village councils, joined local mosques to mobilize massive participation in the voting. Perhaps the most ominous threat hanging over non-participants was the risk of being reported as counter-revolutionary by the neighbourhood vigilante committees, which Khomeini himself had entrusted with the sacred duty to function as 'the eyes and ears' of the Islamic regime.

The result of these massive efforts was hardly unexpected. Rajai was declared the winner by a landslide. Nearly 90 per cent of eligible voters reportedly participated, with Rajai receiving 13 million votes or 88 per cent, thus surpassing the 10 million secured by Banisadr in his election over nineteen months earlier.[7]

No matter what one thinks about the fairness or authenticity of these elections, the Islamic Republic viewed them as its final consolidation of power. Boycotts by opposition groups and armed attacks by the Mojahedin on various polling stations, though causing about fifteen deaths amongst the Pasdaran, did not seriously disrupt the elections. Banisadr's clandestine radio message from his hideout banning the elections was of no more consequence. A combination of repression, threat and the government mobilization techniques used frequently in the past, supplied the magical 90 per cent participation and the overwhelming 88 per cent vote for the IRP candidate. However, not even government authorities were convinced that their troubles with the opposition groups were over. Even on election day and for days following it, the firing squads in the infamous Evin prison and in other Iranian cities were busy putting to death anti-government activists. The brunt of the reign of terror continued to be borne by the Mojahedin.

But the bloody reprisal against the apparently popular guerrilla organization by no means silenced the group. Daily in Tehran and other cities bombings and explosions reminded many that neither the new reign of terror nor the total monopolization of power by the fundamentalists was capable of bringing the tranquillity and peace which the Islamic Republic so direly needed. The ousting of Banisadr, which the IRP had hailed as its third revolution, following the February insurrection and the November hostage-taking, did not signify the end of violent turmoil in the country.

Realignment of the Anti-Khomeini Forces

In the meantime the centre of opposition to the regime shifted to the Mojahedin's hideouts in the capital, where Banisadr and the Mojahedin leader Massud Rajavi joined forces to co-ordinate the anti-government campaign. Between 17 and 20 July 1981 the formation of the National Resistance Council was announced. In an exchange of letters between the two, Rajavi accepted the invitation of Banisadr, calling himself the People's Elected President of the country, to head the executive committee of the new resistance movement. Banisadr regretted his past failure to comprehend and appreciate the true anti-imperialist and mass-oriented direction of the Mojahedin and appealed to all patriotic and truly Moslem Iranians to join the crusade against the dictatorship of the reactionary forces. He also, for the first time, criticized Khomeini by accusing him of having renegued on many of the promises he had made shortly before the revolution. 'The Khomeini of before the revolution and the man now are different personalities, having lost touch with the masses and subjected to the influence of a few power-hungry and reactionary Mullahs,' stated Banisadr.[8]

Several points stand out from an examination of the pronouncements of this new alliance. Its chief significance is that for the first time since the revolution the forces of opposition, apart from dissident ethnic minorities like the Kurds, had organized a base of resistance inside the country. Many exiled groups had been active outside Iran, from Turkey and Egypt to various West European countries and the United States. These groups, whether those who had fled from Iran with the triumph of the revolution or the many more who had broken away from Khomeini as his regime had become increasing despotic, had little impact in fomenting opposition inside the country. But now the opposition had finally found a home within Iranian territory.

Of further significance was that the Mojahedin, with its impeccable record of struggle against the monarchy, had put all its resources and experience at the disposal of the new National Resistance Council. To be sure, the Mojahedin had not been the sole guerrilla organization fighting the Shah. But partly because of their heavier casualties in over 12 years of urban guerrilla warfare against the Shah, and in part due to the splits in the rank and file of its chief rival, the People's Fedayeen, the Mojahedin added a credible weight to the anti-Khomeini opposition. To quote one of its leaders:

> With no more than a few hundred poorly armed members we made the SAVAK and the Imperial Army desperate. Now with several thousand well-armed Mojahed and hundreds of thousands of genuine supporters throughout the country, we are a power to reckon with.[9]

Impressive and confident as these statements sounded, many Iranians were mindful of the fact that the Mojahedin were now fighting a much more brutal foe. The Islamic Revolutionary Guards Corps, as the arm of the revolutionary courts and committees on which the regime depends for survival, have shown the savagery of their treatment of the opposition since the Mullahs' monopolization of power. If the outcome of the impending struggle cannot be predicted with certainty, there is little doubt that the struggle will be as violent and bloody as anything the country has witnessed even since the 1979 revolution. Consequently, many moderate opponents of the regime have chosen silence while violence persists.

A final point about the new alignment is the systematic effort to broaden its popular appeal to the maximum possible extent. The alignment has not only emphasized its anti-imperialistic, hence anti-Western stance, but has also dedicated itself to establishing a genuine and humane Islamic Republic. The intention is clearly not to alienate the Moslem forces in the country. Whether out of conviction or for tactical reasons the new alignment seems to seek out the very groups in Iranian society who responded so effectively to the mobilization efforts of the revolutionary clergy in the year-long turmoil of 1978-9.

The Second Bomb Blast

The victory of the triumvirate of Rajai-Rafsanjani-Beheshti over Banisadr became even more short-lived than had first appeared. As previously noted, after the bomb blast at IRP headquarters in June Khomeini moved quickly to replace Beheshti with two of his close associates. Ayattolah Ardabili, the Prosecutor-General, was named the new Chief Justice, and Hojatolislam Mohammadjavad Bahonar, Minister of Education, became General Secretary of the IRP.

These appointments signified that Khomeini had decided against giving the head of the judiciary control of the IRP and through it control of the Majlis. But soon after the election of Rajai as President, Khomeini decided that Bahonar as the new General Secretary of the party should head the new government. The new Prime Minister was among the central group of Moslem fundamentalists who, ever since February 1979, had worked closely with Khomeini. He was appointed a member of the initially secret Revolutionary Council which for over a year and a half had effectively governed Iran. A close lieutenant of Ayattolah Beheshti, he had joined the first anti-Banisadr triumvirate which had finally forced Banisadr from the Presidency in June, and set out to intimidate other government foes. As a former theology student, he had studied under Khomeini in Qom, and in 1962 had helped organize the anti-Shah clergy who a year later incited the bloody religious uprising in Qom and Tehran. In the critical stage of the revolution he was in charge of organizing strikes against the Shah and later joined Beheshti to bring about the surrender of the armed forces to the revolutionary authorities. His imprint on the Islamic Republic's constitution was made possible when he was elected to the Assembly of Experts and became one of the principal drafters of the constitution. Additionally, he had joined the Provisional Government of Bazargan as Deputy Minister of Education and had served as Education Minister since March 1981.[10]

The decision to appoint Bahonar as Prime Minister also meant that Iran had now moved closer to the concept of one-party government. Fundamentalist newspapers hailed the nomination and appointment of Bahonar as a genuine parliamentary move. Since the IRP had the clear majority in the Majlis, what could be more logical or even 'democratic' than asking the General Secretary of that party to head the Cabinet? The Bahonar government, therefore, could expect to have no problem with the Majlis. In short, the legislative and executive powers would now be fused to assure the smooth functioning of the governmental machinery.[11]

Another significance of the move was that the pretence of non-clerical government was finally abandoned. For the first time the head of government was a member of the Shia clergy. The experience of combining secular and clerical personalities was given up as far as the institutions of parliament and Cabinet were concerned. As far as the new President was concerned, although a non-cleric, he had proved so subservient to the leadership of the IRP that for all practical purposes he could be considered a member of the fundamentalist religious clique which appeared to be in full control of the country. Thus emerged a new triumvirate of Rafsanjani, Rajai and Bahonar which proudly proclaimed the viability of the Islamic Republic's constitutional legitimacy and political continuity despite the heavy odds against it. At the inauguration of Rajai as President, Khomeini warned him that the more than 13 million people who had voted for him would turn against him if he took one foul step. 'They will shout "death to Rajai" tomorrow if you should default on putting into effect the cannons of Islam. That is the way of the revolution.'[12]

The day after his investiture Rajai appealed to the Mojahedin to lay down their arms and return to Islam. Invoking the Iranian sense of nationalism, he reminded everyone that the main issue continued to be the war and that as long as the enemy was present 'on our land, killing our fellow countrymen, destroying their homes, ruining our economic resources and finally as long as our revolution is menaced, the main issue for us will be the war.'

On 13 August Bahonar introduced his Cabinet to the Majlis, and among other things promised to purge Iranian society of the factionalists. 'The government is resolved to stand against the factionalists and not to allow society to become a haven for factions attached to imperialism and international Zionism.' Bahonar, who had gained administrative experience by serving in different capacities from the inauguration of the revolutionary regime, also promised to restore security and order to the country. But acts of violence and armed struggle against the officials of the Islamic Republic continued unabated.

On Sunday 30 August the armed opponents of the regime dealt it a second serious blow. As the Supreme Defence Council was meeting in the office of the Prime Minister in downtown Tehran, a powerful bomb blasted the building, killing both Rajai and Bahonar as well as seriously injuring Chief of Police Colonel Vahid Dastgerdi, who died some days later from his wounds. In a matter of a few minutes the new triumvirate was reduced to one. Rafsanjani, the Majlis Speaker, who had miraculously escaped the blast at IRP headquarters in June, was absent from the Prime Minister's office at the time of the Defence Council meeting. The government accused the two prominent exiled leaders Banisadr and Bakhtiar, as well as the Mojahedin, for the plot. It also declared, 'these agents are working for the United States and Iraq, and the Great Satan in particular is capable of any crime against the Moslem people of Iran.'[13]

As expected, revenge was quick in coming. Within twenty-four hours of the blast 40 more people, including 23 Mojaheds, were executed, bringing the total of reported executions to over 800 since the ousting of Banisadr on 24 June. The Council of Supreme Justice clamoured for even harsher revenge. It urged all court officials speedily to end the lives of all traitors to Islam and the Islamic fatherland, after a rapid review of their cases. A Cabinet statement boasted, 'The Ship of Revolution is sailing at full speed even on rough seas, as its leader, Imam Khomeini, is the Noah of our time.' At a massively attended funeral, indicative of Khomeini's continuing popularity with the poor and the destitute, cries for revenge and condemnation of the USA were shouted. Though no specific group had claimed responsibility for the blast, it was obvious that it was an 'inside job', for the building was extremely well protected and access to it could have been possible only by planting agents amongst the Revolutionary Guards or the civil servants who served in the Prime Minister's office.

Apart from the Mojahedin, the minority faction of the Marxist Fedayeen, the Trotskyite Peykar and the Maoist Ranjbaran (Toilers) were other prime suspects. The precision and the technical know-how necessary for the successful infiltration of the building made the military also suspect. In view of the already demonstrated ability of the

Mojahedin to convert some Army officers, the possibility that this was a combined effort of civilian and military members of the Mojahedin could not be ruled out. Indeed the pilot who had flown Banisadr and Rajavi, head of the Mojahedin, to Paris on 29 July had joined the group along with two other crew members.[14]

Be that as it may, the assassination of Rajai and Bahonar led to the emergence of yet another triumvirate. Under the constitution the Presidential Council, composed of the Majlis Speaker, the Chief Justice and the Prime Minister, took over, except that with the death of Bahonar it had become a two-man council. But in the kind of quick move which had by now become quite familiar, Ayattolah Mahdavi Kani, for long in charge of the Ministry of the Interior, was appointed acting Prime Minister until a new president could be elected within 50 days of that office becoming vacant.

However, unlike Bahonar who had also led the IRP, this time Ali Khamenei, himself a recent victim of an attempt on his life, was made the IRP's General Secretary. The new triumvirate of Rafsanjani, Kani, and Ardabili, acting as the Presidential Council, represented the full domination of the clergy, even though Kani's Cabinet, which was confirmed by a vote of 178 to 10 with 8 abstentions, had a majority of non-clerical personalities.

Many opponents of the regime hoped that this second decimation of the senior government leaders would lead to the regime's downfall. Banisadr, barely a week earlier, had singled out five senior leaders whose elimination would cause the collapse of the regime. With the assassination of Rajai and Bahonar the members of the new triumvirate constituted the remaining three on Banisadr's list.

These expectations, just as those expressed after the June bombing of the IRP headquarters, turned out to be premature. Despite heavy odds, Khomeini's personal magnetism and the availability of scores of clerical leaders willing to serve, despite clear threats to their safety, helped the regime to overcome the immediate crisis. Showing supreme confidence in his regime's survival, Khomeini expressed no anxiety over the deaths of Rajai and Bahonar, declaring that although they had been valuable, 'We have a long line of committed people willing to become martyrs for the revolution.'

Several days later when Ayattolah Ali Ghoddusi, Prosecutor-General of the revolutionary courts, was assassinated, Khomeini boasted that despite the bombings and the assassinations the Islamic Republic was one of the most stable governments anywhere in the world. 'Where else could an assassinated Prime Minister be replaced so promptly and smoothly as occurred in our Islamic country within a few days?'[15] The government's efforts to reinforce an impression of continuity and normalcy was accompanied by a continuing hard-line towards dissidents. Rafsanjani, the leading member of the triumvirate, declared that all counter-revolutionaries should be put to death. Defence Minister General Mussa Namju, echoing the same sentiments, boasted, 'Iran's soldiers of Islam will not rest until the revolution achieves victory.' These exhortations were dutifully heeded by the revolutionary courts and the Pasdaran. After every act of violence by the opposition groups, the revolutionary courts would retaliate promptly and mercilessly.

Yet Another Election

The Islamic Republic was also preoccupied with assuring the continuity of its institutions. Shortly after the appointment of Mahdavi Kani as interim Prime Minister, the IRP met and elected Ali Khamenei as its General Secretary. Unlike the second presidential and party nomination, this time it was decided that the President, rather than the Prime Minister, and the party secretary should be one and the same. The date for the new presidential election was fixed as 2 October in addition to by-elections for scores of Majlis constituencies.[16] Mahdavi Kani, who was approved as one of the four candidates, withdrew from the contest shortly before the election and threw his support behind Khamenei. Even though he had had considerable administrative experience, since he had apparently left the IRP and a decision concerning the fusion of the party leader and the President had been made already it was logical for Mahdavi Kani to withdraw.

The election results were not much different from previous results; a combination of mobilization and threat once again produced the near 90 per cent support for the IRP candidate, Ali Khamenei. Though he had previously declared that Mahdavi Kani would be retained as Prime Minister, he now recommended a fundamentalist non-clerical IRP member of the Majlis for the post. This candidate, Dr Velayati, was rejected by the Majlis and this was interpreted as a sign of friction within the party leadership. However, the President's second nominee, Hossein Mussavi, who had served briefly as Foreign Minister, had no problem securing the necessary vote of confidence from the Majlis. This third Prime Minister since the formation of the Islamic Majlis had a long record of devoted service to the IRP of which he was one of the non-clerical founders as well as editor of its official organ, *Jomhuriye Islami*. More importantly, he was a half-brother of Khamenei, leading some observers to believe that the nomination of Velayati was a ploy by the President designed to compel the Majlis to accept his third choice after Mahdavi Kani and Velayati.

As a matter of fact, it is perhaps no accident that the current senior leaders of the Republic, the Chief Justice, the President and the Prime Minister, all hail from Azarbayjan. Not a few non-Azarbayjani Iranians believe that there is a specific reason for Khomeini's choice of so many Azarbayjanis, particularly at a time when armed resistance by the guerrillas continues unabated. The reason is a desire to exploit the sense of hostility that Azarbayjanis have long harboured against their Farsi-speaking fellow citizens. By putting Azarbayjanis in charge of the judicial and executive branches of government, so goes the theory, Khomeini enables them to retaliate against the non-Azarbayjani majority which has discriminated against them for such a long time.

Be that as it may, with the confirmation of Mussavi total control by the IRP of the three branches of government was re-established. It now seemed that Khomeini had come around to the initial position of the late Ayattolah Beheshti — that it was not sufficient merely to be ideologically 'Maktabi' or Shia fundamentalist. It was also indispensable for senior government leaders to belong to the Islamic Republican Party if Shia theocracy were expected to meet the challenge to its stability from within and without.[17]

The apparent failure of the attempts at the physical elimination of the senior leaders of the Islamic Republic and to shake Khomeini's grip on power has had demoralizing effects on opposition groups both in Iran and abroad. A review of the exiled Iranian groups indicates that practical measures to achieve unity of purpose and organization, as a means of overcoming this sense of despair, continue to evade them.

Expatriate Iranians

On the assumption that political challenge from within the country is much more serious to the regime than the activities of Iranian expatriates, not much attention had been given to these opponents of the Islamic Republic until the flight of the Mojahedin leader and the deposed President to Paris at the end of July. However, since Khomeini's experience in the autumn of 1978 played an important role in the mobilization of anti-Shah forces, the potential for a repeat performance by one or another of the expatriate leaders needs consideration.

Somewhat akin to the overthrow of the Russian Tsar, which led to several waves of political refugees from Russia to Europe and beyond, the overthrow of the Shah had led to the departure of at least three waves of exiles from Iran. The first occurred during the final stage of the revolution in the winter of 1978–9 when close associates of the Shah, including civil servants, military, academic and diplomatic officials either left Iran or refused to return after February. These were joined by such people as Dr Bakhtiar, who had co-operated with the Shah for a brief period between the Shah's departure and the overthrow of his last Cabinet. A second wave of exiles trickled out of Iran as Khomeini began to monopolize the power of the fundamentalist groups, and the Islamic Republic institutionalized itself as a one-party theocratic state. Men like Hassan Nazih, Admiral Madani, Baniahmad, all opponents of the Shah, and some collaborators of the Provisional Government under Mehdi Bazargan, were often just one step ahead of their pursuers in their clandestine flights out of the country. This second wave consisted of the secular and old-fashioned liberal politicians who, like the followers of Kerensky after the overthrow of the Tsar, believed the revolution could and should lead to a constitutional democratic regime. These Iranians believed that the Shia fundamentalists, like the Bolsheviks in Russia some seven decades earlier, were robbing the revolution of its original democratic goals by imposing a new form of autocratic control.

The third wave of exiles started with the flight of Banisadr, Rajavi and other Mojahedin activists to France at the end of July 1981. In previous chapters reference was made to the goals and tactics of the Mojahedin and their allies. Numerous organizations and publications both in Western Europe, the USA and Canada represent these expatriates. Some have merged together and have made their new homes permanent by abandoning any hope of returning to Iran. Others are actively seeking to mobilize their fellow expatriates against the Islamic Republic.[18]

Needless to say, their degree of success and their optimism about the future is proportionate to the turmoil within Iran. As Khomeini's regime continues to manifest tenacity against very heavy odds, some of these expatriates sink deeper into despair. At several critical junctures since the revolution, however, they have seemed genuinely hopeful about 'doing to Khomeini what he did to the Shah from his Paris exile.' Thus, for example, the day before the Soviet invasion of Afghanistan

Dr Shahpour Bakhtiar, Iran's last pre-Khomeini Premier, was confidently predicting the downfall of his successor within the next two months. The headline in the Iranian weekly, *Faryade Azadi* (Scream of Freedom), published in London, declared that units under General Palizban, a supporter of the Shah, were training the Kurdish troops who were poised to strike at the very heart of the Ayattolah's establishment in Qom. ARA (Iran Liberation Army) announced a seven-point plan to overthrow Khomeini's reactionary regime and his 'theocrats.' A rival group of nationalist officers in exile calling themselves NEMARA, the acronym for the Iranian Revolutionary Liberation Armed Forces, echoed Bakhtiar's line that the trio of Bakhtiar, Ayattolah Shariatmadari and the nationalist army would shortly free Iran from the claws of the reactionary Mullahs.

Other Iranian exiles were wondering aloud how long the USA would wait before intervening militarily in Iran. Their sense of anxiety had been heightened by the recent assassination of Shahriyar Shafigh, the deposed Shah's nephew, who was reportedly involved with ARA. Rumour had it that General Hossein Fardoust, the Shah's closest associate who 'betrayed' him and now heads the Iranian National Security and Intelligence Organization, had flown to Paris for this mission.

In a two-week survey of West European capitals before and after Christmas 1979, the author had found that interest in Iranian events surpassed the concern in the USA. Proximity to the Middle East, a longer historical association with it, a more vital dependence on oil, and the activities of Iranian exile groups all partly explain the Western European preoccupation with the Iranian crisis. Prospects of a global war resulting from the inability of the super-powers to keep the Iranian crisis and the Afghan conflict localized had evidently aggravated this sense of anxious concern.

A measure of wishful thinking pervades the prognosis of most of the exile groups about Iran. The French-educated, urbane and sophisticated Shahpour Bakhtiar saw US intervention as inevitable. This would so discredit Khomeini's regime that the forces of opposition, including Shariatmadari followers and the remnants of such secular groups as the National Front and the National Democratic Front, would join the two guerrilla groups to topple his regime. Would the armed forces play a role? Bakhtiar thought the nationalist officers, for whom he was taping a message, would surely join this new coalition of anti-Khomeini forces. As for the royalist officers, he was not quite so sure.[19]

How far do Iranian exile groups support him in his quest for a return to power? What are his ties to the deposed Shah's family or his close associates? Prior to the Iraqi invasion, the Bakhtiar organization was the best financed and perhaps the strongest amongst the expatriates. Bakhtiar's visit to Baghdad shortly before the invasion and an ambiguous statement which he made about the war played into the hands of his rivals, who thought he had taken an unpatriotic stand. With the lengthening of the war that criticism has abated. The failure of his supporters and indeed of the guerrilla groups to do anything tangible, such as establishing a base in parts of Kurdistan or waging commando raids on the Iranian coast, has also caused despair among them.

There are other matters of dispute among the Iranian exiles. Even though a common agreement on hostility to Khomeini exists they are divided on strategy and tactics. One common criticism of Bakhtiar echoed by exiled secular and moderate opposition groups, is that he has not fully accepted the revolution as an indigenous, popular, anti-dictatorial uprising, for he insists on offering Iranians a constitutionally limited monarchy. Is this for tactical reasons, disguised to rally the deposed Shah's supporters in the broadest possible anti-Khomeini coalition? Bakhtiar insists it is a matter of principle. 'I am a true social democrat,' he has said. 'I believe that option which I personally do not espouse should be given to our people in a genuinely free referendum.'

Do the Shah's supporters appreciate this? Could Bakhtiar not assure the same freedom of choice by advocating a pluralistic party system including a monarchist party? He was not sure about the first question. He has no contact with the former royal family and is embarrassed by the activities of some personalities exiled in France. Yes, he has said, it could have perhaps been better to support the notion of a constitutional monarchy in a multi-party political system. But is Bakhtiar the man to lead a political move to oust Khomeini? Much disagreement exists among Iranian exiles and European scholars and officials.

Royalist groups believe that in the first stage of the process of replacing Khomeini a strong and probably military man willing to shed blood and risk fratricide is needed, for they are convinced the Mullahs both in and outside the government cannot be removed from power without violence. Non- or anti-royalist exiles, while conceding that the Shia Mullahs cannot be removed peacefully, do not agree that Bakhtiar should be regarded as a kind of politician in reserve to be called back once a strong military leader forcibly removes the Mullahs. Indeed, they wonder why such a leader should voluntarily relinquish power in favour of a civilian politician. Reza Khan, father of the deposed Shah, had staged a coup in association with the civilian politician

Seyed Zia, only to oust Zia shortly afterwards and become the new Shah in 1925.

By the end of 1980, with the arrival of the second wave of exiles in Europe and the US, Bakhtiar had found some important rivals. In extended interviews with the leaders of these groups, the author found that the election of President Reagan had considerably boosted the morale of the more traditional and conservative groups among them. Many were convinced that soon after the release of the hostages the United States would actively support all anti-Khomeini forces in exile.

Early in 1980 Dr Ali Amini, an elderly statesman who had served as Prime Minister in the early 1960s when President Kennedy was pressurizing the Shah to initiate reforms, tried to unify all opposition groups in a movement for the liberation of Iran. He believed a provisional government of national reconciliation should be formed. Disavowing any role for himself, he was predicting that the disunity of the opposition to Khomeini would render it completely ineffective.[20] But Dr Bakhtiar did not welcome that initiative. He thought his own organization had been much more consistent in opposing Khomeini and rightly predicting the course of events under the Khomeini theocracy 'while many of these late-comers have either actively supported him or remained silent when murderous crimes were committed against our people.'

Dr Amini had no illusions about the effectiveness of civilian opposition alone. He believed that two simultaneous moves, one by the anti-Khomeini military and one by the civilian opposition, should be launched with the goal of a progressive infiltration into the country. Somehow he thought the United States would come around to accepting and encouraging such a move before it was too late.

Opposition groups are, of course, not confined to those in Western Europe. Many of the above-named groups have their branches in major US cities, Washington, DC, Houston, New York and Los Angeles in particular. A fairly recently organized military group called *Kanoune Sarbazan Iran* (Iranian Soldier's Society) consisting mostly of US Navy-trained officers is active in Arlington and other suburbs of Washington, DC. The group is professional and extremely nationalistic, but like its counterparts in Europe, unsure about affiliation with any political party and personality. When in the autumn of 1981 representatives of the different exiled military groups tried to draft a common statement concerning the armed struggle against Khomeini, they could not even agree on whether the armed forces should be termed Imperial or National.

However, in the wake of the flight of Banisadr and Rajavi from Iran, some of these groups were compelled to move towards more unified words and deeds. General Bahram Aryana, an exile of pre-Khomeini vintage who had had his own dispute with the late Shah, assumed the leadership of *Azadegan* (Farsi for free-spirited). The group quickly became a household word among Iranian expatriates when it successfully hijacked the French-built missile boat, *Tabarzin*, in mid-August. Admiral Habibollahi, who led the operation, was one of the second wave of refugees who had joined Azadegan and was dedicated to the slogan 'deeds speak louder than words'. The surrender of the boat to the French and ultimately to the Iranian authorities showed that the action was not an integral part of a larger plan to undermine the Islamic Republic. Ninety per cent of the crew of the boat chose to return to Iran, and Iran's military naval officers aboard did not declare allegiance to Azadegan.

The arrival of Banisadr and Rajavi in France forced many exile groups to clarify their attitudes towards the two and their so-called 'Covenant for a free and independent democratic Islamic Republic.' Dr Bakhtiar, the royalist groups and Azadegan declared their opposition to Banisadr 'who after all sat quietly in the Revolutionary Council while brave officers and civilians were ordered butchered by the Council.' Dr Amini, on the other hand, thought anyone who was willing to contribute to Khomeini's downfall should be welcome. The liberal and democratic groups which had greatly admired the audacity and dedication of the Mojahedin and other guerrilla groups in their armed combat against the Islamic Republic, wondered if democratic freedoms could be established in their country with the victory of these groups. Undoubtedly some within the military groups do not forget the critical role of the guerrilla forces in the 1979 insurrection. Nor can they ignore the political platforms of the Mojahedin and Minority Fedayeen which are opposed to the established army and seek to emulate some models of the communist countries' People's Armies. Finally, the acceptance of the Covenant entails the recognition of the Islamic affiliation of the projected republic, which does not sit well with the secular forces.

Other organizations dedicated to overthrowing the regime must also be noted. *Etehad baraye Azadi* (Unity for Freedom) represents the support of Bakhtiar in Europe. *Irans Azad* (Free Iran) is led by the daughter of the late Shah's twin sister, Azadeh Shafigh, with a weekly newspaper of the same name published in Paris. Other members of the late Shah's family are also active in such widely dispersed locations as New York, where Ashraf Pahlavi has his headquarters, or Cairo where the Shah's son, Reza, declared himself the 2nd Reza Shah in October 1980 on attaining the legal age of 21. Also supporting the former royal family is *Bonyad Azadi Iran* (Iranian Freedom Foundation) in Washington, DC.[21]

In recognition of the weakness of the exiled groups due to their ideological and political discords, efforts at reconciling their differences have come from many sources. President Sadat, during his state visit to France early in 1981, tried his hand at bringing the diverse forces of opposition together. He met with Dr Bakhtiar to assure him that the way was open for the late Shah's family to co-ordinate their efforts with those of nationalist and democratic forces to pursue the common goal of working against the Islamic Republic. In the summer of 1981, when Rajavi and Banisadr installed themselves in Paris, many leftist, secular European and Arab politicians tried to achieve the same purpose. Ahmad Ben Bella, the recently released leader of the Algerian revolution and the first President of that country, reminded the Mojahedin leader how the diverse factions within the Algerian Front for National Liberation had put off their very serious differences until after independence, and how important it was for the Iranian secular revolutionary forces to do the same if they wished to succeed.[22]

For the time being, it is commonly agreed among Iranian expatriates that independently of the domestic opposition, the exiles cannot achieve much in the way of overthrowing the Islamic regime. However, once the internal opposition forces succeed in doing so, undoubtedly the exile groups will clamour for the spoils in proportion to their militancy while in exile. In sum, neither the present internal Iranian situation nor the background and experience of the various exiled personalities are similar enough to 1978 to allow for much optimism about a repeat performance like that of Khomeini from his exile in Paris.

In the final chapter a prognosis of the current crisis, the prospects of the viability of the regime and the chances of its opponents will be offered. While domestic turmoil has dominated Iranian politics since immediately after the revolution, Iran's relations with the world at large have also experienced many vicissitudes. The severance of diplomatic ties, the renunciation of treaties, war, isolation and a desperate search for a genuine non-alignment have taken turns in dominating Iran's external relations with both neighbouring and distant countries alike.

Notes

1. 'A chronological survey of the Iranian revolution,' in *Iranian Revolution in Perspective*, Iranian Studies, Vol. XIII, Nos. 1–4, 1980, pp. 327–57.
2. *Le Monde*, Paris, 30 June 1981.
3. *Ibid.*
4. Statement by Ayattolah Ghoddusi in *Jomhuriye Islami*, Tehran, 30 June 1981.
5. Armed clashes between the Pasdaran and guerrillas opposed to the government date back to 7 February 1981, when on the eleventh anniversary of the attack on the Siyahkal outpost about 5,000 members of Minority Fedayeen held a rally in Tehran. Government sources gave the resulting casualties as one dead and 50 wounded, while the Fedayeen reported five killed and nearly 100 wounded. *Jomhuriye Islami* and *KAR*, Tehran, 9 February 1981.
6. *Le Monde*, Paris, 30 June 1981.
7. *Keyhan*, Tehran, 4 July 1981.
8. *Enghelabe Islami* (Clandestine and abbreviated version), Tehran, 21 July 1981.
9. Mussa Khiyabani, who took over the leadership of the Mojahedin after Rajavi's flight to Paris, made this and similar statements, published in the clandestine *Mojahed*, 31 July and 5 August 1981.
10. *News Letter*, Washington, DC, No. 32, 1–18 August 1981. (Published by Islamic Student Association.)
11. *Jomhuriye Islami*, Tehran, 10 August 1981.
12. *News Letter*, Washington, DC, No. 32, 1–18 August 1981.
13. News of the death of the President and Prime Minister was broadcast ten hours after the blast on the state-controlled radio. On 5 September the office of the revolutionary prosecutor identified one Masud Keshmiri, a Mojahed, as the secretary of the Prime Minister's office who had taken the time-fused bomb into the meeting room hidden in an attaché case. *Jomhuriye Islami*, Tehran, 6 September 1981.
14. *Transcript*, MacNeil–Lehrer Report, Washington, DC, 31 August 1981.
15. *Ettelaat*, Tehran, 4 September 1981. A few days earlier the Majlis deputy and IRP leader in Khorassan Hojatolislam Abdolkarim Hasheminejad, had been assassinated in Mashad. Like Ayattolah Madani of Tabriz, who was killed in September, Hasheminejad was the *de facto* proconsul for Khomeini in the religiously significant north-eastern province. *Jomhuriye Islami*, 1 October 1981.
16. A total of 44 candidates were considered by the twelve-man Council of Custodians which declared only 5 as qualified. Apart from Khamenei, they were Ayattolah Mahdavi Kani, the interim Prime Minister, Aliakbar Parvaresh, Minister of Education, Hassan Ghafourifard, Minister of Energy, and Reza Zarvarei, a former Deputy Minister of the Interior. *Keyhan*, Tehran, 22 September 1981.
17. Mir Hossein Mussavi was confirmed by a vote of 115 to 39, with 48 abstentions. *Ettelaat*, Tehran, 18 October 1981.
18. The best available data, based on personal interviews and sources at US consulates in Europe, indicate that since shortly before the revolution close to 175,000 Iranians have sought refuge in different West European countries. Another 250,000 have joined nearly the same number who had settled in the United States in the decade preceding 1978. In all nearly 3 million Iranians are now in semi-permanent exile.
19. Interview in Paris, 27 December 1979.
20. Interview in Paris, 21 February 1981.
21. Aliakbar Tabatabi, Director of the Foundation, was assassinated in the spring of 1980 in the Washington, DC area, reportedly by Khomeini's agents who had recruited several black Moslems for this purpose.
22. *Khabarnameh*, newsletter of the *Enghelabe Islami* published in Paris, 18 October 1981.

9 THE ISLAMIC REPUBLIC AND THE WORLD

The triumph of revolution in Iran created a new atmosphere for determining and articulating the country's international posture. Although
the highly fluid and radical nature of its internal developments is
hardly conducive to a rational analysis of Iran's relations with the outside world, the Islamic regime has been compelled to adopt policy
position regarding a whole range of issues in the last 30 months. The
hostage crisis, the Soviet invasion of Afghanistan, and above all Iraq's
invasion of Iran, were matters of profound domestic political connota-
tions forcing the revolutionary regime to take a specific foreign-policy
stance. American–Iranian relations, however, have had more serious
effects on all the other aspects of Iran's place in the world at large.

The USA and Khomeini in Power

Iran's attitude toward the United States was evidently influenced by
American policy towards Iran in the post-Shah era. Earlier in this
study an examination was made of the American connection with the
Iranian revolution. Aspects of US policy during the hostage crisis were
reviewed in the chapter devoted to that crisis. What must be considered
now is American policy towards revolutionary Iran both before and
after the hostage crisis. It is important to note that the hostage crisis
was an exceptionally tumultuous event in the relations between the two
countries and as such did not permit a balanced examination of US–
Iran relations. Once it was over, the assumption of power by President
Reagan put these relations in a new context.

The victory of the revolution confronted the United States with
several positions concerning Iran. Each of these related to a specific
interpretation and comprehension of the revolution. One position
interpreted the overthrow of the Shah as an agonizing setback in terms
of US strategic, economic and a whole range of other goals and interests
in the region. The logical conclusion of that interpretation was to
recommend a policy designed to reverse the situation, something which
had been accomplished in August 1953 with considerable ease. This
hardline position found its advocates among the 'old hands' of the
Pentagon, the CIA and the State Department, as well as those Iranians

who had a stake in such a reversal. Specifically they wished for the prompt severance of diplomatic relations after the first assault on the US embassy on 14 February 1979, together with an end to military and commercial relations. In sum, they felt 'the loss of Iran,' very much like the 'loss' of China some three decades earlier, must be responded to by a policy of isolation and punitive measures against the new regime which would contribute to its eventual overthrow. Could this policy play into the hands of the Soviet Union? Had not the Chinese, Cuban and Egyptian experiences shown that active hostility toward a revolutionary regime would be promptly exploited by the Soviet Union?

The advocates of a hard-line posture toward Khomeini believed that either the Soviets would be extremely prudent in Iran or else they would attempt to subvert its revolution. A cautious Soviet policy need not evoke America's concern. An aggressive policy should be dealt with using the kind of toughness that the USA had demonstrated during the 1962 Cuban missile crisis. This school of thought seemed to view the revolution as much a setback for the Soviet Union as it was for the United States. The Soviet Union had acquired a stake in Iran's political stability. It had developed mutually beneficial commercial ties with the Shah's government.[1] It was also ill-disposed toward a Shia fundamentalist regime next to its Moslem-populated regions. This line of thinking acquired considerable credibility with the assault on the US embassy and the prolongation of the hostage crisis. All the evidence indicates that the counsel of these hardliners fell on deaf ears in the Carter Administration.

A second view of the Iranian revolution was basically an optimistic one. It held that the overthrow of the Shah must be accepted by the United States as at least a blessing in disguise. It was the logical conclusion of the US human-rights policy. There was general agreement on two fundamental questions: the Shah had lost the determination to rule and the opposition to him had acquired, by the end of 1978, a gigantic popular dimension. The United States would be hard put to oppose a popular revolution so soon after its own clamour for the respect of human rights. Was not the political right to change a regime, even though by violent means, one of the most sacred of these rights? Furthermore, had not extreme pressure on Cuba and Egypt from the West been responsible for their adoption of radical pro-Soviet policies? Moreover, pragmatism dictated that the USA should seek to accommodate the new regime. Its anti-American rhetoric should be viewed as just that and as basically for domestic consumption. There were no reasons to suspect that the Islamic Republic would knowingly accept Soviet domination. If anything its religious accent could bolster its resistance to Soviet communism. Moreover, the broad coalition which made the revolution a success included many democratic, nationalistic and even anti-Soviet Marxist groups. Iran of 1979 was in no way similar to post-World War II period, or the Mossadegh era, when a pro-Soviet party seemed to monopolize the allegiance of much of the politically articulate Iranians. Thus if the USA lowered its sights and concentrated on a minimum goal of assuring the security of the oil-rich Persian Gulf *vis-à-vis* direct or indirect Soviet inroads, it could hopefully coexist with the Islamic Republic. If the new regime manifested a disregard for the very human rights which the Carter Administration had espoused, the USA could always return to its fall-back position of non-intervention.

The position of the accommodationists appeared to prevail prior to the hostage crisis. Not only was the lowering of the US profile in Iran gradually reversed, in the summer of 1979 when several ethnic uprisings began to threaten Iran's territorial integrity, the USA quietly resumed the shipment of some military hardware which had been paid for by the previous regime. Ledeen and Lewis quote from a diplomatic cable to Washington dated 30 July speculating that the urgency of the Iranian defence officials' request was associated with events in Kurdistan.[2] Those in the United States who favoured accommodation with Khomeini's regime believed the resumption of military aid was justified in terms of US strategic interests, irrespective of the nature of the Iranian regime or its hostility toward the United States. Mindful of the Soviet establishment of a Kurdish Republic in Iran's Khuzistan in 1945 in association with the setting up of a similar regime in neighbouring Azarbayjan, the supporters of the resumption of military ties with Iran felt failure to do so would be tantamount to encouraging Iran's territorial disintegration. Even though the dominant Kurdish political party was the KDP, under the leadership of Sheikh Ezzeddin Husseini and Dr Abdolrahman Ghassemlou, both non-communist and nationalist, the lure of autonomy was so strong that they could have solicited active Soviet support. Indeed, in 1945 the Kumeleh Party had been led by Ghazi Mohammad, a religious nationalist leader who had become a willing agent of the Soviet Union when he saw co-operation with the occupying Red Army as the only means for establishing an autonomous Kurdish republic.[3] The accommodationists in short believed the renewal of military ties with Iran was necessary in terms of the need to contain the Soviets at a time when the new regime was encountering serious troubles in literally holding the country together.

A third position *vis-à-vis* the Islamic Republic was associated with those who believed Iran needed to be left alone. A 'benign neglect' rather than active hostility or deliberate accommodation was prescribed. The dangers of adopting either of the first two positions were underlined. To try to overthrow the Islamic regime would simply compound the 'loss of Iran.' To accommodate the revolutionary regime would be to entail surrendering to humiliating demands which could set precedents and damage US interests elsewhere. The advantage of a posture of benign neglect would be that with the passage of time, when revolutionary turmoil had subsided, the new Iranian regime might decide that correct relations with the United States would be in its own interest. Though not stating so publicly, the supporters of this posture seemed to relegate Iran's strategic significance to a much lower level. The loss of Iranian oil to the West did not seem to be as catastrophic as some had predicted. Internal chaos in Iran had not automatically transformed it into becoming a target of opportunity for the Soviet Union. The United States could never reinstate another Shah-like regime in that country, so should leave Iran to its own devices and instead concentrate on such countries as Saudi Arabia, the Gulf states, Turkey and Egypt, where active American support was sincerely welcomed.

The substance of this analysis seemed to be that not only the loss of the Shah, but even the loss of the country to the Soviet Union were eventualities that the United States must learn to cope with calmly and without excessive anxiety. If need be perhaps an understanding with the Soviets concerning a *de facto* partition of the country into zones of economic influence could be achieved. What was regarded as the absolute minimum US objective had to do with the Persian Gulf and the Arabian Peninsula, and not with Iran. This concept was of course at the root of the so-called Carter Doctrine announced in the wake of the Soviet invasion of Afghanistan in December 1979.

Some of those favouring 'benign neglect' were quite optimistic in their outlook, believing that the worst possible likelihood, namely Soviet control of Iran, would not materialize. Others were convinced that the logical outcome of a prolonged period of benign neglect would be a progressive Soviet encroachment. This outcome did not bother the latter group. As such, their position was closer to those who advocated a retaliatory policy towards Khomeini's regime. Hostility toward him, especially after the hostage crisis, was so intense that even

Iran's Sovietization was not considered too high a price for Khomeini's downfall.

Once the shock of the Iranian revolution had begun to dissipate, the Carter Administration embarked on a policy of accommodation with Khomeini. Ambassador Sullivan was allowed to stay until April. Sympathetic American scholars were reportedly recommended by Foreign Minister Ibrahim Yazdi and his son-in-law, Shariyar Rouhani, to replace Sullivan. Most frequently mentioned were Professors Richard Cottom and James Bill, both reputable Iran specialists many of whose predictions about events in Iran had proved accurate. Sullivan himself reportedly favoured a policy of accommodation and thought if the new regime wanted someone like Professor James Bill the USA should oblige.

But the policy of reconciliation suffered several setbacks in the spring and summer of 1979. In May the US Congress passed a resolution criticizing some of the executions carried out in Iran.[4] The response was a well-orchestrated barrage of anti-American propaganda. This Congress resolution was interpreted as intervention in domestic affairs, particularly in view of the fact that the United States had given political refuge to a large number of military and civilian associates of the Shah. The United States should decide whom it wanted to accommodate, the officials of the fallen regime or the new Islamic government. If it was the latter then it should keep quiet about the practices of Khomeini's justice. Secondly, the State Department refused to consider an academic for the position of US Ambassador and instead recommended Walter Cutler, a career diplomat, to the Iranians. In June the Islamic Republic rejected that nomination on the grounds that Cutler, as US Ambassador to Zaire, had interfered in the internal affairs of that country. By now it had become apparent that the Islamic Republic wanted a very gradual normalization of relations with the USA on its own terms. Thus, when Foreign Minister Yazdi came to New York to attend the UN General Assembly in October, in a secret meeting with Secretary Vance and Ambassador McHenry the Iranian voiced strong doubts about US sincerity. Interviews with former Iranian foreign ministry officials revealed that Iran had demanded three things from the USA as concrete evidence that they had genuinely accepted the revolution. One was that the USA should absolutely cease and desist from expressing concern about the trials and punishments of officials of the former regime. Secondly, that the United States should agree to extradite at least some of the more notorious military and civilian officials of the Shah who had been granted refuge. Thirdly, the USA should abandon any idea of sheltering the Shah and indeed should co-operate with the Iranian authorities to recover some of the Shah's assets in the United States. The Iranian Foreign Minister skill-fully played up the anti-communist theme of the Islamic regime, arguing that any undermining of that regime would simply strengthen the hands of those who wished to bring the leftist groups to power.[5]

Every account indicates that the USA was most conciliatory on all these scores, literally accepting Khomeini's terms for accommodation. Only on the issue of the extradition of the Shah's officials did the American diplomats remind Yazdi that as a former Iranian expatriate in the USA he should know that the laws of the United States would not permit such an action. Otherwise neither the issue of a new ambassador to Tehran, nor the question of the purge of the former Iranian officials should be allowed to impede the process of normalization. Thus, in June Bruce Laingen became the US Chargé and was reportedly in line to become the new ambassador when and if the situation improved. In mid-October Henry Precht, the State Department Country Director for Iran, paid a visit to Tehran. Informal talks between Bazargan, Yazdi and Brzezinski in Algiers in the same month gave another indication of US adherence to a posture of accommodation.

This posture was severely tested by the admission of the Shah to the United States in October. The chain of events that it unleashed had two serious results. As far as the Khomeini government was concerned that act simply proved that the US protestation about accepting the revolution and accommodating the new regime was a blatant deception. The USA pretended to pursue the second option in its relations with revolutionary Iran, but in fact it was biding its time and preparing itself to achieve Khomeini's downfall. A second result related to the perception of US policy. How could the USA be unaware of the potential reactions of radical and fundamentalist forces in the new regime to the admittance of the Shah to the USA? If the failure to predict the Shah's downfall had been the first dramatic US failure, the inability to comprehend the difficulties of accommodating Khomeini might surely be considered as a second disastrous US error.

Nor could this error be attributed to a lack of understanding of the Iranian position due to the failures of the American diplomats in Iran. Bruce Laingen, the new Chargé who in September had vigorously supported a policy of accommodation with Khomeini, had a month earlier sent a revealing cable to Secretary Vance. Among his observations were the following:

(1) Never assume that your side of the issue will be recognized, let alone that it will be conceded to have merits. Persian preoccupation with self precludes this. A negotiator must force recognition of his position upon his Persian opposite number.

(2) Should not expect an Iranian readily to perceive the advantages of a long-term relationship based on trust. He will assume that his opposite number is essentially an adversary and will seek to maximize benefits for himself that are immediately available.

(3) Interlocking relationships of all aspects of an issue must be painstakingly developed. Linkage will be neither readily comprehended nor accepted.

(4) One should insist on performance as the *sine qua non* at each stage of negotiations. Statements of intention count for almost nothing.

(5) Cultivation of goodwill for goodwill's sake is a waste of effort. The overriding objective should always be to emphasize mutuality of the proposed undertaking.

(6) One should be prepared for the threat of breakdown in negotiations at any given moment and not be cowed by the possibility. Given his cultural and psychological limitations, he is going to resist the very concept (from the Western point of view) of a rational negotiation process.[6]

Despite this and similar warnings the United States appeared to be quite optimistic about its chances of a negotiated accommodation with the regime. From all accounts, in Algiers Bazargan and Yazdi had succeeded in portraying a positive image of their intentions towards the United States to Brzezinski. At a time when reports from Iran and indeed recent public statements by Bazargan himself had shown great tension between the government and the Revolutionary Council, the United States seemed to put considerable trust in the ability of Bazargan to protect America's interests.

The rude awakening to the accommodationists came with the assault on the US embassy and the taking of the hostages. The more obstinate the revolutionary regime became, the more untenable the position of those who advocated appeasement toward Khomeini appeared. But as was noted in the coverage of the hostage crisis in Chapter 3, the Carter Administration was as yet not able to comprehend the intricacies of Iran's domestic political developments. Consequently, its policy toward Iran was marked by intended or unintended errors of judgement, which resulted in the prolongation of the crisis. Except when the ill-fated

rescue attempt was made the position of the hard-liners seeking retaliatory measures against Khomeini's government did not gain acceptance.

Once the crisis was resolved the United States finally seemed to
abandon the accommodationist position toward Khomeini's regime.
The new administration was left with only two of the positions described above concerning Iran, i.e. either try to penalize, and thereby
destabilize the Iranian regime, or neglect it, whether benignly or otherwise. The latter posture alarmed many of the Iranian exile groups who
believed a benign neglect would easily become malignant, and that
Iran's independence and territorial integrity would be threatened if the
USA decided to 'write off' the country. As the internal turmoil aggravated, many Iranian expatriates expressed utter amazement at the
refusal of the United States to make any policy-declaration concerning
Iran. In particular it was distressing to these Iranians that the blatant
violation of basic human rights and the brutal repression of opposition
groups did not evoke any official condemnation by a government that
only two years earlier had clamoured for the support of human rights
everywhere.[7]

Even though few comprehensive policy statements concerning the
non-Arab Middle East have been made by the Republican Administration, it is not difficult to identify the general trends of the US position
concerning Iran. For one thing the USA seeks to learn from mistakes
made in 1953, in 1978 and during the hostage crisis. For another,
America's new concept of a strategic consensus for the Middle East
seems to exclude Iran, at least as long as the present regime remains in
power. The first constraint on the United States will no doubt lead to
excessive prudence and most likely to no policy at all because no consensus exists as to what precise lessons must be learned from these three
crises in US-Iran relations. Because of the wide range of opinions
on the causes and effects of these crises, it is impossible to draw identical lessons which could act as a policy guidance. Hence the temptation to do nothing, lest doing something might entail repetition of old
mistakes, appears irresistible.

As to the concept of strategic consensus, it is obvious that the
Reagan Administration is moving toward a preclusive posture towards
Iran. Such friendly countries as Egypt, Turkey and Saudi Arabia
will be included in attempts to form a consensus on a common threat
perception from the direction of the Soviet Union. The exclusion of
Iran will continue as long as the government in power there does not
share that perception. To some extent the present US position seems

to combine elements of the first and third positions enumerated above. That is to say, while a hard-line policy of destabilizing the Iranian regime has not been promulgated, the present posture of neglect is not unlikely to generate the consequences desired by the hardliners. Put anther way, the critical question of Soviet exploitation of Iran's chaos and the US response to it remains unresolved. To the hard-liners possible Sovietization of Iran may appear as the kind of just punishment which its present regime richly deserves. To others, including many Iranian nationalist and liberal groups, the West's acquiescence to such development is short-sighted and highly immoral.[8]

Caught in a web of contradictory concerns and pressures, the United States appears incapable of initiating active new policies towards Iran so long as Khomeini's regime holds a radically different perception about Iran's security. It is that perception which must be understood in order to analyse Iran's international posture in the revolutionary era.

Three Foreign-policy Considerations

Since its inception the new regime has been influenced by three predominant considerations in determining its foreign-policy goals. First, its attitude towards the major powers was influenced by its perception of their support of the deposed Shah. The timing and degree of sympathy for the revolution, and since 1979 the real or imaginary intervention in Iran's domestic affairs, notably at the time of various ethnic uprisings during 1979, have combined to determine the nature of Iran's relations with these powers. A second consideration has been the internal function of foreign policy. The need for an identifiable external enemy as a means for retaining revolutionary momentum has figured prominently in shaping Iran's attitude towards the superpowers. The United States, as was noted in the coverage of the crisis in American–Iranian relations, could perform that function not only because of its close association with the deposed Shah, but chiefly because Iran was secure in the knowledge that the USA could not afford to retaliate in kind. Iran on the other hand could not afford to select the other super-power as a target for its hostility, for compelling strategic and political reasons.

A third consideration for the new regime, as for the deposed one, has been the threat-perception which foreign-policy objectives seek to contain and overcome. The Islamic regime naturally revised that perception just as soon as it came to power. Unlike the old regime, the Islamic regime did not consider the threat as emanating from the Soviet Union and the radical regimes in the region. Instead it came from the United States and regional regimes aligned with it.

As to the first determinant of Iran's new international posture, it is significant to note that although the USA was the main target of Iran's hostility, other Western powers and the Soviet Union also fared poorly with the new regime. The undeniable fact was that the deposed Shah had established cordial and normal relations with nearly all countries across the broad ideological spectrum.[9] Furthermore, few countries were able to foresee the course of events in 1978 so that they could initiate an anti-Shah position sufficiently early in 1978 to expect tangible rewards from the new regime. Thus, for example, France which had given refuge to Khomeini in October, even though with the consent of the late Shah, none the less pursued a correct policy with Iran until the triumph of the revolution. Its expectations that because of granting asylum to Khomeini, it would reap rich rewards in terms of huge contracts and expanded trade relations soon proved futile and certainly by the time the US hostage crisis had come to overshadow everything else.

Today, precisely because the same political sanctuary has been offered the key opponents of Khomeini, Franco-Iranian relations have sunk to their lowest depth. When in early August 1981 the ruling Socialist Party condemned the mass executions of Khomeini's opponents and appealed for moderation and reconciliation, the Islamic regime waged a massive anti-French campaign reminiscent of the anti-American hysteria of a year earlier.

Similarly communist China, whose former party chairman Hua Fung had paid the Shah a state visit in the early autumn of 1978, found itself the target of vengeful Iranian hostility after the revolution. In a memorable meeting with Khomeini in Qom in March, when the ambassador of the People's Republic of China tried to persuade the new regime of the perfidy and unreliability of the Soviet Union, Khomeini scornfully reminded him of that ill-timed visit. The pro-Tudeh press dutifully exploited this event, concluding that the Soviet Union had at least provided sanctuary for communist opponents of the Shah ever since 1949 and 1953, either in Russia or in other East European countries.[10]

As for the rest of the world, the new regime found all of them guilty of befriending the Shah and decided either to reduce its diplomatic missions to a low consular level or simply to recall entire missions without notifying the formal severance of diplomatic ties. Egypt and

Israel were the two notable exceptions when complete severance of all relations were effected almost immediately after the revolution.

As to the second determinant of Iran's immediate post-revolution foreign policy, the United States fitted admirably the role of the revolution's public enemy number one. It is, however, important to note that not all the Iranian leaders and political groups who acquired power or influenced its exercise after the revolution believed in a prolonged and non-selective anti-American posture. At least up to the overthrow of Banisadr in June 1981 the following positions concerning Iran's policy toward the United States and consequently toward the Soviet Union could be identified.

(1) First was the position of the Islamic fundamentalists, whose hostility towards the USA stemmed as much from that government's identification with the Shah as it did from close US–Israel ties. This position was embraced by the younger clerics such as Rafsanjani, Khoeini and Khameini. Outside the Revolutionary Council, the government and the Majlis, the Mojahedin were also identified with it. The advocates of this position did not fear Iran's isolation. Indeed, they cherished what may be described as a siege mentality which would put the Islamic Republic at the centre of a sea of hostile regimes and unfriendly countries. In sermon after sermon these young clerics preached to the faithful that isolation and loneliness on the international scene were virtuous, and superior to being in league with immoral and oppressive regimes.

(2) A second position was articulated by former Prime Minister Bazargan and the first President, Banisadr. While they had understood the initial outburst of anti-Americanism, at least after the Shah's death in July 1980 and the Iraqi invasion in September of that year, they wished for an even-handed policy toward both super-powers. They were quite concerned that a major cornerstone of Iran's century-old tradition of reliance on a distant great power as a counterweight to its proximate great power, be permanently and irreversibly abandoned. Bazargan and Banisadr both reflected the views of a considerable sector of Western-educated Iranians who, irrespective of their social status or religious-ethnic affiliation, viewed this as a dangerous departure from the past, since in critical times this reliance had served Iran's interest whether *vis-à-vis* Tsarist or Soviet Russia, or in relations with Imperial Great Britain. This was particularly so in view of the Soviet-Iranian Treaty of 1921 of which Article 5 justified Soviet intervention to protect its legitimate security interests in Iran. These Iranian

nationalists remembered how the treaty had last been used in connection with the Anglo-Soviet invasion of 1941, and how repeated efforts for its bilateral abrogation or revision had failed.

Khomeini's regime, like the Shah's before him, declared the treaty null and void in the wake of alleged evidence of the Soviet arming of some Kurdish dissidents. This unilateral abrogation of the 1921 Treaty proved ironic, for the threat of Soviet reaction could not be used in the hostage confrontation with the USA. Indeed, at the height of the hostage crisis Soviet references to their legitimate security interests as a means of discouraging American military intervention were rather played down in the state-controlled media, at least until the Soviet invasion of Afghanistan.

(3) A third position, with which Beheshti, Behzad Nabavi and Rajai were initially identified, was reliance on the Third World and co-operation with genuinely non-aligned countries. Followers of this line of thinking believed that Iran should insulate itself from super-power rivalries, but they opposed total isolation from the international community. They believed as Iran progressively de-emphasized its ties with both super-powers it should seek closer identification with the Third World. As will be noted later, in the wake of the settlement of the hostage crisis this line became fully identified with the government's position. Both Rajai as Prime Minister and Nabavi as Minister of State articulated this position at the United Nations in October 1980 and at the conference of Non-aligned Nations in February 1981, respectively.[11]

Considerable overlapping of these positions occurred when the country faced such major crises as the Soviet invasion of Afghanistan and the war with Iraq. What is evident is that advocates of all three positions gradually became aware that a third consideration, based on a valid perception of the sources of threat to the country and its regime, should be attended to.

The Changing Threat Perception

The third determinant of foreign policy had to undergo important revisions at the beginning of the revolutionary era. There is no doubt that as long as the Shah was alive and not physically too distant from Iran, the Islamic regime considered the United States capable of restoring him to power. The new regime therefore justified its anti-Americanism on the basis of a valid perception of this threat to its existence.

The Soviet Union, on the other hand, was viewed as incapable of direct intervention in Iranian affairs, for such an intervention had to be supported by domestic political forces. An outright invasion was out of the question. Just as the Soviets would not tolerate a US occupation of Iran, the Islamic Republic was convinced that the United States would not permit a Soviet invasion. Although to acknowledge this publicly would have run counter to the regime's policy, some of the closest associates of Khomeini had openly underlined this reciprocal constraint on the super-powers. Mostafa Chamran, the former Minister of Defence, made it clear that US inability to intervene militarily at the height of the hostage crisis was largely based on that implicit mutual Soviet–American restraint.[12]

If a direct Soviet invasion could be ruled out, an indirect intervention in support of pro-Soviet political groups inside the country was considered even less likely. The Islamic fundamentalists held such groups as the Tudeh Party in utter contempt. Not only had their contribution to the revolution been marginal, but they were forced to support the regime loyally and out of fear of total destruction if they failed to do so. The Soviet invasion of Afghanistan at Christmas 1979 was the first serious test of the validity of Iran's new American-focused threat perception.

That invasion placed the regime in a quandary. On the one hand, it could not ignore the triumph of the Soviet-backed Afghan regime over an Islamic rebellion which the Iranian government had fully supported on religious and political grounds. On the other, it could not afford an abrupt shift of attention away from the United States and towards the Soviet Union; the first would have eroded its credibility as the champion of all oppressed fellow Moslems; the second would have created a tacit alliance with the United States at a time when the hostage crisis was continuing to serve the domestic need of rallying the diverse forces of leftist opposition in support of the regime. At least until the presidential election of 25 January and perhaps the Majlis election of 7 March, the regime needed the maximum possible support from all political forces, in particular those which had proved their mobilization skills. The Soviet putsch in Afghanistan could also be viewed as a blessing in disguise, for not only did it moderate the United States' threat of severe sanctions, including a possible blockade of the Khark oil terminal, but it caused a considerable toning-down of Shariat-madari's opposition in the strategic Azarbayjan province.

Faced with these divergent and often contradictory considerations, the regime opted for a policy of procrastination and indecision lasting until the election of Banisadr on 25 January. Prior to that government spokesmen had made ambivalent pronouncements about the Soviet invasion. On the other hand, they dealt decisively with the state of near-insurgency in Tabriz, where the Moslem People's Republican Party, the chief pro-Shariatmadari organization, was forcibly outlawed and some eleven of its militants tried and executed. When the occupation of the Soviet embassy in Tehran by Afghanistan's Iranian sympathizers appeared imminent, Khomeini bowed to the strong protestations of the Soviet Ambassador and saw to it that no such meddling with the Soviet diplomatic mission was attempted.

Indeed, on the first day of the demonstration outside the Soviet embassy, during which the Soviet flag was lowered and burned, the ambassador requested an immediate meeting with Khomeini in Qom. Reliable reports indicate that the ambassador had given the government eight hours to secure fully the safety of the embassy and its personnel, 'or else an independent country called Iran will simply be erased off the face of the earth.'[13] Irrespective of the absolute reliability of this report, the fact remains that ever since that encounter, even when the Soviet attitude towards the Iraq–Iran war became suspect, no further anti-Soviet demonstrations have occurred outside the embassy.

Related to Iran's threat perception is the regime's view of its own viability and survival. Devoid of its rhetoric, it seems that the revolutionary regime's foreign policy is intimately linked with that view rather than with its ideological or Pan-Islamic aspirations. This concern also explains Iran's reluctance to apply its Pan-Islamic exhortations to its northern neighbour. The revolutionary regime also seems aware of the sensitivity of the Soviet Union to the Pan-Islamic dimension of the Iranian revolution with regard to the Moslem-dominated regions of the Caucasus and central Asia. It, however, does not exaggerate the significance of this factor as a determinant of the Soviet attitude towards Iran, for it feels, unlike Iran's other Moslem neighbours, that these Moslem areas are securely controlled by an efficient totalitarian system.

A further point concerning Iran's view of how the West perceives the revolution has to do with the notion of the so-called Arc of Crisis, which establishes a linkage amongst Moslem countries on the southern periphery of the Soviet Union, stretching from Iran deep into southeast Asia. The assumption that turmoil in one is destined to have a domino effect on the rest of the region was, of course, complimentary to the revolutionary leaders, but questionable in certain respects.[14]

It was so because it underestimated the fundamental socio-economic differences of Moslem countries like Turkey, Pakistan and Iran, and disregarded other equally critical religious schisms between predominantly Shia Iran and these predominantly Sunni countries. Its other flaw was that in a real sense it was a fall-back to the Cold War and the mid-1950s era when the Northern Tier concept endeavoured to formalize precisely such an alliance under the sponsorship of the USA and Britain. The Central Treaty Organization (CENTO) Treaty was based on similarly fallacious assumptions and thus failed to achieve any of its implicit or explicit aims. Khomeini's awareness of the above accounts for confining his Pan-Islamic objective to rhetorical statements rather than performing concrete deeds.

As to changes in Iran's regional foreign policy since 1979 it should be noted that just as under the Shah, regional foreign policy was determined by Iran's threat perception. Now that the main source of threat was considered to be the United States, Iran's attitude toward the region obviously had to be decided by the closeness or remoteness of each country in the region towards the United States. But the same rule did not apply to the Soviet Union, or Iraq as one of its closest allies or Afghanistan since December 1979, should have become Iran's closest friends. As we shall see later Iran became quite hostile to both countries.

Almost from the beginning the new Iran became entangled in disputes with nearly all its neighbours. Although the interim government of Bakhtiar had already abrogated Iran's membership of CENTO, the revolutionary regime branded any neighbouring country remaining in it as a lackey of American imperialism. Turkey was thus branded as a hostile country and with which relations cooled down considerably. Even though the trade route via Turkey was essential for Iran's economic survival, especially after the imposition of American and West European sanctions, Iran showed no reservations in branding the military coup in Turkey on 1 September 1980 as 'made in America'.

Clearly Iran's regional policy was not merely determined by its threat perception, but also by its solidarity with Islamic fundamentalist groups, many of whom were targets of hostility by the new military regime in Turkey. Indeed, some of Iran's fundamentalist leaders had boasted about direct support for militant Turkish Moslem parties just as they had done concerning other Arab countries within the region. Thus, Saudi Arabia, the Persian Gulf states and even Pakistan, as far as new Iran was concerned, suffered from two interrelated liabilities. One was that they were non-radical and often ruled by a dynasty, and the other was their close ties with the United States. Needless to say, a third test was hostility to Israel, but that by itself did not suffice in terms of cultivating Iran's support for such an anti-Israel state as Iraq, which suffered from other, more significant liabilities.

Arab-Iranian relations as a whole also were negatively affected by the way Arab states, particularly those in the Gulf, viewed the revolutionary regime in Iran. These states, which had come to view a pro-Western Iran as a source of stability, were now forced to revise their own threat perceptions. Ethnic uprisings amongst the Kurds, the Baluchies and Arab Iranians in Khuzistan aggravated the mutual sense of distrust. Not only the Pan-Islamic proclamations by Khomeini, but instances of Iraqi–Palestinian incitement of Iranian Arabs and Kurds compounded an already tense situation. The outbreak of the war with Iraq was thus the culmination of tensions in Arab–Iranian relations which could no longer be contained.

To move beyond the confines of neighbouring countries, the tensions in Saudi–Iranian relations stem from factors similar to those affecting Iraqi–Iranian ties. Additionally, the overriding concern in Saudi Arabia, much more than in neighbouring Iraq, was with the prospect of the radicalization of the Iranian revolution, which they perceived inevitably as a gain for the Soviet Union. Here again, such provocative measures by revolutionary Iran as Khomeini's appeal to the pilgrims to promote the Iranian–Islamic revolution amongst all Moslem brethren, a powerful radio station in Khuzistan trying to reach the masses of non-Saudi Arab workers in the region, and the systematic expression of contempt for 'the failure of the oil-rich Arab state to face the challenge of a few million usurping Zionists,' were of course bound to aggravate the existing tension.[15] Divergent views on oil policies between the two countries are not of post-revolution origin, but have become intensified over the last year with Iran bent on reducing production and maximizing profit, and the Saudis pursuing a moderate policy favouring the industralized consuming nations. Iran's exploitation of an oil policy designed to destabilize the Saudi royal regime by branding it a puppet of the West, has further contributed to the growing mutual suspicion and recrimination, the façade of normalcy notwithstanding.

The Gulf states share similar misgivings and concerns about revolutionary Iran. Iran's susceptibility to such reckless attempts as renouncing the 1969 Bahrain Settlement, or utilizing Iranian and other non-Arab Shia workers to subvert these traditional regimes from within, are perceived by them as inherent dangers, despite the erosion of the credibility of Iran's military capacity.

Iraqi aggression elevated regional policy to a much higher level. Since September 1980 Iran's attitude towards nearly all foreign countries as well as toward international organizations has been determined by their attitudes towards the war. In a sense Iran's foreign relations since then have been basically determined by Iraq's threat to the survival of the regime and the territorial integrity of the country.

The Iraqi–Iranian Conflict

Relations with Iraq began to deteriorate almost immediately after Khomeini's seizure of power. Some long-standing historical reasons as well as specific immediate causes brought the two countries to the brink of war early in September and actual hostilities broke out on 22 September 1980.

First, in the last few years of the Shah's regime the two countries had managed to normalize their relations. Outstanding issues such as sovereignty over Shat-al-Arab, the demarcation of boundaries and the relations of each government towards the Kurdish people within their territories were all resolved in the historic Algiers agreement signed in 1975.[16] As far as the new regime was concerned Iraq was a pro-Shah regime, and since it was determined to reverse the basic premises of the Shah's foreign policy, it was obvious that sooner or later Iraq's Baathist regime would be placed on Khomeini's enemy list. Secondly, the Iraqis too felt strong reasons for suspicion and increased enmity toward the new Iran, which was not only espousing an international dimension for its Islamic revolution, but displaying strong hostility towards the Baathist regime as secular and, not the least, ideologically pro-Western. Moreover, Saddam Hossein, who by the time of Khomeini's triumph had consolidated his hold on Iraq, was concerned that his Shia population, roughly 50 per cent of Iraq's population, might respond to Khomeini's Islamic fundamentalism and challenge his regime from within.

Although Iraqi nationalism had for some time built up a strong component of Persophobia, Hossein was not confident that his Shia compatriots would be totally impervious to Khomeini's agitation from across the borders. Of all Iran's Moslem neighbours, Iraq was the only country with over half its population Shia, and was the land where the most holy Shia shrines, namely Nejaf and Karbala, were located. When in December 1979 the Islamic constitution was approved, the principle of Pan-Islamism became an official doctrine of Khomeini's Iran. Consequently, Iraq became convinced that given the opportunity Khomeini would not hesitate in the least to take active measures for exporting his brand of Shia fundamentalism into Iraq.

A third reason for the outbreak of hostilities between the two was that in a real sense the Iraqis felt that the 1975 agreement had been imposed on them by a more powerful Iranian regime under the late Shah. Although Saddam Hossein had been the architect of this accord, and objectively speaking the agreement favoured each side equally, the fact remained that it had been concluded with an Iranian ruler at the zenith of his power and prestige. Now that Iran was undergoing the chaos of revolutionary turmoil, was not the time opportune for Iraq to renegue on the agreement? A successful abrogation of that treaty accompanied by the 'liberation' of the three Persian Gulf islands occupied by the Shah in 1971, could only help elevate Iraq to the status of leadership in the Persian Gulf rivalling that of the deposed Shah at the height of his power. The Iraqis felt that since both these actions had been taken by a hated Shah, the new regime would have no difficult in sanctioning their revocation.

Fourthly, there was the perplexing and still unsettled question of the Kurds. Under the 1975 agreement the Shah had stopped his less than clandestine backing of the Kurdish insurgents in Iraq and shortly afterwards the Baghdad regime had crushed the insurrection. Since late 1975 that major burden had been lifted from the shoulders of the Iraqi rulers. The considerable measure of self-rule granted the Iraqi Kurds had additionally made the region less hostile to the central government in Baghdad. Historically, Kurdish turmoil in one country had a way of spilling over into the other. Iran and Iraq could be confident of the tranquillity of their respective Kurdish regions only if both regimes pacified their Kurds by whatever diplomatic or military means were deemed necessary. With the collapse of the Shah's regime this equation began to change.

Because the new regime had embarked on a systematic decimation of Iran's armed forces, the chief instrument for the pacification of the Iranian Kurds was effectively undermined. In the best tradition of their forefathers the Kurds launched a new insurrection in Iran, just as soon as they became convinced of the weakness of the central government, as well as of the genuine sympathy of some secular leftist revolutionary forces for a limited Kurdish autonomy in the context of a federated Iran.

The Kurdish problem since the revolution has been covered elsewhere in this study. Suffice it to stress that the resurgence of the struggle of the Iranian Kurds against what they perceived to be a weak central government, had a major influence on the outbreak of the war with Iraq. Objectively speaking, Iraq had a vested interest in a tranquil Iranian Kurdistan, for if the Kurds there could successfully secede from Iran, their compatriots across the ill-defined borders would not long delay in embracing that cause. As long as Iran possessed sufficient military strength to keep the Kurds in check, Iraq had restrained from provocative actions with regard to the Iranian Kurds.

But with the near collapse of the armed forces and their partial replacement by the Pasdaran, whose fundamental Islamic ideology was suspect to Iraq, and finally with the successful insurgency in the summer and autumn of 1979, Iraq felt a reassessment of its policy in this matter was essential. If the Iranians could not restore tranquillity to their Kurdistan, then Iraq would ensure that a stretch of its common border with Iran would be protected by its own military forces. This need not be a permanent solution and could be reversed as soon as Iran could acquire the military leverage necessary for retaining its Kurdistan. Throughout the autumn of 1979 repeated border skirmishes took place between the armies of the two countries as the Iranians were attempting to put down the new Kurdish insurgency. In the meantime, the ideological and propaganda warfare between Baghdad and Tehran was intensified, with Iran openly calling on the Shias and other Moslems all over the Arab world to rise up and overthrow their 'corrupt rulers,' and the Iraqis inciting the Arab Iranians of Khuzistan to secede from 'the racist Persia and rejoin their Arab brethren.' In mid-December, at the height of domestic and foreign turmoil in Iran, serious clashes along the common border almost brought the two countries into an undeclared war. However, as yet the Iraqi regime was not ready to risk an all-out invasion. The assault on the US embassy, the uncertainties of the US response and ambiguities about the Soviet attitude concerning Iran and Iraq, treaty obligations notwithstanding, combined to dissuade Saddam Hossein from striking before September 1980.

On 22 September 1980 Iraq struck along its 300-mile border with Iran. Iraqi armoured divisions moved towards Kirmanshah, Dezful and Ahwaz, and most significantly towards Khoramshahr and Abadan in the Shat-al-Arab shores.

Iraq's Political Aims

Having declared the 1975 treaty null and void, Iraq announced the acquisition of complete sovereignty over Shat-al-Arab as its primary objective. The acquisition of the two disputed border enclaves which under the 1975 treaty were conceded to Iraq but never actually relinquished by the Iranians was their second demand; and the return of the three Persian Gulf islands to Arab sovereignty, which meant the restoration of the 1971 *ante bellum*, was their other initial aim. Implied, though not openly declared, Iraq's overall objective was to topple Khomeini's regime at a time when it seemed totally isolated and facing formidable challenges both from inside the country and abroad. On the face of it the Iraqis seemed to be insisting upon their share of the 1975 agreement while simultaneously declaring that agreement invalid.

Be that as it may, in the first three weeks of the war the Iraqis gained some of their military objectives. A strip of land ranging in depth from 10 to 35 miles was captured along the common border. But no quick political concession was forthcoming from Iran. The important cities of Ahwaz, Dezful and Abadan put up a determined resistance. The Iranian Air Force reached deep into the heart of Iraq and flew spectacular sorties against Baghdad as well as against such port facilities as Basra and Ummul Qasr. The Shat-al-Arab was blocked by some seventy stranded ships, but its western shores could not be completely taken over by the Iraqis because of their inability to capture Abadan, although the port city of Khoramshahr was recaptured after three weeks of bitter street fighting.

Despite the incredible propaganda warfare on both sides, by the third week of the hostilities it became quite obvious that Iraq's original time-table could not be achieved. Documents taken from Iraqi prisoners-of-war had disclosed a timetable of 10 to 14 days during which, apart from Khoramshahr, Abadan, Ahwaz, Dezful and Masjed Soleiman, the main centres of oil-rich Khuzistan had to be captured. One-third of neighbouring Kurdistan, including the region of Ilam and Kirmanshah, was to be under Iraqi control by the end of the third week. At no time during more than a year of warfare did the Iraqis succeed in attaining more than 30 to 40 per cent of their territorial goals. Why? What went wrong?

Some important miscalculations marred the attainment of Iraq's initial military and political objectives. First, they had underestimated the power of nationalism, which even in Islamic Iran meant the rallying of most of the political forces to the central government, however weak and unpopular it had become. Secondly, it had vastly underestimated the ability of the Pasdaran to resist the invading Iraqi forces and to help defend cities in and around such major targets as Dezful and Ahwaz, as well as Abadan. Thirdly, the Iraqis had over-relied on a spontaneous uprising by dissident Arab-speaking Iranians in Khuzistan, or for that matter by other Iranian dissidents in the border regions. Fourthly, it had overestimated the significance of the Abadan refinery to the Iranian economy. The sharp decline in oil revenue was no more crucial for the country than had been American and West European sanctions, imposed during the hostage crisis, since November 1979. These miscalculations caused the war to drag on, despite optimistic initial signs that the hostilities would be short-lived. At the end of the spring, nearly nine months after the offensive had been launched by the Iraqis, the war had settled into a low-key war of attrition while peace missions continued their slow and cumbersome efforts. In early April two such missions, one from the Islamic Conference, the other from the non-aligned countries, reported some limited progress. Some accounts from Baghdad suggested that Iraq's objectives had been considerably toned down. Some reports indicated that all they now wanted were the two tiny border enclaves granted them under the 1975 agreement, and sovereignty over the whole Shat-al-Arab waterway.[17]

Fifteen months after their invasion the Iraqi armies continue to hold a narrow strip of land about 5–30 miles along the border, with their deepest penetration in the Abadan front at about 45 miles. Repeated attempts by the Iranians to dislodge them from these positions have been futile. In February 1981, responding to the pressures from his clerical rivals, Banisadr ordered a counter-offensive near Susangerd, south of Dezful. The attack was a disaster, resulting in hundreds of casualties and the capture of scores of tanks and other heavy weapons by the Iraqis. Some press accounts describe the details of this offensive as evidence of Iraq's ability to sit tight and simply wait the Iranians out. *The Economist* reported that some 400 Iranian tanks had broken out of the town, crossing the river to its west. The Iraqis retreated about a mile and then sent in their aircraft to destroy the bridges. While the Iranians were rebuilding the bridges, the Iraqis crossed the river on either side of the Iranian tank force and cut it to pieces as it tried to return to Susangerd. Iraq claimed the capture of 30 tanks and the destruction of another 270. There has been no other such massive counter-offensive since then in this region. But the Iraqis have not been faring much better either. Despite their repeated claims of capturing Ahwaz or Dezful, these major targets have so far withstood the daily shelling and occasional probing assault by the Iraqis. More significantly, Abadan with its shattered refinery has not been seized, and as long as it remains in Iranian hands Shat-al-Arab will be within their artillery range and therefore closed.

For several reasons the Iraqis seem to have been reluctant to launch a determined offensive against the city. Above all, the experience of

Khoramshahr, which took the Iraqis 24 days to capture, must be mentioned. The Iraqis acknowledged that only about 3,000 regular army and Pasdaran were defending the city. The house-to-house battle for its capture took a heavy toll of the Iraqis — estimated at 2,000 dead and three times as many wounded. Abadan, on the other hand, is defended by about 10,000 regular troops — a mechanized brigade, a mechanized battalion, a naval battalion, an armoured brigade with some 50 tanks, in addition to about 5,000 battle-tested Pasdaran.

During the spring much was said about an imminent attack on Abadan, for the Iraqi President was allegedly in need of a major military gain to please his people. To attack Abadan the Iraqis must overcome formidable problems. The island city has many defensive advantages. To its north directly across the Karun River lies Khoramshahr. To the west lies Shat-al-Arab and to the east Bahmanshir River which is a tributary of the Karun. To the south-east there are huge marshes. In between these two natural defensive obstacles lies a single road to Khosrowabad. Early in the autumn the Iraqis crossed the Karun by laying down four pontoon bridges, but they have neither crossed the Bahmanshir nor cut off the road to Khosrowabad. It is via this road that Abadan is being supplied.

Iraqi field commanders have cited political reasons for not having completed the noose around Abadan before the winter turned the marshes into huge lakes. None the less, the stalemate has been sustained because the Iranians too had failed to open up additional connecting roads to Abadan. Between November and January the city garrison twice tried to link up with an advancing column coming down the road from the east, but faced tough Iraqi resistance and had to turn back.

A week after the first anniversary of the war, 22 September, the Iranians launched a successful counter-attack to lift the siege of Abadan. After twelve hours of heavy fighting they succeeded in pushing the Iraqis to the western shores of the Karun River. Close to 2,000 prisoners were taken and scores of tanks and armoured personnel-carriers were captured. The Iraqis acknowledged their withdrawal to the western shores of the Karun for 'tactical' reasons and have instead resumed the heavy shelling of the city, with considerable civilian casualities.[18]

This successful counter-offensive has not radically altered the standoff in the war. In the central sector around Susangerd, the stale-mate resulting from the unsuccessful counter-offensive by Iran in February, persists. Likewise the stalemate in the air war seems to hold. After some spectacular bombing by both sides, in which the Iranian US-equipped war planes gave a more impressive account of themselves, the air war has literally ended. The supply routes to Iraq from Jordan, Turkey, Saudi Arabia and Kuwait work to full capacity. Iraq's two pipelines across Turkey and Syria carry between 600,000 and 100,000 barrels of oil daily. Despite the destruction of the main Iraqi offshore terminal in the Gulf early in the war, the Iraqis have not destroyed the main Iranian pipeline sending oil from Khark Island to Tehran. Either because most of the pipeline is underground or because of political considerations, this aspect of the war is also stalemated.

There is no doubt that if this is the result of mutual restraint it is also due to the casualties and destruction of the first three months of the war. Iranian sources acknowledge that nearly 2 million people from Khuzistan have either become homeless or have moved out of threatened towns and villages.[19] Iran's military and civilian casualties, according to the best estimates, range from 20,000 to 30,000 dead and several times that many wounded.

The Iraqis have lost from 6,000 to 10,000 in the war and several more thousands as a result of the early bombing by the Iranian Air Force of Basra, Baghdad, Mosul and Kirkuk. Some 100,000 civilians have also reportedly been evacuated from Basra and its surroundings. This being the case, at the end of the autumn of 1981 and in the absence of any major Iraqi offensive and Iranian counter-offensive, the question as to why a truce cannot be arranged has puzzled officials and military analysts alike.

The Divergent Positions on a Truce

From the outset Iran viewed the war as an act of aggression and demanded not only the total withdrawal of the invading Iraqi army, but condemnation of Hossein's regime as an aggressor and compensation for damages to Iranian towns and installations. Thus, any suggestion of a cease-fire while the Iraqis were still on Iranian soil was adamantly rejected until recently. In April 1981 the Iranians seemed to have agreed to a cease-fire as a first step for an Iraqi pull-back. On the question of sovereignty over Shat-al-Arab, the idea of arbitration by an Islamic committee has been implicitly accepted by both sides, but there is disagreement as to when this should be done, with Iran insisting that this should follow the complete withdrawal of Iraqi forces and Iraq demanding that it be done simultaneously with the cease-fire. Furthermore, Iran wishes the committee to determine who was responsible for the war, which suggests some modifications of the original demand that

Iraq should admit its responsibility for doing so.

The Iraqis have not accepted these terms. They seem to be genuinely willing to return all their occupied territories in return for the two border enclaves and the recognition of their sovereignty over Shat-al-Arab. They are on record as pledging that unless Iran recognizes their sovereignty over the Shat they will not begin pulling back, even though a cease-fire can be agreed upon. Although Iraq's continuing occupation of some Iranian territory appears to give it the upper-hand, the situation has presented the Iraqi government with a certain dilemma. If Iraq launches another offensive, say to capture Abadan, Dezful or Ahwaz, it must risk heavy casualties. If it accepts the Iranian terms to settle the dispute it must abandon nearly all of the political and military objectives for which it launched the offensive in the first place.

Despite growing internal conflict within Iran, Iraq could not confidently rely on an internal revolt in the non-occupied areas of Khuzistan by Arab Iranians. The so-called Arabistan National Liberation Front, which supposedly represents the dissident Arab Iranians of Khuzistan, has not been able, and is not likely in the future, to function as a fifth column for the Iraqi Army. This is not to say that militarily the Iraqis are in a desperate situation. Since the outbreak of the war, eight of its twelve army divisions have been fighting Iran; one division is located on the Syrian front and the other three are guarding Kurdistan, even though since the 1975 agreement usually six divisions had been used to guard the still-disgruntled Kurds.

Despite what some military analysts regard as an overstretching of its military forces, Iraq has ample sources of material and financial support from Arab and European sources and therefore has the capacity to prolong the existing stalemate. None the less, since the destruction in June 1981 of Iraq's nuclear facilities by the Israeli Air Force, a more sober mood seems to mark the Iraqi attitude. In a rare news conference at the end of June 1981, Saddam Hossein sounded an extremely conciliatory note towards Iran at the very time that internal chaos had reached a new height in the Islamic Republic. Reviewing the status of the war with Iran, he acknowledged that his troops had pulled back in several areas including 2.5–3 miles from its furthest advance to the outskirts of Ahwaz. He pointed out that these retreats had little to do with the Iranian counter-offensive, but were necessary for guaranteeing better offense and reducing their losses. Only in two areas of Gilan Gharb and Sare Pole-Zahab have the Iranians been able to regain some lost territories in combat, according to Hossein. More significantly, he made some very sophisticated statements about the war suggesting that it would be very bad if Iran felt it had taken a beating from Iraq, for it would simply hunger for another war, just as Germany had done after World War I, so that it could avenge its defeat. 'We hope that the war will not end under circumstances in which Iran pays a high price, since this would give it a historical complex where we are concerned. When I am talking about a high price, I am referring to its unity.'[20]

What is apparent is that having learned from the serious miscalculations in the initial phase of the war, Hossein is extremely reluctant to repeat his mistakes. Internal considerations may also play a role, for although the war does not seem to be unpopular in Iraq there is no assurance that the military leaders will support a 'neither war nor peace' situation indefinitely. Furthermore, the Kurdish variable may also change in an unexpected way which could upset the present equation. More than Iraq, perhaps the internal vicissitudes of Iranian politics may force each side of the present deadlock to change heart.

Both the new Iranian President and Prime Minister elected after Banisadr, had hardly served a month before their assassination at the end of August. Their replacements could not be expected to go beyond the April modifications of Iran's position. The Islamic Republic can neither enable the still-suspect armed forces to defeat the Iraqis militarily, nor accept the terms for a cease-fire and pull-back of the Iraqi Army that it had frequently and systematically rejected in the past.

A major change in this equation is necessary before the war can formally end. This can come as a result of either a radical change in the Baathist regime or the collapse of Khomeini's government. Both so far have shown an extraordinary staying power, irrespective of heavy odds.

At the time of writing the armies of the two countries are in a stalemate on either side of the Karun and Karkheh Rivers in Khuzistan province. The strength of the Iranian Army in this area is estimated at four and a half divisions, withdrawn from the northern garrisons between Tabriz and Mashad, thus leaving the Soviet–Iranian border virtually unprotected.

On the Iranian side numerous political problems plague the relations between the regular army and the Revolutionary Guards. Apart from a profound suspicion of the regular army, the Pasdaran are ill-equipped for conventional war and reluctant to accept the command of the former. They may, however, have learned the lesson of the February 1981 counter-offensive, for no new attempt had been made since that disastrous experience until the lifting of the siege of Abadan at the end of September. The Iranian Air Force, despite heavy losses, still has about 100 operational combat aircraft, but in the wake of Banisadr's and Rajavi's spectacular flight to France, with the complicity of certain Air Force personnel, the Air Force has been virtually grounded. When and if this constraint is lifted, the US-trained Iranian Air Force could exploit some natural advantages over Iraq such as the closeness of Iraqi targets to the Iranian front line, often only ten minutes' flying time, contrasting with Iranian targets which are dispersed over a much larger area.

It is the Iranian Navy which has denied Iraq the fruits of its limited victory on land. While taking some losses in the initial phase of the war, the Navy has literally bottled-up the Iraqi ports of Basra and Ummul Qasr. They have also kept up supplies to Abadan and have shelled targets across Shat-al-Arab. Compared with Iraq, whose only access to the Persian Gulf is via these ports, Iranian ports on the Gulf and the Arabian Sea have not been put out of action.

In terms of military supplies, both sides have been able to diversify the sources of their arms procurement. France continues to be Iraq's main supplier as evidenced by the recent agreement to sell the Baghdad government 150 tactical ground-support Alpha jet fighters plus 60 Mirage jets. Some Arab states like Egypt, despite political differences, also supply Iraq with Soviet-made spare parts. The Iranians have received some supplies from Moscow, Syria, Libya and North Korea. In July and August 1981 reliable reports indicated the sale of some spare parts for the Iranian Air Force by Israel.[21] But Iran's major problem remains its inadequate overhaul and rebuilding capacity, even though a tank-repair factory in Masjed Soleiman in Khuzistan remains operative.

Neither West nor East

The protracted war with Iraq has compelled the regime to tone down its radical rhetorics and to seek to articulate its foreign-policy tenets. This, however, could not be done as long as internal conflict prevented the regime from speaking with one voice. Once the hostage crisis was resolved the Cabinet, as opposed to the President and the Majlis, acquired ascendency in the area of foreign policy. In one of the most authoritative statements on Iran's new international posture, Minister of State Behzad Nabavi, the architect of the final hostage settlement, reviewed Iran's views and policies at the conference of Non-aligned

Nations held in New Delhi on 12 February 1981.[22] His address was particularly significant because by then Nabavi had become closely identified with the Islamic Republican Party. Previous spokesmen on foreign policy like Banisadr, Ghotbzadeh and Ibrahim Yazdi had all been pushed into oblivion. Nabavi had weathered the storm of protest over the hostage settlement raised by the secular opponents of the regime, including the above personalities.

In his address Nabavi began by criticizing the way non-alignment had been practised until recently. In its former form the concept had become meaningless because many of the professed non-aligned countries could not in practice follow a policy independent of the super-powers. Furthermore, their attempts to play one super-power against another had proved futile because in the process they had been forced to accept many kinds of dependency. How real independence could be achieved and how the non-aligned movement could pursue its original thesis depended on the understanding of major changes in the Third World. According to Nabavi,

> Today in many of the Third World countries a movement has been set afoot that has profound cultural and ideological overtones. The growth of liberation and anti-colonial movements in many nations has placed the foreign-affiliated governments of these nations at a crossroad. One course of action open to them is to change their methods and align themselves with the aspiration of the masses, and let them grow in freedom and acquire self-confidence so that they can lay the foundations for a truly independent and non-aligned foreign policy. The other course, in the wake of this onslaught is to further enlist the support of the super-powers and thus guarantee their survival through them. Sadly enough, the names of a number of nations which have chosen the second alternative appear in the roster of the non-aligned member states. The only remedy for the problems of non-aligned nations is to be sought in the first alternative, that is to say, in returning to self-reliance. If the non-aligned movement were able to recover its true identity and evolve into a real political power, it surely can then fulfill its objectives, or else it cannot claim even a better position than the one presently enjoyed by the innocuous United Nations.

Hostility towards the United Nations was directly related to Iraq's aggression against Iran, although the memories of what Iran regarded as silent acquiescence with regard to the Shah's oppressive policies also played a significant role. Indeed it was because of the ineffectiveness of the UN's specialized agencies in dealing with violations of human rights under the Shah that the new regime made every effort to blunt UN participation in resolving the hostage crisis. When the Security Council refused to condemn Iraq as an aggressor the Iranian regime had even more pronounced grievances against it.

Nabavi recalled that in the mid-1960s at the height of international tension and prestige of the non-aligned movement, there were some leading nations which thought the movement should replace the UN as the protector of the security of the Third World countries. This suggestion did not materialize for several reasons.

First, the charter of the non-aligned movement was weak and directed at preventing super-power influence rather than positive response to them. Secondly, quantity rather than quality had been used as the criterion of membership, thus permitting admission to a number of pro-Western or pro-Soviet nations. Thirdly, the criterion of membership was superficial and confined to non-membership in formal military political alliances, whereas in reality a number of states were fully aligned with either of the blocs without formal treaty relationships. Fourthly, the movement had been unable to arrive at any collective and practical decisions. Fifthly, the spirit prevailing in the organization had been that of compromise and accommodation with the super-powers.

The Iranian minister had concrete suggestions to transform the movement into 'a strong arm in the service of the oppressed people and capable of challenging the dominant position held by the super-powers.' One suggestion was a change in the name of the movement, which as it stood emphasized a negative role rather than something denoting a constructive role. Another was a purge of the movement of countries which were non-aligned in name only. Apart from these two general ideas he offered the following set of proposals for consideration and adoption by the conference.

(1) Financial assistance to be rendered to the poor members of the movement as well as to liberation movements through the creation of an international fund to be established by the member states.

(2) Efforts to be directed for the purpose of reaching economic self-sufficiency and the satisfaction of economic needs of the member nations through mutual co-operation, with a view to accelerating the process of sheltering the member states from the economic pressures of the super-powers through participation in international common markets and other mutual economic and financial devices.

(3) Efforts should be launched with a view to establishing a banking apparatus in order to cut off financial dependency of the member states on the Western banking system. I may call your attention here to the Iranian experience which brought home the lesson that no bank belonging to international money dealers can safely be entrusted with the earnings of the small nations. As soon as these nations initiate the smallest move contrary to the interests of the super-powers and their bankers, their assets become immediately exposed to the threats and vagaries of these international usupers.

(4) The creation of an international news agency to be put at the service of the deprived nations for the purpose of doing away with the propaganda monopoly in the hands of the super-powers.

Iran and the Three Aggressions

Nabavi also took the opportunity to pronounce his government's views on what he called three instances of international acts of aggression. These consisted of the continued aggression against Palestine, the Soviet occupation of Afghanistan and the Iraqi invasion of Iran. On Afghanistan he echoed the hard-line position initially adopted by Sadegh Ghotbzadeh in December 1979. The Islamic Republic considered Barbak Karmal's regime illegal and imposed on the people of Afghanistan by foreign military forces. The total withdrawal of foreign forces was indispensable to finding a political solution. Iran therefore demanded the unconditional withdrawal of Soviet forces so that the Moslem people of Afghanistan could be free to choose their own destiny and install a political order congenial to their national aspirations.

Nabavi urged the conference to oust the Afghan government delegation in favour of representatives of the opposition movement. He did not, however, go as far as Ghotbzadeh, who a year earlier had included a number of Afghan representatives in the Iranian delegation. That action had caused considerable consternation among the Tudeh and other pro-Soviet groups in Iran at the height of the state-sponsored anti-American radicalism. Soviet pressure, added to that of the influential IRP leaders who were suspicious of the ties of the secular former Foreign Minister with the West, had cost Ghotbzadeh his post. Almost a year later, Nabavi could only repeat a general condemnation of the Soviet occupation and a pledge of not becoming a party to any scheme to settle the Afghan crisis which was not compatible with the principles of non-intervention and respect for popular sovereignty. In early November the new government of Mir Hossein Mussavi proposed the formation of an Islamic peace-keeping army to replace the Soviet Army and prepare for a referendum. The Karmal regime promptly rejected the plan as impractical and insane.[23]

Iran did not clarify its position concerning a Soviet proposal about tripartite negotiations between herself and Pakistan and the present Kabul regime. This proposal had been turned down by Pakistan on the grounds that its acceptance would give legitimacy to the Soviet-installed Karmal government. Instead, the Pakistanis wanted four-way negotiations in which the Kabul regime and the Afghan Mojahedin would participate. There were strong indications to suggest that the Iranian attitude was dictated by its desire not to antagonize irreversibly the Soviet Union.

Moscow's attitude towards the Iraqi–Iranian conflict was obvious enough to encourage Iran to secure maximum concessions from the Soviet Union in return for a more restrained position on Afghanistan. Indeed, three significant developments during the first three months of the war showed Soviet susceptibility to Iran's machinations. First was the interruption of the delivery of military hardware to Iraq, the treaty of friendship with that country notwithstanding. Second was permission for flights by Libyan, Iranian and third-party cargo planes carrying sorely needed ammunition and weapons over East European and Russian territories around the Black Sea.[24] A third gesture was the Soviet condoning of close military ties between Iran and North Korea which had been flourishing to an amazing degree in the recent past.

Be that as it may, it was the Iraqi invasion about which Nabavi complained bitterly to the Non-aligned Conference. Denying that Iran had received any military aid from any quarter while Iraq was receiving billions of dollars' worth of all sorts of aid from the 'West and its puppets in the area,' he reiterated that the Iraqi invasion was part of a greater international plot to destroy the Islamic Republic. In reviewing the background to the conflict the Iranian Minister found himself defending the sanctity and inviolability of the Algiers agreement which the Shah had negotiated with Iraq in 1975. As noted elsewhere, the treaty signed on 13 June 1975 was supplemented by four additional agreements signed on 2 December 1975 and duly registered with the UN secretariat. Articles 5 and 6 of the main agreement commit the contracting parties to recognizing the inviolability of the new frontiers and the negotiated settlement of any dispute concerning its interpretation and implementation.

The New International Posture

As noted previously in the analysis of its constitution, the broad principles of Iran's international posture such as non-alignment and Pan-Islamism are laid down in the document. In the wake of the second anniversary of the revolution several authoritative statements concerning this matter became available. In a detailed commentary the organ of the Revolutionary Guards Corps *Message of Revolution* gave some insights into the Islamic Republic's perception of contemporary international relations and Iran's position therein.[25]

According to this analysis the contemporary world is fragmented into territorial entities called countries. In each of these countries a power rules which is called 'Political Supreme Power.' Under this definition over 150 countries have been introduced, which are members of the United Nations Organization. In practice, however, the absolute and total independence of these countries has become restricted. Since World War II two political poles or two social systems have governed the world: the Washington pole and the Moscow pole. Due to their economic and military power, each of these poles has attracted several countries to itself as satellites. Naturally, these countries no longer have the total independence indispensable to a government. For this reason, while the two poles were being formed and strengthened, certain mindful politicians attempted to found a 'Third World.' Marshal Tito in Yugoslavia, Doctor Sukarno in Indonesia, Gamal Abdel Nasser in Egypt, and Nehru in India expressed similar ideas when forming the famous Bandung Conference in 1955, and later the Movement for Non-aligned Countries. They decided to modify the two main poles of capitalism and communism and prevent the obliteration of the independence of smaller countries.

The commentary further claimed that the history of the past quarter of a century had revealed that the efforts of this group had failed as a result of the lack of a totally 'independent' ideology. The non-aligned countries were unable to safeguard themselves against the two well-known poles of East and West because they did not present independent social, cultural, economic and political programmes based upon an ideology separate from capitalism and communism. A study of the 1979 Conference showed that although close to one hundred countries outside the military blocs had joined the Movement, almost every one of them was, in one way or another, dependent upon the superpowers.

For instance, though the Cuban government had been able to

abolish US domination of Cuba in the 1960s, it was today in the hands of the Soviet Union. Cuban soldiers fought where Russia wanted them to and the ideology of the country was also nourished by Russia. Cuba was in practice one of the active satellites of Russia on the continent of America. Saudi Arabia, an Islamic country which was possessed of a focal point for the Moslems of the world and must naturally serve as a promoter of Islamic ideology, had so intermixed with the West that it could hardly be called independent. The entire resources of oil in Saudi Arabia were indisputably controlled by American trusts, the government executed West-dictated policies and strove to stabilize the economic situation of Western industrialized countries.

Cuba and Saudi Arabia were only two examples. Other non-aligned countries in Africa, Asia and the Far East were in a similar condition. Iran before the revolution had also been a secure link in this universal chain of servitude. Its Army and weapons had been under the direct control of the United States and its thousands of advisers. No Iranian military unit could act unnoticed by American agents, and by the American research and military bases which had been discovered only after the revolution. Economically the country had been so permanently dependent that it was assumed the Islamic regime in Iran would yield or collapse immediately after the economic sanctions imposed by the USA and its allies.

Having attacked the non-aligned movement as ineffective and not genuinely independent from the super-powers, the commentary then turned to the foundations of the Islamic Republic's international position. 'The most basic of these foundations is ingrained in the slogan of "neither East nor West". This policy has been successful not only regarding domestic affairs, but it has also guaranteed the perpetuation and continuation of the revolution.' As Iran viewed this concept, it was the culmination of a prolonged quest by the Third World for a solution to the cultural and political domination of the super-powers. However, not only because of the military superiority of the super-powers, but owing to their cultural oppressiveness, those efforts had not succeeded in opening an independent path for the Third World countries.

This independent path was needed because both Western and Marxist ideologies were inappropriate for the Third World countries. According to *Message of Revolution*, the Western ideology of liberalism and capitalism emphasized individualism and materialism. They were based on universalism and the superiority of Western values and denied any validity to other civilizations and cultures. The logical outcome of Western thought in relation to other nations was the invention and propagation of a special economic and ideological system. This system encompassed such phenomena as big-business corporations, multinational companies, assembly industries, consumer goods, propaganda for tourism, communication media, educational systems and so forth. Marxist philosophy, on the other hand, was a collection of ideas and principles expressed sometimes in a scientific jargon and sometimes in a politico-ideological nomenclature. Taking advantage of the egalitarian, justice-seeking spirit of mankind in general, and of the new generation in the Third World countries in particular, Marxism had gained some popularity. The commentary charged that Marxism, like liberalism, believed in an absolute universalism for the philosophy it presented. For this reason Marxism did not regard other modes of thought and ideologies as valid or possessed of any message. Taking advantage of pseudo-scientific analyses, Marxisim tried in particular to impose its own solution on every society. Today, however, it had become clear that this ideology was extraordinarily weak, and one could safely say that it was devoid of any scientific value.

Exporting the Revolution

Was the Islamic Republic dedicated to exporting its revolution beyond the territorial context of its origins? Yes, but not through violence and conquest. The commentary claimed that the Iranian revolution had been the starting point for a fundamental change in the political, economic and social conditions of the region. Considering the *raison d'être* of this revolution, it could never remain confined within the geographical borders of Iran.

> Our revolution overturned a despotic regime which in the course of long years had divested the Iranian people of the majority of social and individual rights, and because of its numerous deviations, had placed itself in a complete deadlock. Political and cultural dependence on the West had led Iranian society into complete stagnation and had turned it, economically, into a purely consuming society.

According to the commentary, the Moslem nations had for long been afflicted with despotic regimes because of the influence and domination of colonialism. Freedom of thought and speech could not be found in these countries as befitted humanity. The Third World,

and the Moslem countries in particular, thirsted for a political and
social renaissance and liberation from the bondage of regimes which
were completely out of contact with the masses.

That is why the redeeming message of the Islamic Revolution has
been swiftly received, in the light of whose progressive logic the
obstacles and barriers created by the expansionists' dissemination
of nationalistic ideas have begun to fade away. The exportation of
the Islamic Revolution is a fact which has encountered broad recep-
tion by the Moslem nations even before we ask for it.

Similar views have been frequently reflected by Khomeini himself.
For example, in a well-known speech given on the occasion of the
'Eyde of Qorban' (Feast of Sacrifice), at a gathering of envoys from
Islamic countries, he explicitly rejected armed measures or military
conquest as a means for the exportation of the revolution. While
expressing a firm belief in the necessity of such an undertaking,
Khomeini reasoned that Moslem nations should learn of their rightful claims. If they did they would not hesitate to take government
back to the people and to liberate them from the influence and domination of the super-powers. The Islamic Republic believed that revolutions were not merchandise to be easily exported from one country to
another. Experience had shown that every social change required the
formation and emergence of ideological grounds and predispositions.
Revolutions were not *coups d'état* to be completed by changing a few
generals as heads of an army. The mission of revolutions was a fundamental transformation of the political, economic, and above all,
cultural systems of the people. Moreover, the exportation of the Islamic
Revolution, or any other ideology for that matter, relied more than
anything else on success within its own natural boundaries. In
Khomeini's view, Iran since 1979 had achieved such economic, political
and cultural independence that it could act as a model for other Islamic
countries. In a sense this could be called exportation of the Islamic
Revolution by emulation rather than by imposition. Whether the
Islamic Republic could serve as a model for emulation by other Moslem
countries depended on its political viability.

As has been shown in this study, numerous domestic forces currently
reject its legitimacy and seriously challenge its survival. What are the
prospects of the opposing sides in this continuously escalating struggle
for the control of Iran?

Notes

1. Mohammad Reza Pahlavi, *Answer to History* (Stein & Day, New York, 1980).
2. M. Ledeen and W. Lewis, *Debacle: The American Failure in Iran* (Alfred A. Knopf, New York, 1981), p. 224.
3. S. Zabih, *The Communist Movement in Iran* (University of California Press, Berkeley and Los Angeles, 1966), pp. 98–115.
4. 'A Chronological Survey of the Revolution,' in *Iranian Revolution in Perspective*, Iranian Studies, Vol. XIII, Nos. 1–4, 1980, p. 357.
5. Interview with former Iranian Foreign Ministry officials, Paris, 20 February 1981.
6. *New York Times*, 26 January 1980.
7. Shahpour Bakhtiar, Hassan Nazih and Ali Amini were among prominent Iranian leaders in exile who sent telegrams to the United Nations Secretary-General appealing for a world condemnation of the mass executions in Iran. *Iran Post*, Los Angeles, 2 September 1981. Also see Parvis Radji, 'The Chaos in Iran,' *Sunday Times*, London, 5 December 1981.
8. Editorial in *Khabarnameh*, newsletter of *Enghelabe Islami*, 12 October 1981.
9. Pahlavi, *Answer to History*.
10. *Mardom*, organ of the Tudeh Party, 12 March 1981.
11. *Message of Revolution*, publication of the Islamic Revolutionary Guards Corps, Tehran, No. 1, May 1981.
12. Chamran later became the Commander of anti-Iraqi guerrilla forces and died in early summer 1981 in mysterious circumstances. The above quotation from *Mizan*, 12 November 1980.
13. Interview with former Deputy Foreign Minister of Iran, Paris, 21 August 1980.
14. Fred Halliday, *Soviet Policy in the Arc of Crisis* (Institute of Policy Studies, Washington and Amsterdam, 1981), pp. 77–99.
15. During the occupation of the Grand Mosque in Mecca in December 1979 and again during the annual pilgrimage in October 1981, there were several exchanges of letters between Khomeini and Saudi leaders. On the second occasion Khomeini vigorously protested against the action of Saudi police in dispersing and arresting Iranian pilgrims who had demonstrated in favour of Khomeini and the Islamic revolution. 'Their only guilt was to shout slogans against the satanic USA and imperialist Israel,' wrote Khomeini to King Khaled. *Jomhuriye Islami*, Tehran, 21 October 1981.
16. For background see Zabih, 'Iran's Policy towards the Persian Gulf,' *International Journal of Middle East Studies*, No. 7, Los Angeles, 1976.
17. *The Economist*, London, 9 May 1981. Reports on the war are based on daily communiqués of the Islamic Republic Armed Forces as well as those by the Islamic Revolutionary Guards Corps quoted in *Jomhuriye Islami, Keyhan* and *Sobhe Azadegan*. (The last named is the organ of the Pasdaran.)
18. *Keyhan*, 29 September 1981. A week later four senior military commanders who had flown to Abadan to celebrate the occasion died when their military plane crashed near Tehran. The crash, which exiled opposition groups claimed to be sabotage, killed General Valiollah Fallahi, acting Chief of Staff, General Mussa Namju, Defence Minister, General Javad Fakuri, former Air Force Commander and Mohsen Kolahduz, acting Commander of the Islamic Revolutionary Guards Corps. *Ettelaat*, Tehran, 2 October 1981.
19. On 12 September, Asghar Samet, a spokesman for the Interior Ministry, said the war had created 1,870,000 refugees. The Ministry had set up 20 tent cities, the largest being near Jiroft in Kirman province with the capacity of 70,000. According to him only 10,000 refugees had agreed to move there. His figures

indicated that in all 30% of refugees lived in tent cities, 50% in public buildings and mosques and 20% in private houses. He also stated that 60% of the total populations of Ahwaz and Dezful had fled those war ravaged cities. *Statement of Refugee Foundation* (Islamic Republic Ministry of the Interior) Tehran, 12 September 1981.

20. *The Economist*, 9 May 1981.

21. Iranian exile sources in London identified Yousef Nimrud, a former military attaché to the Israeli mission in Iran, as a major figure in arranging military purchases for Iranian emissaries, having good contacts in Greece, Cyprus and other points well known for weapon black-marketeering. Personal interview, 12 April 1981.

22. *Message of Revolution*, No. 1, May 1981, pp. 41–5.

23. *Jomhuriye Islami*, Tehran, 1 November 1981.

24. The shooting down of an Argentine cargo plane by Soviet fighters in August revealed that Cyprus was used as a pick-up point for the transfer of spare parts to Iran. Exile sources in Europe claim to have details of this black-market operation in arms. *Iran Post*, Los Angeles, 21 September 1981.

25. *Message of Revolution*, No. 1, May 1981, pp. 46–50.

10 A PROGNOSIS

Since the outbreak of armed struggle against the regime in June 1981 many questions have been raised about the viability of the Islamic Republic. After every major act of assassination and bombing involving the leaders of government and the ruling IRP, the ability of the regime to survive has been put to the most critical scrutiny. The temptation to compare the revolutionary turmoil of three years earlier with the summer of discontent for Khomeini has been almost irresistible. Any analysis of the regime's survival in the face of a determined armed struggle must first raise the question of how and through what instruments Khomeini exercises power. Secondly, his determination to retain power at almost any price should be understood. Thirdly, the strengths and weaknesses of opposition groups, whether inside the country or in exile need careful probing.

War on Three Fronts

That the regime is in serious trouble can hardly be disputed. In a real sense the embattled Khomeini regime has long been engaged in a three-front war. For over a year it has been trying to throw the Iraqis out of occupied Iranian territories in Khuzistan and Kurdistan. For over two years it has been engaged in the pacification of Kurdistan and more recently Sistan and Baluchistan in the south-eastern regions of the country. The battle against the urban guerrillas which was formally unleashed on 20 June 1981 is the third front. On no front has the regime been able to act conclusively.

As recently as July 1981, while all attention was focused on the bombings and executions in Tehran, Baluchi tribesmen attacked a gendarmerie position outside Zahedan, killing 33 members of the government forces and compelling the authorities to send reinforcements from the capital. Some estimates indicate a total collapse of government authority in these two provinces bordering Pakistan. Baluchi guerrillas, who now number about a thousand, have declared their aim of increasing their strength seven-fold before the end of the year. The Baluchies have three fundamental grievances against the Islamic Republic. As Sunnis they are unhappy with the constitutional recognition of the Twelfth-Imam Shia

196

Jaafari as the official religion. As an ethnically identifiable minority they are dissatisfied with government failures to grant minorities even limited autonomy. As a political force they are distressed at their inability to organize freely political groups in opposition to the IRP single-party monopoly. The proximity to Pakistan and the absence of frontier check points, has made Baluchistan a favourite haven of the regime's opponents. The Freedom Front of Baluchistan, while as yet not a significant threat to Khomeini's regime, is just another characteristic of the third war which began to endanger Iran's territorial integrity almost immediately after the Shah's downfall.

In coping with this seemingly interminable war on three fronts the regime has given priority in accordance to its perception of the immediacy and seriousness of the threat posed by each. There is no doubt that at least since June the highest priority has been given to problem of the urban guerrillas, for the government is fully aware of the role they played in staging the successful insurrection against the Bakhtiar government in February 1979. Once this source of danger had been identified all available means were targeted to contain and eliminate it. The government's ability to do so has depended, to a large measure, on its skill in utilizing its instruments of power. These are diverse, and both coercive and non-coercive and designed to retain the regime in power and to maximize its security.

What are these tools of power? It is above all evident that Khomeini governs through legitimate institutions. No matter what one thinks of the constitution of the Islamic Republic, there is little doubt that with the conduct of the two referenda, one general election, three by-elections for the Majlis, and three presidential elections, the regime has achieved legitimacy. To be sure, each successive election has received less support from the public. The age limit was progressively lowered to encourage maximum participation of the population. In the best traditions of Iranian electoral politics, many illegal means to influence the results of these elections were also utilized. Members of the revolutionary committees throughout the country threatened confiscation of various rationing coupons if identification cards did not show evidence of voting. Khomeini, as we noted, designated voting a religious duty of all 'good Moslems.'

Despite all this, it is important to note that Western democratic standards should not be applied to these procedures, which were used to set up all the institutions of the Republic. As long as the regime is protected by the mantle of legitimacy, such important institutions as the bureaucracy and the military will most probably remain loyal to it. The bureaucracy, through which the day-to-day activities of the government are carried out, has been traditionally reluctant to switch allegiance from any government safeguarded by constitutional legitimacy. Indeed, during the 1978-9 turmoil the bureaucracy was the last institution to join the massive popular anti-Shah movement, and it did so only after the legitimacy of the regime had been questioned by large numbers of political groups and almost all senior clergy leaders. The Shah's regime itself raised the question of its own legitimacy when it tried to co-opt the revolutionary forces at least after early November riots and the inauguration of the short-lived Military Cabinet of General Azhari. As yet nothing of the kind has happened. Although, as noted earlier, senior clerical leaders have voiced harsh criticism against some aspects of Khomeini's regime, they have not yet gone to the extreme of rejecting its legitimacy.

Similarly, the Army has traditionally accepted the legitimacy of the central government and has been slow in joining popular movements clamouring for its denial. Thus, even towards the end of Mossadegh's regime in 1953 the Army's leadership remained by and large loyal to the Prime Minister. It was only when the Shah's decree for his removal was publicized that regional commanders switched their allegiance from Mossadegh to the *coup d'état* regime. This is not to make a definite prognosis about the military's future role in the Iranian crisis. It is simply to point out that the institutionalized armed forces are keenly aware of their oath of allegiance to the Islamic Republic and its supreme leader, Khomeini. Thus, in the crisis over Banisadr's dismissal, the Army Command had no difficulty in accepting Khomeini's order of dismissal of the President as C-in-C, and reaffirming its allegiance to the Imam.

To be sure, an argument could be made that this personal allegiance, reminiscent of Hitler's *Führerprinzip*, is ephemeral and will not survive Khomeini's death. However, the constitution which legitimized Khomeini's supreme command of the armed forces also provides for the process of succession if the *Faghih* dies in office or otherwise becomes incapacitated. The army's attitude toward such an eventuality may therefore depend on whether or not an heir-apparent to Khomeini will be nominated during his life-time. In September 1981 new evidence pointed to the emergence of Ayattolah Montazari as Khomeini's successor. The legitimacy of his office could in this fashion be extended to Montazari and make both the bureaucracy and the Army reluctant to challenge such a transition of power.

The second instrument of Khomeini's power is the Islamic Revolutionary Guards Corps. The corps, known by its Farsi name as Pasdaran, has been the critical means by which Khomeini has tried to (a) counterbalance the regular armed forces, (b) enforce the ruling of the Islamic revolutionary courts, (c) participate in crushing the rebellions of the ethnic minorities, (d) unite the regular armed forces in the war against Iraq, and (e) fight against the guerrilla organizations which since June have carried out armed struggle against the regime.

The Pasdaran has undergone significant command and structure changes designed to improve its efficiency and performance. Whereas at the outset all members of the guerrilla groups who had fought in street battles to defeat the Army and topple the Bakhtiar government were welcome to join, since the summer of 1979 this has no longer been the case. First, members of the Mojahedin and Fedayeen groups were purged, for by then their loyalty to Khomeini had become suspect. Secondly, the necessity of intensive training in both Islamic principles and the military arts became evident when in clashes against the Turkomans in April, and the Kurds in July and August of that year, the Pasdaran gave an extremely poor account of itself. Thirdly, the war with Iraq also showed the need for high military discipline, as well as ability to co-ordinate military operations with the regular armed forces.

For all these reasons the Pasdaran has now become an elite group. Its members are recruited from the partly literate urban poor and the lower middle class. They are given an intensive six-months training in the ideology of the Islamic Republic which includes reading and the passing of tests on three primary texts: the *Qoran*, Imam Ali's *Nahjolbalagheh* and Khomeini's *Velayate Faghih*. Young officers of the regular army have now replaced Palestinian-trained Iranians, and occasionally some Palestinians, as instructors — particularly since the Iraq–Iran war when the regime has become suspicious about the Arab ties of some prominent leaders of the Pasdaran. In November 1981 there were talks about setting up a college-level academy for advanced military education for the Pasdaran.

As a result of the conflict between Banisadr and the Islamic Republican Party, Pasdaran loyalty was heavily taxed, but once Khomeini had sided decisively with the IRP, the Pasdaran turned its back on the President. In the wake of the bomb blast at IRP Headquarters at the end of June 1981, it was the Pasdaran which took prompt action to surround all Army garrisons in the capital in case the blast was part of an attempt to stage a *coup d'état*.

The Pasdaran has nearly 100,000 members organized into brigades and regiments. The High Command is picked directly by Khomeini. In the process of the changes described above Abusharif, a Palestinian-trained Iranian, was replaced by at least three other commanders — each later dismissed as being pro-Arab, pro-Banisadr or pro-Mojahedin. When the armed struggle was declared in June about 20,000 Pasdarans were summoned to the capital city, leaving just over 10,000 of their number in charge of security in the provincial centres. The Pasdaran also frequently provides the firing squads responsible for carrying out the death sentences handed down by the revolutionary courts. Ever since its creation the Pasdaran Commander has been in effect under the direct control of the radical Mullahs who have acted as the Prosecutors-General of the Islamic revolution or as heads of the revolutionary courts in the capital. At the present time Hojatolislam Hossein Mussavi Tabrizi occupies the former position. Because he is a high-ranking member of the IRP, the Pasdaran is thus linked with the ruling party. Close associates of Khomeini believe that the IRP and the Pasdaran compete for the Imam's support and that Khomeini uses one to counter the excessive concentration of power in the hands of the other. Occasional criticism of the Corps by Khomeini is thus related to his effort to retain it under tight control.

The next instrument of the regime is its total control of the media, press, radio and television. Before the revolution Iran had succeeded in establishing a fairly modern network of state-controlled TV and radio stations. Apart from the capital city, 12 provincial cities had regional TV stations and as many as 50 cities and towns operated radio stations. In a country as vast as Iran, with a rate of literacy not exceeding 40 per cent, the state-controlled TV and radio functioned as the most effective medium of communication, and were under the control of the Ministry of Information at the centre and the Departments of Information in the provinces. In the year-long turmoil foreign broadcasts beamed to Iran became a powerful weapon in the hands of exiled opposition groups, and above all Khomeini. As noted in the account of the negotiations between Army leaders and Khomeini's representatives, encouraged by General Robert Huyser, Deputy Commander of NATO forces in January and February, the cessation of the Persian programme of the BBC was one demand that the army leaders insisted upon in return for a pledge for concluding an agreement with the revolutionary forces. Throughout the summer and autumn of 1978, Western European Persian broadcasts, in particular the BBC's, functioned as a channel of communication between opposition leaders and the Iranian population. Announcements of meetings and rallies, and the contents of Khomeini's recorded cassette messages were thus communicated to a much broader cross-section of people than would have been possible by relying solely on the underground press.

For all these reasons, ever since his return to Iran, Khomeini has been keen to assure his control of the state-managed TV and radio network. The directors of the network were changed at least five times before Khomeini found in the person of Hashemi Rafsanjani, brother of the Majlis Speaker, a reliable and totally dedicated manager. Over the past two years access to provincial radio and TV stations has always been the target of ethnic minorities in rebellions against the government. At the end of November and early December 1979, when the Azarbayjanis rose up against the Islamic regime, control of the Tabriz TV station changed hands several times until a battalion of Pasdaran was flown in from Tehran to secure it. Similarly, in Kurdistan bitter fighting has taken place in and around the TV and radio stations in such cities as Mahabad and Orumiyeh.

Khomeini has been extremely skilful in using radio and TV. After every major event, when he needs a mass demonstration, either personally or through his son Ahmad, his appeals will be broadcast and impressive rallies – and more recently funeral processions – will be organized. The radio and TV were equally skilfully utilized by the Militant Students who occupied the US embassy throughout the hostage crisis. Aware of the utmost significance of the media as his only contact with the Iranian masses, Khomeini has ordered special units of Pasdaran to be assigned to guard the headquarters of the Tehran TV and radio stations. Several efforts by the Mojahedin to sabotage the buildings or to infiltrate them have so far failed. A co-ordinated effort to paralyse the government must, and undoubtedly will, include seizing control of the capital's TV and radio stations. In September precisely such a plan was reportedly discovered in one of the 'safe houses' captured from the Mojahedin in the neighbourhood of the TV headquarters. Since then the building has been placed under heavy protection, reportedly equalled only by that of Khomeini's own residence in north Tehran.

Khomeini's control of the treasury is the next significant means of retaining power. This is done in two ways. First, as part of the legitimate government his treasury receives sufficient funds from internal and external sources to meet the payroll of the still vast and largely untouched bureaucracy, and the Army. Additionally, government revenues are used for paying for the importation of foodstuff via the two land routes from Turkey and Pakistan. Despite the considerable deterioration in the country's economic situation, as long as the current level of oil production of about 1 million barrels a day can be maintained, the treasury's revenue of $1.2 billion to $1.6 billion will help sustain Iran's basic needs. The opponents of the regime are acutely aware of this: when the Kurds succeeded in interrupting railways and road links from Turkey to Iran, albeit briefly, last February, the Army recalled its mechanized division from the northern sector of the war front with Iraq to clear these vital links. For similar reasons the government has concentrated all its efforts to keeping the Pakistan–Iran route open by evacuating many of its outposts in the interior of Baluchistan and Sistan, thus giving the tribesmen a free hand to control the hinterland.

Control of the treasury is exercised secondly through the organization of *Vaghf* or religious endowment. The vast network of mosques and religious schools or Madreseh have been traditionally financed from the incomes of religious endowments and government handouts. Indeed, in 1977 when Prime Minister Jamshid Amuzegar reduced the government subsidy by about 40 per cent, clerical opponents of the Shah interpreted the move as an attempt to starve the Shia clergy into submission. Both these sources of income have increased substantially with the advent of the Islamic Republic.

Additionally, Khomeini controls the contribution to the clergy which is known as *Sahme Imam*, or the share which the Imam donates to his representatives, namely the Ayattolahs and lower-rank Mullahs. This control has been a powerful weapon for retaliation against some of the senior Ayattolahs who have gradually turned against him over the last two years. This is done by forcing the Bazaaris and other contributors to pay their donations to the Friday Prayer Imams, who are invariably appointed by Khomeini and loyal to the IRP. In a sense Khomeini is doing to his clerical opponents precisely what the deposed Shah attempted in 1977. Denied adequate contributions, these Shia leaders will be unable to support the schools, charities, hospitals of which they have been the 'holy custodians' ever since these were established in Qom and in Mashad at the turn of the century. Another consequence will be the loss of divinity students, whose room and board have also been paid from these contributions. Knowing the inner system of the finances of the clergy, Khomeini has been merciless in utilizing this 'power-of-the-purse' against his opponents. When he finally broke with senior Ayattolahs Shariatmadari, Qomi and Shirazi, Khomeini appointed new Friday Imams for Mashad, the residence of the latter two. His heir-apparent, Ayattolah Hassanali Montazari in Qom, was given full power over the finances of all clerical establishments in that city.

The successful exercise of the 'power-of-the-purse' evidently depends on the general economic condition of the country. That economic conditions have greatly deteriorated since 1979 is a matter of little dispute. What evades a consensus of opinion relates to the impact of this deterioration on the regime's political viability. Annual reports by the Central Bank both during the Shah's regime and after his downfall, for example, reveal a fairly steady rate of inflation until 1972. For the next five years the rate showed an upsurge of 17 to 25 per cent. Monetary measures, some quite unpopular with the Bazaar, reduced the rate to 13 per cent in 1978. Two years after the revolution the most reliable estimate puts the rate at around 85 per cent, making Iran along with Israel, Turkey and Argentina one of the four countries with the highest rates of inflation. The chief culprit for this high rate is not an increase in demand, because the purchasing power of the public has decreased dramatically since 1979. It is rather the decline in productivity and services to which the political turmoil has contributed immensely.

Unemployment always accompanies low productivity, and between 1972 and 1977 there were about 350,000 unemployed in a work force of 10.6 million, representing 3.5 per cent. In 1978 there was literally no unemployment, considering that about one million foreign workers were employed in the country. By 1981 Iran had about 4 million unemployed in a work force of 11 million, or about 37 per cent. National productivity in the decade of the sixties increased by an annual average of 8 per cent and in the next decade by about 32 per cent. But over the past two and a half years, the best-available data show an annual decline of between 37 and 42 per cent.

By Western standards the deterioration of the Iranian economy has indeed been devastating, causing many analysts to wonder about Iran's economic survival. However, all the evidence suggests that the country has somehow managed to muddle through. Undeniable economic hardship has not generated its negative political imperatives. The large numbers of unemployed workers and the displaced residents of the war-stricken provinces, not only are not starving, but are intimately identified with the 'have nots' (Mostazafin), whose cause Khomeini has championed. The upper middle class and even the middle classes are those most adversely affected by the poor state of the economy and the even more distressing political turmoil. This disaffection has been turned into a political advantage for the regime, which blames Iran's present economic plight on the former regime and its policies, and which allegedly benefited only the 'haves' to the detriment of the 'have nots'.

In short, Iran's economic plight, instead of undermining the regime's ability to sustain itself, has been used as a powerful weapon for intensifying class antagonism by pitting the poor against the better-off. Only if the regime had failed to provide the necessary food staples for the masses of the people, including the millions of unemployed, could one realistically consider economic decline as a challenge to the regime's viability.

The availability of a whole host of tools of power cannot explain their successful utilization. The Shah had as many, if not more formidable resources to exercise authority, yet he was overthrown with considerable ease. In seeking an answer to the question of how Khomeini has been able to govern so far, one should rank his personal determination to retain power as the most compelling reason. This is particularly so if he is compared with the late Shah – at least during the last four months of the latter's rule. All the evidence, ranging from the memoirs of his generals in exile, testimony at revolutionary tribunals, the accounts of some of the nationalist leaders who were in touch with him and co-operated with Khomeini in early 1979, acknowledges that towards the end of the previous summer the late Shah had lost the will and the determination to retain power. Whereas the Shah tried to accommodate the opposition, to form a coalition government with their leaders and, at one point, even to invite Khomeini to return, the Imam has by contrast shown an iron determination to destroy his opponents, to monopolize power totally, and to brand the dissidents as anti-Islamic and even anti-God.

In the body of this study it has been seen how he forced Bazargan out of office, how he purged a secular President, and how by midsummer he decided that even a loyal and truly Maktabi or fundamentalist non-cleric would not suffice in office, and that the hierarchy of power should be filled exclusively by clerics, many of whom had served as his students and were now in their late forties and early fifties. The most brazen manifestation of Khomeini's determination is, however, his brand of Islamic justice which has surpassed some of history's most brutal precedents.

Khomeini's Islamic Justice

As the armed struggle against the regime intensified, the vengeance of Khomeini's retribution increased. During one weekend at the end of September 1981, 128 men and women were executed in Tehran and four provincial centres. The crime of insurrection against the regime was added to two previous categories of crime, namely 'corruption on earth' and 'war against God'. Together they covered a whole gamut of political opposition, ranging from distributing the leaflets of the anti-regime groups to shooting members of the Pasdaran. Government officials showed no inhibition about the scope of retribution. Prosecutor-General Hojatolislam Hossein Mussavi Tabrizi, who had replaced Ayattolah Ali Ghoddusi, assassinated a month earlier, declared that in the future a smaller number of arrested protestors would be imprisoned to save the treasury the expense of their internments. 'There will be street trials at which the testimony of just two Pasdars will be sufficient for death sentences to be carried out on the spot.' Ayattolah Mohamadi Gilani, the Chief Judge of Tehran's revolutionary courts, declared that those who were wounded in the course of resisting arrest or attacking the Pasdaran should be shot on the spot. A third clerical leader serving as a revolutionary prosecutor in Tehran said that even twelve-year-old youths arrested in any protest march against the Islamic regime would not be spared either. In defending this unprecedented vengeance against the opponents of the regime all three had invoked the name of Islam. To them, opposing the Islamic Republic was equivalent to opposing Islam, for which the death penalty had been traditionally sanctioned.

Khomeini himself, several days after issuing a fairly mild statement urging the full and careful application of Islamic justice against prisoners, made sweeping analogies between his regime and that of Shia's First Imam Ali. 'The glorious Imam killed in one day 4,000 of his enemies to protect the faith.' *Time* magazine reported that on 15 September when the notorious Evin prison began to become over-crowded, about 150 prisoners were moved out in the middle of the night by the Pasdaran, shot, and secretly buried in unmarked mass graves. On 22 September a mother betrayed her son to the revolutionary court as a member of the Mojahedin. When arrested she bade him farewell and said, 'First you pray and then you face ultimate justice.' He was executed for having carried a 'Molotov cocktail'. The state radio congratulated the brave mother, wishing that more would follow 'her heroic Islamic example.' Since June examples of Khomeini's

justice have been broadcast daily by the state media. Untold brutalities
are also reported by occasional travellers or from long-distance telephone conversations, all pointing to a determined and systematic plan
literally to kill off the active opponents of the regime.

Justifying harsh retribution in the name of Islam is of dubious
validity. Many Islamic scholars believe Khomeini's standards of justice
are incompatible with Islam. When in September he made the statement
that the Prophet Mohammad brought people round to his way of
thinking by 'incessant sword strokes to the head,' prominent Shia
scholars protested that such action was not recorded in any of the bio-
graphies of the Prophet. *The Economist* reminded the Iranians that
Mohammad's ideas on promoting the Islamic belief were embodied in
the Qoran. Surah 18, verse 29 says, 'The truth is from your Lord, so
whoever will, let him believe, and whoever will not, let him disbelieve.'
Surah 2, verse 56, declares that there is no compulsion in religion.

Equally repulsive to Islam was Gilani's admonition to finish off
wounded rebels because 'they are at war with God.' Behaviour towards
captured enemies is clearly regulated by the Prophet, who declares
in Surah 47, verse 4, 'So when you meet the disbelievers in war, smite
their necks until you have overcome them and made them prisoners.
Afterwards set them free as an act of grace or let them ransom themselves.' Gilani's other statement about the rejection of repentance by
prisoners taken during armed demonstrations was also suspect as to its
compatibility with Qoranic teachings. Surah 2, verse 190, lays down
that resort to violence should be purely defensive. 'Fight in the way
of Allah against those who fight against you, but do not attack them
first. But if they desist, Allah is forgiving, merciful.' Historical evidence
indicated how meticulously the Prophet observed his own injunctions.
When he conquered Mecca he allowed his inveterate foes, the idolaters,
to leave freely. Similarly, when he conquered Medina the Prophet
allowed the Jewish tribe of Bani al Nadheer, which had tried to assassinate him, to leave unharmed. Many Moslem scholars are convinced
that there is simply no congruence between true Islamic precepts
and practice and the vengeful ferocity of the pro-Khomeini Shia
clerics.

These protestations have scarcely deterred Khomeini. His opponents
amongst the Shia clerics seem to be so intimidated that no common
denunciations of recent mass executions have been forthcoming from
inside Iran. Reports of arrests and executions have been daily broadcast by the state radio for maximum impact on dissidents. An atmosphere
of panic has been created that far surpasses the one of the immediate

post-revolution period when hundreds of the Shah's officials were summarily tried and executed.

Other evidence of Khomeini's dogged determination may be offered. Shortly after the August bomb blast which killed both President Rajai and Prime Minister Mohammadjavad Bahonar, two of the Grand Ayattolahs, Golpaygani and Marashi, who despite many reservations had not publicly criticized Khomeini, were approached by some of the Bazaar's elderly leaders with the idea of sending an appeal to Khomeini from all five Grand Ayattolahs to urge an end to the cycle of violence, by persuading both the Mojahedin and the regime to stop all acts of violence and vengeance. In was contemplated that Bazargan or the veteran National Front leader Dr Gholamhossein Sadighi, would be summoned to form an interim government of national reconciliation, a government of technocrats which would exclude all parties, and above all the ruling IRP.

Two of the Grand Ayattolahs, Shariatmadari and Qomi, tried to ascertain Khomeini's expected reaction to the above initiative. The defiant Imam scornfully responded that those who had left politics to him should remain out of them. That statement gave a further proof of his own personal vendetta against the Senior Ayattolahs for committing the two cardinal sins of opposing the clergy's domination of the Islamic Republic, and objecting to his own assumption of supreme authority in accordance with the concept of Velayate Faghih. Those who know Khomeini well are therefore convinced that as long as his health will permit, his determination to rule will not dissipate. It is, however, not unlikely that with his death, of natural causes or otherwise, precisely the kind of temporary formula for governing Iran described above might be adopted. Very few knowledgeable analysts expect that with his departure from the scene an uneventful transfer of power to his heir-apparent Ayattolah Montazari will take place. Be that as it may, Khomeini's will to retain power has been contested by a variety of opposition groups, the most important of which were reviewed in the body of this study. How they are faring, and what their strengths and weaknesses are, must be considered next.

Problems and Prospects of the Guerrilla Organizations

In June 1981 a *de facto* coalition of guerrilla organizations emerged to wage armed struggle against the regime. Based on the best available data drawn from the list of executed guerrillas, the number of arrests, the identity of 'safe houses' raided by the Pasdaran, and statements by the spokesmen of these groups in European and American exile, the following breakdown of guerrilla groups emerges. Without a doubt the most effective, and consequently suffering the highest rate of casualties, is the Mojahedin. In three months of warfare against Khomeini's regime over 700 of their members have lost their lives either in combat or by execution. Their leader Rajavi has declared in Paris that nearly 10,000 of his followers have been imprisoned in Tehran and provincial cities, notably in the Caspian provinces of Gilan and Mazanderan and areas of Kurdistan. During this period the state-controlled media have declared that 60 per cent of arrested dissidents and over 50 per cent of 'safe houses' located and raided by the Pasdaran also belong to the Mojahedin. Similar data rank the Minority Fedayeen of Ashraf Dehghani as the second most effective guerrilla group, with about a 20 per cent share of arrests and executions. The three other groups which represent the other 20 per cent almost equally are the Trotskyite Peykar (Struggle for the Liberation of the Working Class), the Maoist Ranjbaran (Toilers) and the Kurdish Kumeleh.

This last group is composed of Kurds who do not support the Kurdist Democratic Party and who were backed by the Soviet Union when an autonomous Kurdish Republic was established in Iranian Kurdistan in 1945. A review of some of their literature indicates that while largely Marxist in their outlook they reject Soviet support and affiliation, believing that the Kurdish working class in alliance with the peasantry should be relied upon for a genuine Marxist revolution. Theoretically, at least, they give priority to a class revolution as opposed to an autonomy-seeking one. Most of their casualties have occurred in clashes in Kurdistan and Western Azarbayjan, but they are accused by the Pasdaran of providing safe passage for other guerrillas through Kurdistan and helping some of their most wanted leaders across the borders to Turkey and beyond.

Together these guerrilla groups have dealt serious blows to the regime. In three months 120 government and IRP leaders, and twice as many Pasdars have been killed in clashes with the guerrillas. Apart from the Chief Justice, two IRP General Secretaries, revolutionary prosecutors, an incumbent President and former Prime Minister, the guerrillas have targeted Khomeini's chief clerical representatives in such important provincial centres as Tabriz and Mashad. Other data put the total number of executions between June and December 1981 at 1,800, according to the government; at 3,700 according to opposition sources. In the same period nearly 800 pro-Khomeini individuals in and outside the government have been killed.

Remarkable as the guerrillas have been in planning and infiltrating the inner sanctum of government and the ruling party, they have not as yet been successful in promoting a massive uprising on the pattern of the February revolution. Their dedication to their cause, demonstrated by a number of suicidal grenade and bomb attacks on selected targets, has created a measurable sympathy for them. A new cult of martyrdom has been built around the executed guerrillas, some of whom have faced firing squads while still in their early teens. A comparison of the February 1979 insurrection with the present situation leads to some interesting conclusions:

(1) In 1979 a massive popular uprising provided the desirable objective conditions for urban guerrilla warfare by these groups. For the reasons discussed earlier, that mass popular support for the guerrillas has not been forthcoming in the summer and autumn of 1981. Twice the Mojahedin made the mistake of challenging the regime in public rallies, and twice they paid heavily for their mistake. On 20 June they expected their march from Tehran University compound towards the former American embassy to be joined by tens of thousands of fellow-travellers. When the ranks of the young female Mojaheds who formed a protective line around the main body of armed demonstrators were broken by the Pasdaran, the pavements were quickly emptied of the crowds of alleged sympathizers.

(2) In 1979 the guerrillas could melt within huge crowds of demonstrators after each hit-and-run attack on security forces. As of now there is no evidence that a sufficient number of Tehran's population are willing to let the guerrillas use the same tactics. In a sense a major prerequisite for a sustained and successful guerrilla-inspired insurrection is lacking. In the words of Mao, 'Guerrillas need the masses just as fish need the ocean.' For the time being at least, evidence of active popular support for the guerrillas has been lacking. Instead, Khomeini's followers continue to muster large crowds approximating one million as demonstrated recently on three occasions: the funeral processions for Beheshti and 71 other IRP members, the funeral procession for Rajai and Bahonar and a similar ceremony for the senior commanders of the armed forces and the Pasdaran killed in the air crash of 30 September 1981.

(3) The guerrillas' leadership cadres seem to be aware of the fundamental differences between 1981 and 1979 conditions. More recently they

have refused to be drawn into mass confrontations with the Pasdaran and Khomeini's club-wielders. In a sense their tactics have become identical with those used in the course of the 1965-77 underground warfare against the Shah's security forces, rather than with those used in the autumn and winter of 1978-9.

There is no doubt, however, that the scale of their operations, the quality of their arms and their numerical strength surpass those of the 1965-77 era. Nor is there any assurance that they may not ultimately eliminate Khomeini himself. What seems fairly apparent is that unless they can arouse active support among large sectors of Iran's urban population, it is unlikely that they can repeat the February 1979 insurrection. Needless to say, their weakness is directly correlated with the strength of the regime and its determination to retain power. If a prolonged war of attrition starts to sap its determination, as it may yet do, then one can see this third front of warfare seriously plaguing Khomeini's theocracy.

And what about the Iranian military? Will it play a role in political developments? If the answer is yes, what will that role be?

The Military

Despite the decimation of the leadership of the armed forces in the wake of the revolution, the ethnic uprisings throughout 1979 and the Iraqi aggression in September 1980 made the reorganization of the armed forces necessary. Since the start of the armed struggle against the regime the question of the potential role of the military in determining the outcome of that struggle has become a focus of much interest.

Elsewhere it was pointed out that Khomeini's building up of the Pasdaran was designed to counter the regular armed forces and keep them under a tight control. How effective will this control be now that the bulk of the Pasdaran are in open warfare with the guerrilla organizations? Will the Army be encouraged to side with one or the other and tip the balance decisively in favour of one side? Will it sit tight and watch the two sides kill each other off? Is it likely that Khomeini will call upon the armed forces to come to the rescue of his embattled regime? And what about the war with Iraq?

In any attempt to unravel the complex question of the armed forces it should be first borne in mind that the military reflects many of the social and political characteristics of Iranian society. Although concrete evidence of its political orientation is hard to come by, recent Iranian political developments suggest that those members of the armed forces who become politicized for one reason or another, largely correspond to the political line-up of the civilian population. Thus, all the ideological groups from avidly Islamic to Mojahedin, nationalist and pro-Soviet communist, are most likely to have adherents within the military. The opportunity to demonstrate political support for opposition groups will, however, rest on several significant developments:

(1) The war with Iraq has not only preoccupied the military, but has also imposed on it the powerful constraint that any weakening of the central government is bound to benefit the foreign enemy. Traditional nationalism and patriotism have now been infused by Khomeini's *Shiism* to give the war the characteristics of a *Jehad* to defend Iranian Moslems. But what if the war continues indefinitely? Is not history replete with examples of armed forces interfering in politics when stalemate in a foreign war could not be broken by a non-military government?

Whether or not Khomeini deliberately blocks all efforts at mediation in order to keep his military several hundred miles away from the capital cannot be ascertained. Nor is it possible to rule out the counter-productive consequences of a deliberate protraction of the war. However, other important parts of the equation should also be noted.

(2) The military, having suffered greatly at the hands of the revolutionary regime, is most keen to avoid a repetition of the events of the winter of 1979 when, instead of being allowed peacefully to transfer allegiance to the new regime, it became the object of systematic suppression and disintegration.

It is therefore vitally important for the military to have as accurate a diagnosis as possible of the relative strengths of the competing political forces so that it will not end up on the losing side. A poorly planned *coup* such as the one attempted in July 1980 would only result in more massive purges of the armed forces. An analysis of that attempted *coup* has helped both the military and the government to draw concrete lessons.

Close to six hundred Air Force and Army officers who were arrested at the Hamadan Shahrokhi Air Base in Western Iran found that their ranks had been infiltrated by several pro-Tudeh junior officers. So instead of being able to use the base to bomb such targets as Khomeini's residence, the presidential headquarters in Tehran and the Fayziyeh

Seminary in Qom, they were surprised by the Pasdaran on the eve of the unleashing of their plot. The 140 pilots and technicians who were executed also acknowledged that they had planned to release the American hostages and invite Bakhtiar to return to Iran and establish a provisional government, which later would put the issue of a return to monarchy to a public referendum.

The discovery of the plot showed the officers that secrecy and tight security were indispensable to any similar attempts in the future It also showed that any foreign link, however logical in terms of international law or Iran's image in the outside world, was likely to hurt them as long as the xenophobic frenzy of Iranian Shia ideology persisted. The outbreak of the war with Iraq made the military even more vulnerable to the charge of supporting the foreign enemy. For if the attempt to release the American hostages could be justified by the economic and diplomatic harm their imprisonment was bringing to the country, action against the central government could not be defended when Iraqi invaders were in physical occupation of parts of Iranian territory. Indeed, Banisadr was quick to exploit the war and convince Khomeini that some three hundred arrested pilots and technicians should be released to participate in defending the country. The regime seemed equally convinced by the logic of the primacy of Iranian nationalism over all other considerations, even though it chose to ignore it as a concession to Shia fundamentalism.

More than the lesson of the July *coup* attempt and the indecisive war with Iraq, the Iranian military must carefully assess the chances of success by the opposition forces presently engaged in armed struggle against the regime. For the moment neither these forces nor the regime seem eager to involve the military. The guerrilla organizations have carefully avoided attacking Army bases and engaging the regular forces. It is equally apparent that Khomeini continues to rely on the Pasdaran to do the fighting against his internal enemies. The non-involvement of the military in domestic warfare may persist as long as the external war continues. Under two circumstances this enforced non-involvement may end. One is that the guerrillas may be so successful in their war of attrition against the regime that the Pasdaran alone will not be able to safeguard the physical security of government officials, including Khomeini himself. Whether or not in such a circumstance he will ask some units of the armed forces to move back to the capital and assume security duties can be only speculated.

Some of his former associates, including Banisadr, believe that under no circumstance is Khomeini likely to do so. His suspicion of the military is so deeply ingrained that he might risk anything but calling the regular army into action. Indeed, among these risks is the prospect of appealing to the well-organized, pro-Soviet Tudeh Party for help. Unlike Dr Mossadegh, who turned down an offer of support from the Tudeh Party in the desperate days when the CIA-instigated *coup* was about to overthrow his government, Khomeini might show no such reservations. Such an eventuality would be laden with many uncertainties, for it would confront all the political forces with an entirely new set of variables. For one thing it might provoke the Army and the now-silent clerical leaders, together with the Mojahedin, to join in a grand alliance against Khomeini and his communist supporters. This situation in turn may induce the Soviets to intervene in response to the appeal of a fraternal party for help. For another, the military might fragment amongst the various ideological groups, including a small but quite tightly organized Tudeh faction which could support Soviet intervention. Clearly, a state of civil war will emerge if this 'worst-case scenario' materializes. For the time being neither has Khomeini lost his grip on power, which might unleash the above chain of events, nor has the military concluded that the present opposition groups have substantially improved the odds on their victory.

A second development conducive to the intervention of the military has to do with the emergence of popular opposition to the regime reminiscent of the final phase of the 1979 revolution. If and when the bulk of the public becomes alienated from the regime and actively seeks its overthrow, then the military may do what it did in 1979. In other words, the military will join the public rather than initiate action against the government in the conventional fashion. A civilian-military coalition may emerge in a condition of near-anarchy, perhaps with the simultaneous renewal of ethnic uprisings and the total frustration of the urban population at the failure of the government to maintain a modicum of law and order and provide for essential services.

A further factor in such a development is the passive resistance of civil servants and workers through strikes and slowdowns similar to those of the last few months of the Shah. Indeed, the Mojahedin are heavily banking on precisely such a development. They are convinced that once the war of attrition has taken its toll, a mood of desperation and frustration will engulf the country as in the autumn of 1978. The public will then urge the military to intervene and together with the guerrilla groups it will strike to topple the regime.

In view of the above analysis of Khomeini's control of the tools of power and his dogged determination to use them, at the time of writing (autumn 1981) the scenario described is far from being realized. Supposing this second development ultimately emerges, there are no guarantees that the military will welcome co-operation with the guerrilla organizations, some of which, like the Mojahedin, have long advocated the abolition of the present professional army. To prevail, not only will public support for the military need to be overwhelming, but the diehard militant fundamentalists, the pro-Soviet Tudeh Party and the Majority Fedayeen will have to be crushed.

In the midst of these uncertainties, the indisputable fact is that the militant clergy who came to power by the sword can only be overthrown by the sword. The imponderable is not how they may be dislodged from power, but when and at what cost. The safest prognosis is that in Khomeini's lifetime the Shia fundamentalists cannot be dislodged forcibly or otherwise. His life-span could be shortened by a successful act of sabotage or through natural causes. In the vacuum thus created any of the above scenarios has a chance of materializing and various patterns of interplay of the domestic, and maybe even external, forces are likely to emerge.

POSTSCRIPT

Since the bulk of this study was completed in mid-December 1981, Iranian politics have persisted in their tumultuous course. This postscript is intended as a follow-up to the study, dating events since then, and testing when appropriate some of the contents of our final chapter offering a prognosis of the Islamic Republic. To do so we must first review the regime's struggle on the three fronts: the war with Iraq, the resistance against a variety of guerrilla groups and the progressively intensifying struggle for the succession to Khomeini.

In the war with Iraq Iran's fortunes have taken a turn for the better, beginning at the end of 1981. After the lifting of the siege of Abadan, the combined Pasdaran and regular army forces could not immediately take advantage of the significant demoralization of the Iraqi forces. No counter-offensive was launched for the liberation of Khoramshahr, renamed Khuninshahr (city of blood), whose occupation in October 1980 was the high point of Iraq's military success.

Several probing operations in and around the port city evidently convinced the Iranians that without the adequate preparation and re-equipping of their forces, a major counter-offensive for its recapture would end in another catastrophe akin to the one suffered in February 1981 in the Susangerd region.

Instead, the Iranians concentrated on Bostan, a small city midway along the 350-mile war front with Iraq and within 10 miles of Iraq's borders. In an operation code-named *Fathelfotuh* (Arabic for 'victory of victories'), the Iranians succeeded in liberating the town after some of the heaviest fighting since the fall of Khoramshahr. Another 1,000 Iraqis were taken prisoner, and scores of Soviet-made tanks and long-range artillery pieces were captured. Iranian casualties for this operation were quite heavy, but the victory was a significant morale-booster for the Pasdaran and regular army, which were in dire need of some measure of military success.

In the offensive to recapture Bostan the Iranians took full advantage of the element of surprise. A batallion of the regular army was dropped by helicopter 3 miles behind the Iraqi positions. The army then moved through mine-fields which had been cleared by the Pasdaran, several hundred of them having volunteered to risk certain death in carrying out this operation, instead of relying on mine detectors or mules as

215

the army commander had ordered. This operation resulted in the capture of about 1,000 Iraqi regular and irregular forces. To avenge the Pasdaran 'volunteers' who had died clearing paths through the mine-fields, the Iraqi POWs were led through uncleared mine-fields, resulting in the death of approximately 80 per cent of them.

Both governments have since complained to the International Red Cross authorities alleging mistreatment of POWs by the other. In terms of fanatical zeal the Pasdaran have shown a suicidal dedication reminiscent of the human-wave tactics used by the Chinese in the Korean War. With a much larger population supporting them and fighting in defence of their homeland, the Pasdaran clearly enjoyed an advantage over the Iraqis, whose morale is reported to have deteriorated progressively with the lengthening of the war.

Again, this limited military success by the Iranians was not followed up by taking full advantage of its tactical consequences: the Iranians could not reach the border and thus effectively split the Iraqi forces into northern and southern regions. Heavy counter-attacks by the Iraqis were obviously a factor to be considered, but beyond that the operation also underlined the continuous problem of co-ordination between the Pasdaran and the army, as well as the difficulties of the re-supplying and maintenance of arms and equipment.

This latter problem has been compounded by pressing political constraints. From the black market in armaments and from a few friendly countries such as Libya, Syria, North Korea and even Cuba, the regime has been able to acquire a limited quantity of arms or spare parts. But the involvement of such controversial states as Israel or the Soviet Union in these efforts has created negative trade-offs which the Islamic Republic cannot ignore. Additionally, the integration of arms and equipment from such diverse sources into an army which is basically American–British equipped has proved problematical. None the less, in desperation the regime has allowed Soviet technicians to repair Iraqi Soviet-made tanks captured in the clashes in and around Bostan. It has also contracted with North Korea for the supply of shells for heavy artillery, and for Soviet rocket-launchers which were either purchased during the Shah's government or sold to Iran by Israeli and other black-market operators from material captured from the Syrian and Egyptian armies.

All this goes a long way to explain the failure of Iran until recently to expel the Iraqis from all occupied territories, even though this limited success of the Iranians was followed by a more substantial one later.

Next to Khoramshahr the liberation of Qasre Shirin, straddling the common border of the two countries, must be viewed as a test of Iran's military plans. As the anniversary of the revolution, 10–11 February approached, the Iranians tried their best to achieve that military objective, but stiff resistance by the Iraqis and the common problems of inadequate co-ordination and logistics prevented even the highly motivated Pasdaran from presenting the Imam with this greatly prized gift on that auspicious occasion.

However limited the Iranian counter-offensives in early 1982 were, they had serious repercussions for Iraq, as well as for the Arab states of the Gulf, Saudi Arabia and even Jordan. The expulsion of the Iraqi forces from Iran could have serious repercussions for Saddam Hossein. Even if all that the Iranians could achieve was the liberation of the occupied territories, it would totally discredit Hossein and his old (or new) friends in the Arabian Peninsula. Moreover, it would give Khomeini a major boost in his scheme to destabilize the Gulf States and to export his fundamentalist Islamic ideology to the Gulf area and beyond. Khomeini's involvement in the attempt to overthrow the ruler of Bahrain, in addition to the activities of pilgrims to the Haj, to which Saudi Arabia protested vigorously, combined to unsettle these Arab countries.

Responding to Saddam Hossein's pleas, Jordan's King Hossein offered volunteers to fight on the Iraqi side. The Council for Co-operation between Saudi Arabia and the Gulf States moved closer to a defensive alliance to counter Iranian 'designs' for the region. King Hossein presented the war with Iran as a new front endangering all the Arab nations. His supporters in the Arab world pledged generous financial contribution to enable resistance to 'Persian racist aggression' to continue.

The United States was also directly influenced by the apparent turn in the fortunes of the war in favour of Iran. In his visit to Saudi Arabia and Jordan Defense Secretary Caspar Weinberger was given an alarming picture of Iran's potential of destabilizing the Gulf and Arabian Peninsula states. The United States' search for a strategic consensus, so prominently articulated by Foreign Secretary Haig, was subjected to rigorous scrutiny both in Riyadh and Amman. Not only was the threat-perception of these moderate Arab countries basically Israel-oriented, but since the fall of the Shah was increasingly directed at Khomeini's regime, and through it, at the Soviet Union.

What these Arab states pressed upon Weinberger was the necessity of doing 'something' about Khomeini, particularly in view of Iran's recent success in the war and his inevitable disappearance from the scene. Saudi Arabia, as a senior partner of the Gulf Co-operation Council, was adamant in its insistence that the continuation of the present 'non-policy' toward Iran would prove catastrophic for the region and for the United States.

The Saudi concern was conveyed to other Arab countries. Shortly after Weinberger's visit this writer had the opportunity of speaking to US government officials on this issue. The consensus of these officials seemed to be that after a period of neglecting Iran the US Republican administration was now ready to listen to the anxiety of the Gulf States and Saudi Arabia concerning that country. Perhaps it was no coincidence that in early March the American press reported on US government contacts with Khomeini's opponents amongst the military, in Turkey and other countries. The press also confirmed reports of the sale of approximately $200 million-worth of weapons and spare parts to Iran through the intermediary of Israeli secret and not-so-secret agencies.

As far as a peaceful solution to the conflict was concerned, the Iranian government's position hardened in the wake of its latest military success. In mid-March another effort at mediation in the conflict failed. The Islamic Conference mission was told bluntly that the withdrawal of Iraqi forces from Iranian territory remained a *sine qua non* for ending hostilities. On 13 March President Khamenei wrote to Sekou Touré, the head of the Goodwill Mission of Islamic countries, that although the continuation of the war would benefit only the USA, Iran, as the victim of aggression, could not accept Iraq's conditions for ending the war. Reflecting the new confidence resulting from his country's military successes, the Iranian president confirmed that a complete and unconditional withdrawal from Iranian soil, war reparations, punishment of the aggressors and repatriation of the 100,000 Iranians driven out of Iraq were the absolute minimal conditions for ending the war. At no time was even implicit acknowledgement made of Iran's readiness to re-negotiate the 1975 treaty.

The reasons for Iran's persistence in these terms are quite understandable. The war, and all that it entails, continues to preoccupy the armed forces. As related by this writer elsewhere in a syndicated article on the third anniversary of the revolution, the war has revealed a strong sense of nationalism that no amount of Islamic rhetoric by the regime could conceal. The widespread misery, dislocation and heavy casualties have played into the hands of the regime's sense of martyrdom. This has been fully compatible with the Imam Hossein-Karbala syndrome, which the Shia fundamentalists have skilfully exploited. Put differently, the regime has shown that Iran, with about three times the population of Iraq, can afford to sustain the war for as long as minimal military capabilities are available, and for as long as the conditions for terminating it remain incompatible with Iran's territorial integrity. While the near stalemate in the war persisted other problems loomed in the background of the war. One had to do with Iran's initiative in allowing the families of the nearly 7,000 POWs that each held until 21 March 1982 to visit their captured relatives. After much hesitation, partly due to Iraq's reluctance to allow the Islamic Republic to exploit this move on the occasion of its third anniversary, the arrangements were mutually agreed upon. Kuwait, which has misgivings about both countries for their hegemonic tendencies, but none the less as an Arab country is closer to Iraq, used its good offices in this matter.

In a related matter in Bahrain, Khomeini's agents, organized as the *Islamic Front for Liberation* and involved in an attempt to topple the government there, were put in jail. Seventy-three of their leaders, all either Iranian or leftist Shia Bahrainees, were accused of anti-state subversive activities. This and the continued exhortation by the Islamic regime in Iran to the Arab people of the Gulf to overthrow their incumbent governments are being fully exploited by Iraq.

Similarly, the approach of the non-aligned conference to be held in Iraq in September 1982, has compounded the question of the Iran–Iraq war. Reliable reports speak of indirect contact with Israel and the USA for the purpose of assuring the security of the conference.

Apart from condoning or even initiating the sale of arms to Iran, the Israeli Air Force, at least since the autumn of 1981, has played a critical role in events by its virtual grounding of the Iraqi Air Force as far as the war with Iran is concerned. This is done by the overflight of Israeli aircraft of Iraqi air bases in the north-west of the country, and even near the capital city, to distract and preoccupy the Iraqi Air Force. Official communiqués from both sides confirm a noticeable reduction in air sorties in the recent past, even though the Iraqi Air Force has been re-equipped almost to the pre-war level by France and other countries.

In January and February 1982, while Iran launched a diplomatic campaign to persuade the non-aligned countries not to meet in Baghdad as long as Iraqis were in occupation of Iranian soil, Saudi Arabia, Jordan and Egypt were pressurizing the USA to do one of two things: to persuade the Israelis to desist from flying their aircraft over Iraq, or if that failed to provide an umbrella for protection against Iranian air attack on the capital city while the conference was in session.

With the approach of the Iranian New Year, 21 March, the war once more flared up. While peace mediations continued in Iran and Iraq, the Iranian forces prepared for another offensive which proved to be the most successful of more than 20 months of warfare.

The day after the Iranian New Year the combined forces of the Pasdaran and the regular armed forces launched another offensive to free Iraqi-occupied territory, this time to the east of Dezful and Shush, on the southern front. The initial objectives were to reach the pre-September 1980 Iran–Iraq border, and failing that to push back elements of Iraq's 4th Army sufficiently far from these cities to make them secure against Iraqi long-range artillery and surface-to-surface missiles.

During 20 months of warfare these Iraqi weapons had caused great devastation in the two cities and the neighbouring townships and hamlets. However, determined resistance by the Iranian forces, above all the fanatical Pasdaran, had prevented the seizures of these cities, even though on two occasions at least Iraqi forces had reached the perimeters of these prized military and political objectives. Dezful, in particular, was the main target of the Iraqis, for not only did it constitute the main link between Khuzistan province and Ahevaz, its provincial centre, and Tehran, but it also contained one of the most important Iranian Air Force bases, Vahdati.

The operation, code-named *Fatholmobin* (Arabic for 'blessed victory'), was a tremendous victory for the Iranians. In seven days of often bitter fighting the Iraqi 4th Army was decimated. Three of its four divisions were wiped out, losing close to 15,000 prisoners and at least 5,000 dead and wounded. About 700 tanks, armed personnel carriers, heavy artillery pieces and even a few Soviet-made SAM missiles were either destroyed or captured. About 1,800 square miles of land between the two cities and the 1980 border were freed, and the Iranian forces advanced to within 10 miles of the border. The Associated Press reported from Chenareh, near Dezful, that Iraqis were still in control of a 10-mile perimeter encircling the Iranian towns of Samaida and Fuka, and were regrouping west of the Doveriyeh River which runs south along a salient of far-western Iran.

Baghdad acknowledged the defeat by announcing the planned 'relocation' of the Iraqi 4th Army. To be sure, Iranian losses, especially among the Pasdaran, were also heavy, ranging between 3,000 and 7,000 killed or captured, depending on whose account was to be believed. What is, however, beyond any doubt is that this operation was both well co-ordinated and well executed. Unlike the February operation in the Bostan area where the Pasdaran, ignoring the commands of the regular armed forces, brought havoc on themselves and prevented the artillery and Air Force from giving them close-combat support for fear of harming their own forces, this time things went quite smoothly. Nothing could demonstrate the significance of the Iraqi setback better than the panic it caused in Baghdad. President Saddam Hossein urgently appealed for help from supporting Arab countries. Jordan's King Hossein flew to Baghdad where he received a gloomy first-hand report of the Iraqi military fiasco. The Iranians disclosed that a number of Tunisian and Egyptian 'volunteers' among the Iraqi forces had been killed or captured in this offensive. Both Saudi Arabia and Kuwait sounded the alarm in Western diplomatic circles. If the momentum of the Iranian victory was allowed to continue, not only would the Iraqi armies inside Iran be split and possibly surrounded, but nothing could stop the Iranians from advancing beyond the borders toward Baghdad, then a mere 120 miles away from the farthest point of the Iranian advance.

A subdued Saddam Hossein told his countrymen that the question now was not simply on which side of the border their forces were to consolidate, but rather how the defence of the homeland could be assured through correct strategic and military decisions. For the first time the Iraqi leadership was acknowledging the prospect of military advances by the Iranians inside Iraqi territories. Such an advance, however limited and tactical in nature, was precisely what some Iranian military commanders had advocated, on the theory that establishing even a limited enclave across the border near Bostan or Qasre Shirin would have a devastatingly demoralizing impact on the Iraqis. They would be forced to evacuate or otherwise weaken their forces in their prized possession of Khoramshahr; and they would be forced to sue for peace in earnest, just as the crossing by Israeli forces of the Suez into Egyptian territory in the 1973 war had generated the panic which forced President Sadat literally to beg his enemies for peace.

Without ruling out such a military plan the Iranians seemed aware of several possible constraints. One was that moving the battle zone into Iraq proper would give the Iraqi government precisely the kind of advantage that had eventually turned the fortunes of the war in Iran's favour. That is to say, defending their own homeland, however controversial its exact boundaries, would immeasurably bolster the Iraqi stance, by appealing to the innate Arab sense of patriotism and nationalism of the population.

A second possible constraint was that militarily the Iranians had as yet not acquired the degree of superiority which would enable them to pull off such a sophisticated strategic project. Over-concentration on the central and northern sectors of the front could always renew the serious threat to Abadan, which had been effectively under siege for more than a year.

Then there were some important political considerations, both internal and international. Internally the Moslem fundamentalists were patently aware of the possibility of a military challenge to their own authority if the war went too well without being attributed to the Pasdaran alone. Indeed, in congratulatory messages to both the regular army commander and those of the Pasdaran and a newly formed Militia composed mainly of teenagers (Sepahe Basij), Khomeini was careful to give them all equal credit. By the same token he made sure that a fundamentalist, Nategh Nouri, would be his deptuy as C-in-C. Additionally, Colonel Hossein Hassani Saadi, the overall commander of the 21st Infantry Division and the two regiments of Pasdaran responsible for decimating the Iraqi 4th Army, was routinely rotated. A week later reports about the arrest of Sadegh Ghotbzadeh, another revolutionary leader being devoured by the revolution itself, implicated some officers in another attempt to topple Khomeini.

Thus, at the massive ceremony commemorating the fourth anniversary of the Islamic Republic on 1 April 1982, and on the following Friday when over 10,000 hapless Iraqi prisoners were paraded, each carrying a portrait of the Imam, the more responsible government officials, such as President Ali Khamenei, disclaimed any plan to violate Iraq's territorial integrity. That pledge did not, however, cover up Iran's plans to maximize its efforts to topple the Saddam regime. Close to 20,000 POWs are being carefully indoctrinated into the virtues of Islamic government as set up in Iran. The majority of them being Shia, though non-Iranian, are reportedly responding to these efforts, and thereby causing some concern about an exchange of POWs, even though it would benefit Iraq, which holds only about half as many Iranian POWs as its own people held in POW camps in Iran.

This aspect of the war, namely a personal and vengeful campaign to topple Saddam Hossein, is almost fully controlled by Khomeini's political associates with radical fundamentalist beliefs. The less radical in the Islamic government are aware of another political constraint in any concerted move to carry the war into Iraqi territory.

This constraint has to do with Soviet–Iraqi relations, and indeed with regional Arab–Iranian relations in the Gulf. A few days after the *Fatholmobin* operation, President Brezhnev sent a most friendly message to commemorate the tenth anniversary of the Soviet-Iraqi Treaty of Friendship. Though the treaty is not, strictly speaking, a mutual defence pact, it is important to note that it commits the Soviets to co-operation and consultation with Iraq on issues of defence and military policies.

To students of Soviet policy in the region since the war began in September 1980, this could only be construed as perhaps a not-too-subtle reminder that while the Soviets remained by and large neutral when the Iraqis were on the offensive, they would not so remain if and when the Iranian side carried the war into Iraqi territories. Indeed, this writer was told by the highest intelligence sources in Europe early in April 1982 that the Soviets had resumed shipments of military hardware to Iraq. One week after Iran had publicly celebrated the putting of Dezful outside the range of Iraqi land missiles, several Soviet-supplied SCUDs landed in and around that city, making the celebrations somewhat premature.

While one super-power must therefore be reckoned with in any plan to transform a legitimate defensive war into a punitive aggressive one, the other super-power should be considered in terms of the Gulf and Saudi Arabian Peninsula. Thus the United States, which from February 1982 began to pay more attention to 'Iran after Khomeini', was prompt to reassert its long-standing policy of respect for the territorial integrity of all states within the region, and this of course was taken to mean that it would not stand for the military or non-military expansion of the Iranian revolution beyond its borders to the south and south-west.

As noted elsewhere, apart from its important regional and international ramifications, the war with Iraq has many internal implications, of which the most important is the prospect of the army's intervention before or after the disappearance of Khomeini. All the participants in the succession battle are fully aware of that prospect. In April the Majlis passed a law exempting young Iranians from the 2-year draft if they volunteered to join the Pasdaran. Not only are the pay and fringe benefits of the Pasdaran superior to those of the regular conscripted soldiers, but the Pasdaran also exercises considerable political power in terms of neighbourhood control and the distribution of ration coupons throughout the country.

The Mullahs who function as political commissars with every unit of the armed forces have seen to it that, as an additional incentive, the more dedicated Pasdars are able to join the prestigious Air Force and mechanized units. The net result is that the ranks of the regular armed forces are rapidly thinning, and with or without peace with Iraq, according to Iranian military leaders in exile, the army could be effectively replaced by the Pasdaran within the next three years.

What contributes to the continuing concern of the Islamic fundamentalists about the Iranian military is the continuing evidence of the involvement of certain military officers in various reported plots against the regime. In the latest of such schemes, leading to Ghotbzadeh's arrest, scores of officers were implicated, with three colonels amongst the 50 ring-leaders of the conspiracy, in a plot to destroy Khomeini's residence while he was giving audience to the senior civilian and military leaders of the regime.

Other interesting accounts of this episode have to do with the considerable improvement in the counter-intelligence operations of the Islamic regime's security organization. For over three months reports have been circulated about the involvement of Soviet and/or East German experts in running, or advising the officials of, this agency. Though the government has steadfastly denied these reports, there is little doubt that since the end of 1981 the government has been more successful in its fight against the various guerrilla organizations. The discovery of the Ghotbzadeh plot has been also linked to foreign agents, this time the Syrians, who for their own political reasons apparently decided to disclose sensitive information concerning that alleged plot.

According to Iranian sources in exile which have previously proved to be quite well informed, Ghotbzadeh discussed some aspects of the plot with the Syrian foreign minister, who was on an official visit to Tehran early in March. The Syrian wanted to forestall any move by Khomeini in support of Ikhvan al-Muslemin, the fundamentalist radical Moslem organization, whose rebellion in the city of Homs had just been crushed with heavy losses. Khomeini's old ties with and natural sympathies for the Ikhvan should have led to his all-out condemnation of President Assad's government after this event, but the Syrians took several measures to cultivate Khomeini's friendship. One was to sign an agreement to barter Iranian oil for much-needed food supplies. Another was to close their borders with fellow Arab-Iraqis and shut off the pipeline through which 30 per cent of Iraq's post-war (Iran–Iraq War, 1980) crude oil of about 800,000 barrels a day was trans-shipped to the Mediterranean terminal on the Syrian coast. More importantly, when the Syrian foreign minister reported on the information passed to him by his old and once-trusted Iranian counterpart, President Assad ordered that Khomeini's government should at once be furnished with the information which four days later led to Ghotbzadeh's arrest, along with his 50-odd co-conspirators.

Other interesting information on this episode reveals that the Argentine-born French resident, Hector Villalon, who was deeply involved in the US hostage crisis, was acting as a link between the exiled Iranian groups and the Ghotbzadeh plotters. Mohammad Reyshahri, the *Qazi shar*, or Islamic judge of the armed forces, 'had no doubts that Villalon was an operative of the Central Intelligence Agency, and just as the American media had revealed recently, the CIA was financing the military and civilian opposition plotting Khomeini's overthrow.'

Whether these alleged foreign connections in this latest plot against Khomeini prove accurate remains to be seen. What is not in question is that the fundamentalists are using it to remove the last vestige of even the most silent opposition to their regime at a time when they know a fierce struggle for the succession will break out, perhaps even before Khomeini's coming incapacity to continue governing. As noted elsewhere, one of the chief targets is Ayattolah Shariatmadari, the senior leader of the majority of the Azarbayjanis, who constitute about 6 million of the country's population.

In a televised confession Ghotbzadeh reported that Ayattolah Shariatmadari had let it be known that while he could contribute nothing to the execution of the plot against Khomeini, if it succeeded he would consider making a public statement in its support. Reyshahri, himself, stated that he did not believe the senior Ayattolah had been informed of the plot. None the less, an orchestrated effort to discredit and even to defrock him was set in motion at once. The so-called *Howzeye Elmiyeh Qom*, scientific circle of the holy city, which is in full control of Khomeini's diehards, appealed to the Imam that Shariatmadari must be at least demoted from a senior to a regular Ayattolah. The more radical clerics appealed for him to be defrocked, a practice which is non-existent in Shia tradition, although it is a punitive measure used by the Catholic hierarchy. The fear of many Iranians centres on the real intentions toward Shariatmadari. In Khomeini's Iran Ayattolahs have been arrested, exiled and even, it is alleged, killed, but such extreme measures have not been taken against any of the Grand Ayattolahs, even though two of them, Shariatmadari and Qomi, have been placed under a *de facto* house arrest for quite a long time.

As mentioned earlier, it may be that the plot has become so entangled with the struggle already brewing for Khomeini's succession that the real intention of the government toward its most formidable clerical opponent will never be revealed. It is equally clear that physical harm to the ageing Shariatmadari may be averted by the realization that not only would Azarbayjan most probably explode in rebellion, but also that once the precedent of the physical elimination of a senior cleric was established, there would be no way of knowing when and against whom such drastic measures might be taken in an extremely volatile and uncertain future.

The Internal Front

The struggle of the regime against its many armed and un-armed enemies has continued unabated. The massive and ferocious retaliation against armed resistance groups, notably the Mojahedin, was bound to affect the scope and intensity of the armed opposition to the regime. Shortly before its third anniversary the Islamic regime scored some impressive successes in this front. Mussa Khiyabani, the Commander of the Mojahedin, his wife and the wife of Massud Rajavi, the leader of the group now in exile in Paris, were ambushed and killed. An armed attack by guerrillas at the end of January on the Caspian city of Amol was successfully repulsed. In this second incident the Mojahedin were joined by a new guerrilla group called *Sarbedaran* (literally, 'hanged by the head'); all of which indicates that the end of urban guerrilla warfare against the regime is not yet in sight.

Radio Mojahed, the clandestine radio operating from somewhere in Kurdistan, broadcasts daily reports of clashes with the Pasdaran and armed members of various revolutionary committees. The Mojahedin's office in Paris, announcing the ambush and death of Khiyabani and his comrades-in-arms, revealed that new leaders had been appointed, but for security reasons would not be named. Rajavi appealed to the UN for news about three infants, including his own two-year-old son, who were caught in the ambush and were under government 'protection'. By way of a somewhat cruel joke the Islamic regime invited Rajavi to return to Iran and take care of his infant son 'if paternal instinct meant anything to him.'

That the Mojahedin were still capable of waging guerrilla war against the regime became once again obvious when in late March 1982 a limited, but quite dramatic uprising was staged at the Lavizan army garrison in the heart of Tehran. A squad of Mojahedin in army uniforms penetrated the base, and in collaboration with scores of sympathizers among the soldiers and NCOs took over the base and killed ten officers who were actively involved in purging Mojahedin sympathizers from the base. Additionally, the officers in charge of The Islamic Society and counter-intelligence were killed. Before the Pasdaran could reach the base, the Mojahedin infiltrators, together with their comrades within the base, succeeded in escaping.

The Mojahedin continue to pay a heavy price for their relentless armed struggle against Khomeini. In April the author was supplied, at the Mojahedin office in Paris, with irrefutable evidence of the brutality of Khomeini's retaliation. Birth certificates and copies of burial certificates, issued by the Islamic government's coroner's office in Tehran and Ahwaz, showed that a 16-year-old girl and two boys, aged 13 and 17, had been executed by revolutionary courts. In the case of the young girl the judge prohibited her relatives from burying her in the Moslem cemetery.

These documents show that close to 25 per cent of all Mojahedin members executed between June 1981 and April 1982 were teenagers, and that their crimes ranged from simple membership of the group to active participation in guerrilla operations, some of them leading to the deaths of government officials.

The struggle in the domestic front extends to groups other than the Mojahedin or several leftist anti-Khomeini organizations. In the attack on Amol, which coincided with the anniversary of the late Shah's so-called 'white revolution', and in a major bomb blast near Eshratabad military base, which coincided with the anniversary of Reza Shah's *coup d'état* in 1920, other groups were involved. CIA-leaked press reports and personal interviews with reliable sources leave no doubt in the writer's mind that exiled military groups, particularly in Turkey and parts of 'liberated' Iranian Kurdistan, have become increasingly active over the last few months.

Further evidence pointing to the same conclusion is the regime's periodic discovery of plots for *coups d'état*, which are usually 'nipped in the bud because of the alertness of Iran's 20-million-strong network of intelligence operatives.' In early March another such discovery was proclaimed, leading to the arrest and prompt execution of scores of Air Force and other officers.

The most active of these groups continue to be: ARA (Iran Liberation Army) created by General Oveissi and representing, by and large, monarchist officers, *Pars* (Pre-Islamic name for Iran), which is of a more recent origin and reportedly not as committed to the Pahlavi family as ARA, but none the less extremely nationalistic and patriotic. *Ariya*, a recently organized group, mainly of Air Force officers, is active both inside and outside Iran. As to the *Sarbedaran*, indications are that this group is quite heterogeneous in composition and ideological orientation. Its membership is mostly civilian, but it also includes some retired officers.

The Kurdish issue, whether from an internal or from a regional perspective, cannot simply be brushed aside. In early April the KDP leader, Dr Ghassemlou, wrote in *Le Monde* that despite the overall turmoil in Iran, Kurdistan remains a bastion of the democratic forces.

The Kurds are in control of a vast territory twice the size of Switzerland, even though 45,000 regular Iranian troops and nearly same number of Pasdaran continue to harass about 12,000 Pishmargs (Kurdish for 'death welcomers') as well as 20,000 armed peasants. Not only it is a sanctuary for our fellow combatants against the oppressive Khomeini theocracy, but for anyone who is being hunted down by the authorities.

The Kurdish leader stated that in the course of the two and a half years of war the Kurds had lost more than 15,000, of whom 85 per cent were civilian.

Atrocities committed by Khomeini's armed gangs in the name of Islam abound. Such hamlets and towns as Ghalatan, Sofi and Gharne have left indelible memories for our people. None the less, the Kurds in these difficult years have reinforced their unity. Outside the KDP, which is supported by 80 per cent of the people, Kumeleh is the only organized extreme leftist group which has survived the war.

In the liberated area the KDP has organized a network of administrative units of popular councils elected by direct universal suffrage. Numerous villages are now managed by these councils, and by the end of the current year the entire region will be managed by them.

In September 1981 500 primary schools were established to teach 25,000 students in the Kurdish language.

In the medical field the situation is grim, and such international organizations as the Red Cross have not dared to send missions to ascertain the dire medical needs of our people, although a number of French medical teams have been most forthcoming in helping to operate the three main Kurdish hospitals,

wrote Dr Ghassemlou.

Even though the campaign against armed organizations, in addition to the war with Iraq was sufficient to preoccupy the Islamic regime, other 'enemies' of the Shia theocracy were not completely forgotten. With the appointment of Aliakbar Velayati as foreign minister a concerted effort to repress the Bahai community was unleashed. As a member of the secretive *Hojatiyeh* (Arabic for 'Islamic logic') group, Velayati convinced his clerical colleagues that the 300,000 members of the community in Iran should be finally and completely eradicated.

After repeated warnings against holding religious meetings had been ignored, 18 members of the Bahais' national and Tehran assemblies were executed, at the end of December 1981 and early January 1982. The group included two converted Jews, Iskandar and Jalal Azizi, who were reportedly given the opportunity either of returning to the Jewish faith, a recognized minority religion, or, even better, converting to Islam. Additionally, the members of the community were ordered to produce a certificate of conversion in order to be admitted to state schools and to secure government documents. More ominously, as of 21 March 1982 no ration coupons were to be issued to those whose faith was not formally recognized under the Islamic Constitution. Government newspapers carried long columns of announcements of conversion to the 'noble religion of Islam' by hundreds of intimidated members of the Bahai faith.

The outcry by the international media as well as by human-rights organizations, including the New York-based Freedom House, Amnesty International and the prestigious Committee for the Free World, however, appeared to have persuaded the Iranian regime to move back from the brink of a 'final solution' to the Bahai problem. President Khamenei denied that the Bahais were being persecuted because of their religious affinities, but said they were being legally prosecuted as agents of Israel. Since the January executions only two more executions of Bahais have been announced, but the total number of acknowledged executions since 1979 now amounts to about one hundred. Reports from inside the country also indicate that the decree denying ration coupons to the Bahais has not been fully enforced, and that the policy of starving them to death or conversion has been quietly postponed, if not totally abandoned.

It should be noted that these are the only Iranians who are victimized exclusively for religious reasons. In fact, one of the tenets of the Bahai faith prohibits political involvement in any form or shape. During the Shah's reign they were the only Iranians to be exempted from his command of compulsory membership of the Rastakhiz party on pain of expulsion from the country. However, it is also true that some emotional and religious links do connect the Bahais with what is now Israel.

Under another despotic regime in the late nineteenth century the Bahai leaders were banished to what was then Ottoman empire territory. When the British mandate was established in Palestine after World War I, important cities like Haifa and Accra, to which Bahai leaders were often banished, became the centres of the community. With the establishment of Israel in 1948 these centres came under the jurisdiction of Israel, and a natural link involving financial transactions for the operation of the headquarters of the faith, its schools, charities, etc. was established thereby.

In the recent past the faith has been administered from Haifa by a nine-member *Beitoladl* (House of Justice) of which five are American, two Iranian and two of other nationalities. Thus it is obvious that the link with Israel has non-political roots, and indeed the Jewish state does not allow the Bahais to engage in proselytizing activities inside Israel. As far as the Iranian regime is concerned, these distinctions are questionable. Any connection with the Zionist state is *ipso facto* criminal, even though such connections as that for the procurement of the much-needed spare parts for the Iranian army and the Pasdaran have been condoned for quite some time.

The Leadership Struggle

Ever since the election of Ali Khamenei as president, and the confirmation of Mir Hossein Mussavi, his half brother, as prime minister, a behind-the-scenes leadership struggle has also plagued the Islamic Republic. What has made that struggle quite crucial to the political fortunes of the government are the certainty of Khomeini's eventual death and the uncertainties of political jockeying for position, particularly amongst the various factions of the Pasdaran.

Shortly after the election of Khamenei a rift began to develop concerning Mahdavi Kani, who had served as interim prime minister. His failure to be re-nominated by the president led to a gradual emergence of a new triumvirate consisting of Kani, Rafsanjani and, tentatively, Mehdi Bazargan, in opposition to the president, the prime minister and the chief justice. How profoundly this new group are antagonistic to those in power, and whether ideological as opposed to personal differences underlie this new polarization in the leadership struggle are, for the moment, imponderables. In vying for Khomeini's favour neither of the two groups appears at present in the ascendant.

After over three years in power, Khomeini has established his credentials as a skilful exploiter of factionalism within his entourage. But as age and reported ill-health catch up with him, his ability to continue doing so successfully seems to be eroding.

It is in this context that the control of the Pasdaran, as well as some of the revolutionary committees in the capital city and major provincial centres, becomes extremely critical. Both in fighting the guerrilla forces and in achieving an impressive success in the war against Iraq the Pasdaran have increased their power base and enhanced their image as a reliable and dedicated force. Now numbering almost 96,000, the Pasdaran are divided into five basic units: for anti-subversion, intelligence, internal security, public relations, and recruitment. Not only did Khomeini appoint its present commander, Rezai, who took an oath of allegiance to Khomeini as the Faghih and Rahbar (theocratic and political supreme leader), but he has his personal representative in the Command Council of the Corps. Quite clearly in the ongoing jockeying for position in the event of Khomeini's death or incapacity, the allegiance of the Pasdaran as a whole, or at least some of the more critical of the units mentioned above, may prove decisive.

The control of the Pasdaran at a critical juncture is only one of the uncertainties plaguing the regime. A more imponderable question concerns the transition of the leadership once Khomeini is incapacitated or dead. 'After Khomeini, who?' has become a critical question for the regime and the Iranians as a whole. Beginning in January 1982, when the report of his deteriorating health assumed sudden currency, attention was focused on the constitutional and political problems of Khomeini's succession. Constitutionally, if there is no consensus on his dual position as Faghih and Rahbar, each or both could be replaced by a three to five-man council. But how it will be determined whether or not there is such a consensus remains unclear. Although the constitution provides for the setting up of an assembly of experts to determine the question, its language is so ambiguous as to make it open to many interpretations.

However, it is known that Khomeini himself has groomed Ayattolah Montazari to succeed him as Faghih, and perhaps a three-man council including Rafsanjani, Khamenei and Mussavi Ardabili to take over as the leadership council. On both counts many problems exist. First, Montazari, in terms of scholarship in Shia theology, is a somewhat lightweight clerical leader. At least two of the Grand Ayattolahs who have not broken with Khomeini, namely Golpaygani and Marashi, have much higher reputations as ulama, and are more capable of exercising the tremendous power and prerogatives assigned to the Faghih.

Compounding the issue is that several of the anti-Khomeini Grand Ayattolahs, above all Shariatmadari, are equally superior to Montazari. Having broken with Khomeini on the concept and meaning of Velayate Faghih, these Ayattolahs have none the less powerful constituencies within the country or in such populous provinces as Azarbayjan and Khorassan. To put it bluntly, for many of them Khomeini's power and prestige simply could not be transferred to figures of lesser theological and/or political acumen.

While similar reservations extend to Khomeini's political leadership, it is worth noting that important responsibilities have been granted to the offices of president and prime minister, whereas the Faghih shares his power with no-one. Indeed, the very issue of the legitimacy of the Faghih, which was dormant for over two years, has once again surfaced in anticipation of Khomeini's departure. In mid-April Sheikh Mahmoud Halabi, a well-known political cleric, joined some of the early critics of the Velayate Faghih, such as Shariatmadari, and called for the abolition of the concept, at least in its present form whereby it is represented in the person of one individual and contravenes the concept of popular sovereignty.

What is obvious is that Khomeini in death may prove even more of a problem for Iran's political viability than during his life time. His insistence on creating a monolithic Shia theocracy may prove the undoing of the Islamic Republic, in the same way that the late Shah's perseverance in establishing a one-party state contributed to his ultimate downfall. As of this writing, the most reliable information from sources both inside and outside the country points to the following polarization concerning Khomeini's succession.

As far as it can be determined, the president, the prime minister, and the Majlis Speaker see no reason why Montazari should not succeed Khomeini, at least initially. Certainly, the first two prefer to see the powerful office of Faghih occupied by a rather weak and mediocre personality, since the powers of the head of state and head of government will be enhanced in direct proportion to the decline of those of the Faghih. President Khamenei, who is not an Ayattolah because he has not yet completed a *Resaleh*, an original treatise on some aspect of Shia theology, cannot personally aspire to becoming a Faghih. He has instead been pressing for the formation of the Assembly of Experts to select a council of leadership, which indicates a preference on his part for the separation of the two offices, and perhaps even their subordination to those of president and prime minister.

The Majlis Speaker, Rafsanjani, may be motivated by a similar desire in supporting Montazari, for he knows full well that a powerful Faghih will automatically undermine the position of the Islamic Majlis as the legislature of the republic. However, he is also in competition with the president and the prime minister. All accounts indicate that his present position regarding the Faghih is a convenient one, and that sooner or later he will confront the president and his chosen prime minister, Mir Hossein Mussavi. As a matter of fact, before the public discussion of the succession problem reports were current in Tehran of Rafsanjani's move toward some non-clerical members of the Majlis, notably Bazargan, Dr Yazdi and Dr Sami.

Against the above position are aligned some powerful and extremely political clerics who had long maintained a silent opposition to the whole concept of Velayate Faghih, as well as to some features of the Islamic Republic such as the laws on property and criminal justice. For some of them opposition to Khomeini appeared either unsafe or unwise. For others a sense of gratitude for his contribution to the overthrow of the Pahlavi regime required acquiescence to his wishes as long as he was alive. None of these considerations should hold with his disappearance from the scene. The secretive *Hojatiyeh* society is presently calling into question the transition of the Faghih's power to Montazari, or to anyone else for that matter. Whether this is out of conviction or because of hostility towards the president and prime minister is a speculative matter.

Reliable reports at the end of April 1982 indicated that they have been pressing for Ayattolah Golpaygani to succeed Khomeini, but not as the Imam of the Shia community, but rather as the principal Marjae Taghlid. In other words, the society seems to view the concept of Faghih in a much more restricted sense. Rather than as the sole arbiter of theological and political questions, it seems to maintain that the unique qualifications and services of Khomeini must not and could not be simply transmitted to any single Mujtahed. One of the Grand Ayattolahs, such as Golpaygani, could, however, be recognized as the principal Mujtahed to function as the supreme guardian of faith.

In mid-April evidence of the depth of the conflict between the above two positions began to surface. When Sadegh Ghotbzadeh, the former associate of Khomeini and foreign minister during most of the US hostage crisis, was arrested and accused of plotting to eliminate Khomeini, pro-government newspapers and Majlis deputies aligned with the president and prime minister implicated Ayattolah Shariatmadari in a plot to succeed Khomeini. His son-in-law, Ahmad Abassi, along with 70 of the close associates of the aged Ayattolah were arrested in Qom.

The Pasdaran surrounded Shariatmadari's residence, denying admission even to his physician, who had gone to check on the prostate condition from which he had been suffering for quite a while. His own son, Hassan Shariatmadari, denied in Hamburg, West Germany, that the Ayattolah had in any way been involved in politics since the uprising in Tabriz at the end of 1979. None the less, the Islamic Republican Party seems bent on utilizing the Ghotbzadeh affair to advance its position concerning Khomeini's succession. Not only does it aim to preclude reputable clerical leaders from the process of succession, it also seeks to eradicate the slightest semblance of non-party activities from the Majlis. Thus, on the day of Ghotbzadeh's arrest, party spokesmen accused a few remaining secular members of the Majlis such as Bazargan, Yazdi, and Sami of being involved in the plot against the Imam.

Most likely the struggle for the successor to Khomeini will be bitter and perhaps prolonged. When the dust has settled a single individual rather than a group of equal partners will most likely emerge to succeed Khomeini. Neither under the Shah nor under his successor could collective leadership be effectively exercised. Such notions as the establishment of the reciprocal recognition of the limits of power, and of accountability, which the constitutional revolution at the turn of the century tried to introduce to Iran, continue to evade its political leaders.

This reality is borne out not only by the creation of a new cult of personality around Khomeini, surpassing the one that the Shah built up at the zenith of his power, but also by an analysis of the words and deeds of opposition groups. For over three years these groups have been exhorted by their leaders to agree on a minimum common goal of overthrowing Khomeini's regime. Frequently declarations of intention to do so are issued both outside and inside the country, but just as frequently the forces of discord, personal rivalry and petty jealousies prevent a concerted and co-ordinated effort in opposition to a government whose durability has surprised many, and not the least, its own officials.

To conclude, it is apparent that the fluidity of the political situation in Iran will make accurate and precise prognosis impossible. The review of events in this postscript does not necessitate drastic revision of any of the scenarios presented in the preceding chapter. If one remembers that on the last occasion that the Iranian regime was forcibly changed, the new one lasted nearly 70 years, the longevity of the

Islamic Republic so far does not appear exceptionally impressive. The notable difference between the Pahlavi regime and the present theocracy relates to significant changes in nearly all the socio-economic and political conditions of Iran. Both in scope and intensity much more violence has been used to establish and maintain the Shia fundamentalist regime. Its overthrow will no doubt require even more violence, considering the current standard of political struggle in that unhappy land.

SELECTED BIBLIOGRAPHY

Because of the author's heavy reliance on primary Iranian sources in Farsi and English, books, articles, pamphlets and underground publications originating from Iran or abroad will be cited first. English translations of these items will be offered if they do not appear in the notes. Next, Iranian Farsi and English newspapers, periodicals, news magazines will be listed. The last section will list books in English and French. Articles, documents and other publications, some cited in the notes, will not be repeated here, in the interests of economy.

Algar, Hamid 'Mosahebeye Nasr ba Dr Algar,' *Shahed*, Embassy of IRI, Washington, DC, March 1980

Ayattolah Khomeini 'Ruhaniyune Narazi Bedadgah Ehzar Mishavand,' *Iran Times*, Washington, DC, 17 April 1981

────── 'Adl, Tahvil dadane zalem be Adel va Moshrek be Momen ast,' *Shahed*, Embassy of IRI, Washington, DC, 14 February 1980

Ayattolah Mahallati *Elamiyeh*, clandestine, February 1981

Ayattolah Shariatmadari 'Nazariyeh dar ertebat ba Masaele ruz' *Akhbare Iran*, Bonn, West Germany, No. 8-9, 24 December 1979

Ayattolah Zanjani 'Jenayat bename Islam,' *Payam*, London, No. 3, 29 January 1981

Banisadr, Abolhassan 'Americans: What you should know about the present crisis in US-Iranian Relations,' Moslem Student Association of USA, no date

────── *Eghtesade Towhidi* (Unified Economy), Tehran, n.p. 1979

Dehghani, Ashraf 'Mosahebe ba cherike Fadayi Khalgh,' June 1979, n.p.

Enayat, Mahmoud 'Andar Hashiye Eshghale Sefarate America,' *Iran Post*, London, 21 December 1979

Iran Post, '220 Kudak dar Tehran Tirbaran Shodand,' Los Angeles, 24 October 1981

Iranian People's Fedayeen (Majority), 'Statement Regarding the Recent Development in Iran,' 10 July 1981

──────, 'Statement Regarding the Criminal Terror of the President and Prime Minister of Iran', 4 September 1981

Kianouri, Nureddin *Hezbe Tudehe Iran va Dr Mossadegh*, Tehran, Entesharate Hizbe Tudeh, No. 16, 1980

Madani, Ahmad 'Namehe be Imam Khomeini,' West Germany, 1981
Mihandust, Ali 'The Last Defense,' Moslem Student Society of USA, Long Beach, California, March 1981
Nazih, Hassan 'Mullaha az Islam Chehreye zeshti Erae dadand,' *Faryade Azadi*, London, 19 December 1979
Mojahed 'The Content of the Islamic Republic,' vol. 1, No. 5, London, May 1980
———, 'The Pakistan Conference and the Problem of Afghanistan,' vol. 1, No. 4, April 1980
People's Mojahedin Organization of Iran, Shenakht. Takamol (Recognition and Evolution), Tehran, 1975
Peyman, Dr Habib *Osule Sosyalizme Mardome Iran*, n.p. 1979
———, *Kar, Malekiyat va Sarmaye dar Iran*, n.d.

Arteshe Rahaibakshe Iran ARA, Paris, 1979–81
Ayandegan, Tehran, 1979–80
Bamdad, Tehran, 1979–80
Embassy of Islamic Republic of Iran, *Text of the Constitution*, 1979
Enghelabe Islami, Tehran and Clandestine, 1979–81
Ettelaat, Tehran, 1978–81
Faryade Azadi, London, 1979–80
Iran Post, London, 1979–81
Iran Tribune, San José, California, 1980–1
Iran Press Service, London–Paris, 1979–81
Iran Times, Washington, DC, 1977–81
Highlights of Imam Khomeini's Speeches Pars Agency, distributed by Moslem Student Association of USA, 1980–1
Harekat, San Francisco, California, 1981
Iran Voice, Embassy of IRI, Washington, DC, 1979–80
Iran Post, Los Angeles, 1977–81
Islamic Revolution, Monthly, Falls Church, Virginia, 1979–80
KAR, Tehran, 1979–81
Keyhan, Tehran, 1978–81
Khabarnameh Enghelabe Islami, clandestine, 1981
Khalghe Mosalman, Tehran, 1979–80
Jomhuriye Islami, Tehran, 1979–81
Mardom, Tehran and clandestine, 1979–81
Mizan, Tehran, 1979–81
Mojahed, Tehran and clandestine, 1979–81
News Bulletin, Long Beach, California, 1980–1
News Letter, Washington, DC, 1979–81

Newsletter, Iran Center for Documentation, Paris and Falls Church, Virginia, 1979-81
Omide Iran, Tehran, 1979-80
People's Mojahedin Organization of Iran, London, 1980-1
Pardis, Los Angeles, California, 1981
Ranjbar, Tehran and clandestine, 1979-81
Rastakhiz, Tehran, 1978-9
Shahed, weekly, Washington, DC, 1979-80
Tehran Times, Tehran, 1979-81
The Iran Council Grapevine, The Asian Society, New York, 1980-1
Ummat, Tehran, 1979-80

Akhavi, Shahrough *Religion and Politics in Iran: Clergy-State Relations in the Pahlavi Period* (State University of New York Press, Albany, 1980)
Albert, David H. (ed.) *Tell the American People: Perspectives on the Iranian Revolution* (Movement for a New Society, Philadelphia, 1980)
Alexander, Yonah and Allan Nanes (eds.) *The United States and Iran: A Documentary History*. University Publications of America, Frederick, Maryland, 1980
Amnesty International *Law and Human Rights in the Islamic Republic of Iran*. London, 1980
Balta, Paul and Rulleau, Claudine *L'Iran Insurgé* (Editions Sinbad, Paris, 1979)
Binder, Leonard 'Revolution in Iran,' *Middle East Review*, Special Studies, 1, 1980
Braley, Russ 'The Scourging of the Shah,' in C.K. Pullapilly (ed.) *Islam in the Contemporary World*. Cross Roads Books, Notre Dame, Ind., 1980
Brière, Claire and Blanchet, Pierre *Iran: La Révolution Au Nom de Dieu*, Seuil, Paris, 1979
Chubin, Shahram 'Soviet Policy Towards Iran and the Gulf' (Adelphi Papers, 157), Institute of Strategic Studies, London, 1980
Farhang, Mansour *US Imperialism: The Spanish-American War to the Iranian Revolution* (South End Press, Boston, 1981)
Fisher, Michael J. *Iran: From Religious Dispute to Revolution* (Harvard University Press, Cambridge, Mass., 1980)
Flanz, Gisbert H., Nicholas M. Nikazmerad and Changiz Vafai 'Iran ' in P. Blaustein and G.H. Flanz (eds.) *Constitutions of the Countries of the World* (Ocean Publications, Inc., New York, 1980)

Forbis, William H. *Fall of the Peacock Throne* (Harper and Row Publishers, New York, 1980)

Graham, Robert *Iran: The Illusion of Power* (Croom Helm, London, 1978)

Halliday, Fred *Iran: Dictatorship and Development* (Penguin Books, New York, 1979)

—— *Soviet Policy in the Arc of Crisis* (Institute of Policy Studies, Washington, 1981)

Hanks, Robert J. 'Conflict in Iran.' *Conflict* 1, pp. 145–59, 1979

Hoveyda, Fereydoun *The Fall of the Shah* (Wyndham Books, New York, 1979)

Hurewitz, J.C. *The Persian Gulf: After Iran's Revolution* (Foreign Policy Association, New York, 1979)

Ifshayi Impiriyalism *Disclosures of Imperialism*, Vol. I. Danishjuyani Musalmanie Peyrove Khatt-e-Imam, Tehran (Documents in English on Embassy Seizure) 1980

Jabbari, Ahmad and Robert Olson (eds) *Iran: Essay on a Revolution in the Making* (Mazda Publications, Lexington, Kentucky, 1981)

Jansen, G.H. *Militant Islam* (Harper and Row, New York, 1979)

Jazani, Bizhan *Capitalism and Revolution in Iran* (Zed Press, London, 1980)

Katouzian, Homa *The Political Economy of Modern Iran: Despotism and Pseudo-Modernism* (New York University Press, New York, 1981)

Kazemi, Farhad *Poverty and Revolution in Iran: The Migrant Poor, Urban Marginality and Politics* (New York University Press, New York, 1980)

—— (ed.) *Iranian Revolution in Perspective* (The Society for Iranian Studies, Boston, 1980)

Keddie, Nikki R. and Richard Yann, *Iran: Roots of Revolution* (Yale University Press, New Haven, 1981)

Khomeini, Ayattolah Ruhollah *Islamic Government* (Manor Books, Inc., New York). Also available as Khomeyni (Translations on Near East and North Africa No. 1897, 19 January 1979, National Technical Information Service) 1979

—— *Sayings of the Ayatollah Khomeini: Political, Philosophical, Social and Religious* Tony Hendra (ed.) translated by Harold J. Salemson (Bantam Books, New York, 1980)

Ledeen, Michael A. and William H. Lewis *Debacle: The American Failure in Iran* (Alfred A. Knopf, New York, 1981)

McFadden, Robert *et al. No Hiding Place* (New York Times Books,

1981)

Manashri, David 'Iran.' *Middle East Contemporary Survey* edited by Colin Legum, Haim Shaked and Daniel Dishon, 2, 1977-8

Nahavandi, Houshang *Iran: Deux Rêves Brisés* (Albin Michel, Paris, 1981)

Nickbin, Saber *Iran: The Unfolding Revolution* (Relgocrest Ltd, London, 1979)

Nobari, Ali-Reza *Iran Erupts: Independence, News and Analysis of the Iranian National Movement* (Iran-America Documentation Group, Stanford, Calif., 1978)

Noyes, James H. *The Clouded Lens: Persian Gulf Security and US Policy* (Hoover Institution Press, Stanford, Calif., 1979)

Paalberg, Robert, (ed.) with Eul Park and David Wyman *Diplomatic Dispute: US Conflict with Iran, Japan, and Mexico* (Harvard University Center for International Affairs, Cambridge, Mass., 1979)

Pahlavi, Ashraf *Faces in a Mirror* (Prentice-Hall, Inc., Englewood Cliffs, N.J., 1980)

Pahlavi, Mohammad Reza *Answer to History* (Stein and Day Publishers, New York, 1980)

Pakravan, Karim 'The Political Economy of Middle Eastern Oil and the Islamic Revival ' in C. Pullapilly (ed.) *Islam in the Contemporary World* (Cross Roads Books, Notre Dame, Ind., 1980)

Queen, Richard *Inside and Out: Hostage in Iran, Hostage to Myself* (Putnam's, New York, 1981)

Rizvi, Saiyid Athar Abbas *Iran: Royalty, Religion and Revolution* (Ma'rifat, Canberra, Australia, 1980)

Rubin, Barry *Paved with Good Intentions: The American Experience and Iran* (Oxford University Press, New York, 1980)

Saikal, Amin *The Rise and Fall of the Shah* (Princeton University Press, Princeton, 1980)

Semkus, Charles Ismail *The Fall of Iran 1978-1979: An Historical Anthology* Vols. I and II (Copen Press, New York, 1979-80)

Salinger, Pierre *America Held Hostage: The Secret Negotiations* (Doubleday, New York, 1981)

Siddiqui, Kalim (ed.) *The Islamic Revolution in Iran* (The Open Press in Association with the Muslim Institution, London, 1980)

Stempel, John *Inside the Iranian Revolution* (Indiana University Press, Bloomington, 1981)

Stauth, Georg (ed.) *Iran: Precapitalism, Capitalism and Revolution* (Verlag Breitenback, 9 Saarbrucken, Germany, 1980)

Sullivan, William H. *Mission to Iran* (Norton, New York, 1981)

United Nations University *Aspects of the Iranian Revolution* New York, 1980)

US Congress, House Permanent Select Committee on Intelligence *Iran: Evaluation of US Intelligence Performance Prior to November 1978* Staff Report, 96th Cong. 1st sess. Washington, DC, Committee Printing, 1979

US Congress, House Joint Economic Committee *Economic Consequences of the Revolution in Iran* (Government Printing Office, Washington, DC, 1980)

Zabih, Sepehr *Iran's Revolutionary Upheaval: An Interpretative Essay* (Alchemy Books, San Francisco, 1979)

—— *The Mossadegh Era: Roots of the Iranian Revolution* (Lake View Press, Chicago, 1981)

INDEX